DATE DUE

The making of
US foreign policy

The making of US foreign policy

John Dumbrell

with a chapter by *David M. Barrett*

Manchester University Press

Manchester and New York

Distributed exclusively in the USA and Canada by St. Martin's Press

Published by Manchester University Press
Oxford Road, Manchester M13 9PL, UK
and Room 400, 175 Fifth Avenue,
New York, NY 10010, USA

Distributed exclusively in the USA and Canada
by St. Martin's Press, Inc.,
175 Fifth Avenue, New York, NY 10010, USA

British Library cataloguing in publication data
Dumbrell, John, *1950–*
    The making of U.S. foreign policy.
    1. United States. Foreign relations
    I. Title II. Barrett, David M.
    327.73

Library of Congress cataloging in publication data
Dumbrell, John, 1950–
    The making of US foreign policy : American democracy and American
    foreign policy / John Dumbrell, with a chapter by David M. Barrett.
        p. cm.
    Includes index.
    ISBN 0–7190–3187–7
    1. United States — Foreign relations administration. 2. United
    States — Foreign relations — 20th century.   I. Barrett. David M.,
    1951– . II. Title.
    JX1706.D85   1990
    353.0089 – dc20   90–6428

    ISBN 0 7190 3187 7 *hardback*
         0 7190 3188 5 *paperback*

Typeset in Linotron Janson
by Northern Phototypesetting Co Ltd, Bolton

Printed in Great Britain
by Billing & Sons Ltd, Worcester

Contents

Acknowledgements

I would like to thank David Barrett for writing Chapter 3 and for his comments on other chapters. I should emphasise that he is not responsible for views expressed and errors committed in Chapters 1 and 2, and Chapters 4 to 9. Donna Hunter of Manchester University and Jules Townshend of Manchester Polytechnic provided valuable comments on draft chapters. I would also like to record my personal debt to my parents; to Charles Malyon, history master at my old school; and to the late John D. Lees of Keele University. The scholarship and enthusiasm of John Lees were an inspiration to a generation of British scholars interested in American politics. A grant from the Lyndon Johnson Foundation, a sabbatical term, and participation in a four week project on decision-making in US foreign policy (organised by the US Information Agency) also aided preparation of this book. The staffs of the Lyndon Johnson Library at Austin, Texas (especially David C. Humphrey) and the Jimmy Carter Library at Atlanta, Georgia (especially Martin I. Elzy) were extremely helpful and efficient. Thanks also to Jenny Williams, who typed the manuscript, and to Richard Purslow of Manchester University Press.

John Dumbrell
March 1990

Introduction

American foreign policy tends to be perceived outside the United States in negative fashion. It is often characterised as incoherent and, despite its post-1945 internationalist continuity, unpredictable. In his testimony to a House of Commons Select Committee in April 1984, Sir Nicholas Henderson (former British Ambassador to Washington) responded thus to a question about the US 'Administration view' of the situation regarding the Falkland Islands: 'When you say the U.S. Administration, I am sorry to be pedantic but there is the Pentagon view, the State Departmental view and the White House view'[1]

Unpredictablity is held to derive both from this putative institutional incoherence, and from an endemic uncertainty about America's proper role in the world. A familiar theme in (especially) European commentaries on US foreign policy is that of oscillation between the ideals of withdrawal from the world, and of globalistic intervention in order to redeem the world.[2]

Particularly (but not only) in the Third World, US foreign policy is often regarded as militaristic, imperialistic and beyond democratic control. The Central Intelligence Agency, in particular, is regarded with fear and incomprehension. Defenders of American diplomacy regularly find themselves facing an exasperating and frustrating task. David Newsom, for example, described his experience as a US Information Agency officer in Pakistan and Iraq as follows: 'Americans imagine themselves as free, democratic, innovative, generous and peace-loving. They assume others see them that way. They are shocked that there are those outside the Soviet orbit who see them as neo-colonialists, aggressive, insensitive, ungenerous and trigger-happy.'[3]

More recently, American foreign policy has seemed to some Europeans as increasingly irrelevant to their concerns: the atavistic expression of an arthritic superpower.

US foreign policy is the product of ambivalent traditions and forces, and of a policy-making environment characterised by fragmentation. Ambivalence (notably between non-involvement and messianic interventionism) lies at the heart of liberalism, the ideological core of American foreign policy. Ambivalence is also encouraged by the liberal policy system: the US constitutional system itself. It is fundamentally antipathetic to the kind of unitary 'efficiency' associated with the British process, where policy-making elites are generally shielded from criticism and scrutiny.[4] The Constitution itself simply outlines a battleground over which the President and the Congress vie for power. Yet another source of ambivalence lies in the contrast between the historically defined aspirations of American foreign policy-makers, and the demands of contemporary power structures in the United States. American policy-makers tend to see themselves as upholding open, democratic traditions appropriate to the New World. In the early years of the republic, President John Adams denied any 'notion of cheating anybody'.[5] American foreign policy, however, is also the product of a militarised economy, of unaccountable and private power, and of periodic drives towards secrecy which seem to be stimulated by the very fragmentation of its policy-making structures.

Given these various sources of ambivalence, it is perhaps not surprising that US foreign policy so often occasions puzzlement among foreign observers. The primary purpose of this book is to address this puzzlement by providing an account of the structures and traditions which shape American foreign policy.

The book is organised primarily around the major institutions of foreign policy-making: President, Congress, the intelligence community, and so on. It also attempts, however, to discuss the historical and theoretical dimensions of American foreign policy, and to situate it within the context of international politics. This book's preoccupations and outlook have been shaped by three interconnected developments of contemporary international politics. These developments came to centre-stage during the 1980s, and seem likely to dominate the international politics of the 1990s. They are: firstly, the debate about the decline (and, from a European perspective, the relevance) of American power; secondly, the Gorbachev era in Eastern Europe and the putative end of the Cold War; and, thirdly, the burgeoning evidence of interdependence in international relations.

Against this background, this book has three major themes: the interaction between American foreign policy and America's changing position in the world; the interconnection between process and substance in foreign policy-making; and the relationship between foreign policy-making and democratic institutions and practices. The first two of these themes – the debates over American international power and over process and substance – are treated most directly in Chapters 1 and 2. The first chapter offers a discussion of theoretical approaches to the study of international relations generally, and to US foreign policy and its driving ideology in particular; it also deals directly with the debate about America's decline. Chapter 2 discusses theoretical arguments about the foreign policy process, and its relation to the substance of policy. These two themes also, however, inform and underpin Chapters 3 to 8. Nonetheless, these six chapters address themselves more obviously to the book's third theme: the relationship between foreign policy and democracy.

Successful foreign policy has often been presumed to be antagonistic to open, democratic processes: to amenability to the rule of law, to popular accountability through the electoral process and Congress, to significant and positive legislative participation, and to the more than merely formalistic participation of an informed general public. Alexis de Tocqueville thought that it was in foreign policy-making that democracies showed themselves inferior to other forms of government. The anarchic, unpredictable nature of the international environment militates, so it is argued, against democratic due process.[6]

This debate raises questions about the actual and desirable role of Congress and of public opinion, and also about the nature of international politics in an age of interdependence. These questions are addressed throughout this book and also, in a more general way, in the concluding section of Chapter 9. This, final, chapter presents two detailed case-studies, and attempts to relate them to theories about American foreign policy.

To conclude this introduction, special mention should be made of Chapter 3, written by David Barrett. In its focus on the interaction between process and substance (and also on the central importance of the Vietnam experience) this chapter reaffirms the preoccupations and assumptions of the rest of the book. In tracing the rise of Presidential foreign policy, David Barrett, in effect, provides a narrative of modern developments in American foreign relations. (Readers who wish to familiarise themselves with this material might be well advised to address themselves firstly to this chapter.) Chapter 3 also provides valuable background for the case-studies in Chapter 9. David Barrett's chapter is also, however, intended to provide a creative counterpoint to the arguments inherent in the rest of the book. Firstly and most obviously, it presents an American perspective. Even more importantly, it contains an essentially positive judgement on Presidentially-dominated foreign policy, and on the National Security Council system. Other chapters are more critical of this system, and argue for greater Congressional and public participation.

Notes

   1   Cited in Z. Steiner, 'Decision-making in American and British foreign policy', *Review of International Studies*, 134, 1987, pp. 1–18, p. 9.
   2   See the London *Economist*, 1984, cited in D. D. Newsom, *Diplomacy and the American Democracy*, Bloomington (Indiana), 1988, pp. 12–13; also C. Coker, *Reflections on American Foreign Policy since 1945*, London 1989, (ch. 1 on 'exceptionalism', 'redemptionism' and 'exemplarism' as American historical myths).
   3   Newsom, p. 181.
   4   See Steiner, p. 15. On the US constitutional position, see L. Henkin, *Foreign Affairs and the Constitution*, New York, 1972; N. J. Ornstein, 'The Constitution and the sharing of foreign policy responsibility', in E. S. Muskie *et al.*, eds., *The President, the Congress and Foreign Policy*, New York, 1986, pp. 35–65; K. W. Thompson, 'The President, Congress and foreign policy', in R.C. Simmons, ed., *The United States Constitution: The First 200 Years*, Manchester, 1989, pp. 184–202.
   5   Cited in J. B. Moore, *American Diplomacy*, New York, 1905, p. 254
   6   A. de Tocqueville, *Democracy in America*, London, 1875, Vol. 1, p. 237. See also E. A. Mowrer, *The Nightmare of American Foreign Policy*, New York, 1948, pp. 4–5.

1

The United States and international politics

1. The ideology of American foreign policy

(a) *Liberalism* An optimistic interpretation of the relationship between capitalism and democracy is central to the driving ideology of US foreign policy: the ideology of liberalism. It is, of course, conventional for practitioners and defenders of American foreign policy to deny that it has an ideology. It certainly has goals, but ideology, no. Writing in 1945, Thomas Bailey outlined the traditional goals or 'fundamental policies' as: isolation, nonintervention or non-entanglement; the Monroe Doctrine (the protection of a sphere of influence in the Western Hemisphere); freedom of the seas; the Open Door (especially in China) – the 'right of American citizens to engage in industry abroad on an equal basis with other foreigners'; pacific settlement of disputes; Pan-Americanism; and opportunism (minor adjustments without reference to fundamentals).[1] The principal post-1945 goal has been the containment of communism, an objective to be achieved within an internationalist policy context. But, as for ideology, it is, according to Arthur Schlesinger, 'out of character' for pragmatic Americans.[2]

Of course, 'ideology' bears many meanings and, no doubt, the term can be defined so as to separate it from American liberal pragmatism. Such a separation, however, seems to serve little purpose other than the polemical one of being able to characterise opposing positions as 'ideological': over-zealous, dogmatic, undemocratic, totalitarian. Within Marxism, 'ideology' embraces both 'false consciousness' and forms of thought which function to preserve or represent class interests.[3] For the Marxist, obviously, there is no question as to the 'ideological' status of ideas underpinning and seeking to justify US foreign policy. Outside Marxism, 'ideology' may be defined as 'more or less coherent collections of political beliefs and values which take a distinct and identifiable shape', [4] 'a value system' or *Weltanschauung*. [5] In these senses, US liberalism is clearly an ideology among other ideologies, and it is worth remembering that Louis Hartz, the most celebrated modern interpreter of American liberalism, had no doubts about this. [6]

American democratic liberalism, whose main progenitor was John Locke, may be characterised as embodying commitments to the interdependence of democracy and capitalism; to individual liberty and the protection of private property; to limited government, the rule of law, natural rights, the perfectibility of human institutions, and to the possibility of human progress. It is allied with a strong sense of national mission and American exceptionalism: the belief that American democratic history provides a model for the world. At its heart, Lockeian liberalism embraces a commitment both to national self-determination and to the view that the world belongs to the industrious and the rational. [7] Enemies of liberalism are, on the right, conservative ideologies which exude pessimism about the possibility of progress through human agency; and, on the left, ideologies which assert that human freedom may only be realised through a transcendence of private property and capitalism. [8]

As an ideology underpinning US foreign policy, liberalism oscillates between the poles of nonentanglement and interventionist internationalism. Historically, as in President George Washington's farewell address, nonentanglement has been held up as a consequence of American exceptionalism. Nonentanglement would allow the United States to shape its frontier destiny, remain aloof from distant quarrels, and provide a model for the world in the process. (The Swedish ambassador wrote to John Adams in 1784 that he trusted that the United States would 'have sense enough to see us in Europe cut each other's throats with a philosophical tranquillity'.) [9]

With the closing of the frontier and, especially, with US assumption of global leadership after 1945, nonentanglement gave way to the liberal internationalist ideal: the protection and promotion of liberal, capitalist values on a global scale. President Woodrow Wilson appropriated the term 'liberal' to justify American entry into the First World War. Liberal internationalists like President Franklin Roosevelt used the denigratory label 'isolationist' to stigmatise the older, nonentanglement tradition. [10] After 1945, the cause of liberal internationalism became inextricably bound up with the idea of 'containing' expansionist, Soviet-directed communism. Containment, articulated within a culture of self-righteous anti-communism, was always a rather unsatisfactory concept. Its progenitor, George Kennan, came to disagree with the global interpretation of containment advanced by the Truman Administration. When tied to a defensive vocabulary, and particularly when used to underpin 'limited' wars, containment also conflicted with the crusading, quasi-messianic tone of US liberal internationalism. [11]

(b) *Alternatives to liberalism* What alternatives have been presented, within the history of US foreign policy, to liberal ideology? There are at least five candidates: self-interested realism; conservatism; isolationism; Wilsonian idealism; and left liberalism. These will now, very briefly, be considered in sequence, with the underlying implication that they are most appropriately viewed as variants on and tendencies within the overarching liberal ideology. This is not to suggest that there are not real and important differences between these points of view – between, for example, self-interested realism and left liberalism. It is both annoying and absurd to be told that voters in liberal, capitalist democracies are offered no 'real' choice in these matters. It is also the case that both realism and conservatism have the potential to constitute ideologies antagonistic to Lockeian liberalism. Rather, the point is that, at least in the American context, these viewpoints have exhibited a large measure of convergence, and an unwillingness to challenge the dominant liberal ideology.

Even accounts of American foreign policy which stress its moral idealism and evangelising mission generally acknowledge the role of national interest. The dialectical tension between 'ideals' and 'self-interest' lies at the heart of conventional treatments of US foreign relations.[12] Robert Garson puts the point well: 'Foreign policy is the result of the intermingling of preconceived assumptions (ideology if you like) and calculations about the national interest.'[13] A full-blown realist interpretation would hold that US foreign policy achieves rationality and purpose only to the extent that it embodies accurate, power-oriented, calculations of the national interest. Arguing against the legacy of Wilsonian idealism, Nicholas Spykman wrote in *America's Strategy in World Politics* (1942) that the 'preservation and improvement of their power position' constitutes the goal of nations' foreign policies.[14] The point to be made here, however, is that power-based, national interest-oriented realism has been an influence upon, rather than a substitute for, the liberal ideology of US foreign policy.

Realist, geopolitical ideology in recent American foreign policy has operated as a facet of liberal internationalism, which itself embodies a firm (if usually unstated) commitment to the national interest. Realism has had an important effect on the history of the Cold War. Realist critics of the American involvement in Vietnam contributed decisively to the changing public debate over the war. However, when self-proclaimed upholders of *Realpolitik* have guided US foreign policy, they have altered the direction of American diplomacy rather than its underlying foundations and assumptions.[15]

Conservative foreign policy positions in the United States tend to be identified with a strong commitment to high levels of defence spending and an intense level of anti-communism. They also are inclined to romantic notions about the assertion of American power.[16] Burton Pines of the conservative Heritage Foundation applauded President Reagan's foreign policy in 1983 as authentically conservative in its commitment to US security and its recognition of the Soviet Union as the 'focus of evil in the modern world'. Pines also congratulated Reagan on his refusal to sign the Union Nations law of the sea treaty, describing it as a measure hostile to free enterprise.[17] A version of conservatism has also been articulated in recent years by writers like Norman Podhoretz and Irving Kristol. Hostile to the perceived foreign policy practices and legacy of the Carter Administration, these 'neo-conservatives' exhibit a self-consciously tough-minded world outlook; they also have a firm commitment to free market liberalism and a disillusionment with welfare capitalism. Again, such views may be regarded as constituting a variant of, or tendency within, liberal internationalism rather than as an alternative to it. Nonetheless, conservatism, especially in its scepticism as to the perfectibility of human institutions, can (at least in its 'realist' rather than 'romantic' mode) represent a genuine alternative to liberalism. From a 'neo-conservative' position, Jeane Kirkpatrick has berated liberals for failing to acknowledge the existence of human wickedness, taking refuge in 'pale euphemisms and blind theories of inevitable human progress'.[18] An authentic conservative tradition does exist within the history of American foreign policy: anti-imperialist, anxious about American security, sceptical about Manifest Destiny and national missions, concerned above all with the preservation of liberty at home. Defined in these terms, conservative sentiments were expressed by Daniel Webster at the time of the acquisition of California and New Mexico (1846–48). Webster feared the growth of an

American imperialism: 'this country should exhibit to the world the example of a powerful republic, without greediness and hunger of empire'.[19] Henry Clay argued in 1852 that the best way for the United States to show 'to other nations the way to greatness and happiness' was by maintaining liberty at home as a model for imitation.[20] Samuel Flagg Bemis, diplomatic historian and celebrator of American liberty as expressed in its foreign policy, wrote in 1936 that, after 1898, the American people decided to acquire an empire and take their place in the world: 'Actually, the United States had already taken its proper place in the world before 1898. That was in North America.'[21]

Robert Taft, despite occasional lapses into conspiracy theory and partisanship, also developed a coherent conservative position during the Korean conflict (1950–53). One dimension of this concentrated on the domestic effects of war: partly inflation, but also the inevitable domestic militarisation and centralisation of power. Another related to the constitutional issues of excessive executive unaccountability and secrecy. The Republican Senator from Ohio also stressed the dangers of America 'becoming an imperialistic nation', which failed to recognise the moral and practical 'limitations on what the United States can do'.[22] This anti-imperialist strain within American conservatism was to generate a debate in the 1970s on the putative continuity between older conservatives and Vietnam generation – New Left positions.[23] During the Korean war, Taft pointed to the possibility that interventionist liberalism might destroy the rights and lives of people the US intended to defend against communism. In *A Foreign Policy for Americans*, Taft argued that forcing remote peoples to be free ran counter to American democratic ideals.[24]

Taft himself saw these democratic ideals as liberal:[25] individual liberties defined within the context of market liberalism and governmental non-interference. If we define liberalism in these terms, and also note that American liberalism embodies a strong commitment to the idea of America's special mission to protect liberty, we see here a major problem with the articulation of American conservative thought as a genuine alternative to liberalism. Conservative positions tend to spin off in a liberal direction. As Richard Crockatt has put it, the US lacks a tradition which unites the European organicist conservatism of Edmund Burke and the *dirigisme* of Alexander Hamilton.[26] Taftian conservatism, although taken up in later years by conservative intellectuals like Karl Hess, in any case found it hard to survive the Cold War. Anti-imperialist criticisms of the Vietnam war came from the left rather than the right of the political spectrum. In this connection, a comparison of Barry Goldwater's hawkish *Why Not Victory?* (1962) with Taft's fears about the creation of a 'garrison state' in *A Foreign Policy for Americans* is instructive.[27]

Isolationism is often regarded as an attribute of American conservatism, and ex-President Hoover's 'Gibraltar' speech of December 1950 as its post-Second World War high-water mark. In fact, both Taft and Hoover disowned the isolationist label, seeing themselves rather as critics of President Truman's overweening globalism. Walter Lippmann declared at the time of the Vietnam war that, compared 'to people who thought they could run the universe', he was a 'neo-isolationist and proud of it'.[28] Since the promulgation of the Monroe Doctrine (1823) the US has, at the very least, been committed to regional or hemispheric hegemony. 'Isolationism' is an unsatisfactory term, and has become little more than a pejorative polemic. As LaFeber writes: 'The United States has never been isolated or outside the world's political struggles. It was born in the middle of those struggles, and its great problem was – and has always been – how to survive those struggles while maintaining individual liberty at home.'[29]

The debate of the 1930s over American involvement in a European conflict was as much a debate over neutrality as over 'isolation'. 'Corporatist' historians have challenged the whole conception of inter-war American isolation.[30] It also makes little sense to label as 'isolationist' those who would give priority to domestic reform over foreign adventures. Such a view was presented by Charles Beard in 1934 in his aptly titled *The Open Door at Home*.[31] During the Vietnam war (in 1971), Senator Symington of Missouri declared that 'we should express less interest in South Asia and more in South St. Louis'.[32] He echoed and reflected public war-weariness, and the not unreasonable opinion that the US had plenty of problems to deal with at home without seeking out more on the opposite side of the planet. The rhetoric of the Cold War did, at one level, operate to ease domestic tensions and to postpone the kind of reform programme outlined by Chester Bowles in 1946.[33] Such sentiments do not constitute a fully-fledged ideology of isolationism.[34]

The main tenets of the foreign policy idealism associated with President Woodrow Wilson were outlined in Wilson's 1918 'Fourteen Points' speech: open diplomacy, anti-colonialism and self-determination, free trade. This idealistic internationalism was to find echoes in the 'world order' internationalism of the Carter Administration.[35] Clearly, however, neither Wilson's nor Carter's internationalism were outside the ambit of liberal ideology. On the contrary, both were driven by a notion of human perfectibility guided by the example of American democracy and responsive to the needs of American capitalism. Wilson declared in 1912 that US producers had 'expanded to such a point that they will burst their jackets if they cannot find a free outlet to the markets of the world'. T. P. McCormick, summarising the work of 'corporatist' historians, equates 'Wilsonianism' with 'globalised corporatism'; ('Americanised corporatism' is defined as 'a sort of corporate, pro-capitalist reformism').[36] Carter's policies were affected, at least temporarily, by the programme for post-Vietnam inter-capitalist co-operation advanced by the Trilateral Commission.[37] Both Wilson and Carter, in fact, oscillated between 'idealist' and 'realist' versions of liberalism. Wilson intervened in six Latin American conflicts to secure regimes acceptable to the United States government. American troops fought against the Red Army in the Russian civil war. The Carter Presidency, overtaken by events, had by 1980 adopted a confrontational posture towards the Soviet Union.

Left liberalism may be regarded as an attempt to take Wilsonian idealism seriously: to amputate its interventionist and militarist tendencies. Former Vice-President Henry Wallace advocated open diplomacy with the USSR in the late 1940s. He attacked the Baruch Plan of 1946 (to set up an international atomic development authority) as insufficiently generous in its promise to share knowledge of atomic energy.[38] In 1947, he admonished: 'Once America stands for opposition to change, we are lost'. Unthinking counter-revolutionism would lead to America becoming 'the most hated nation in the world'.[39] Wallace was attacked as an appeaser and dismissed as Secretary of Commerce in 1946. He was an optimistic liberal, believing firmly in American democratic values, 'peace and prosperity': the alleviation of distress through post-war reconstruction and the expansion of democracy and free trade.[40] (Wallace resigned from the Progressive party in 1952 in support of US policy in Korea). Post-Vietnam left liberals continued to protest the influence of giant corporations and the 'military-industrial complex', in the name of democratic values.[41] Globalistic ambition had caused political leaders to lose sight of domestic problems. In his 1968 campaign, Robert Kennedy attacked President Johnson's claim that the war presaged 'a

Great Society for all of Asia'. Kennedy urged that 'we cannot build a
Great Society there if we cannot build one in our country'.[42] In 1984,
the Reverend Jesse Jackson delivered a speech to the United Nations
entitled 'Foreign policy – but not foreign values'. He took up,
indirectly, Robert Kennedy's point about the neglect of domestic
reform and linked it to the need to recover America's true liberal
democratic mission: 'If we are to remain the hope of the free world,
our challenge is not military escalation but a worldwide war on
poverty, disease and illiteracy. Domestic policy is foreign policy.'[43]

In *Ideology and U.S. Foreign Policy*, Michael Hunt makes an eloquent
plea for a 'republican' foreign policy rooted in the notion that
'American greatness should be measured against domestic conditions'. He traces the cultural roots and accretions of American foreign
policy ideology, identifying a commitment to American exceptionalism and sense of mission, an acceptance of racial hierarchy, and
hostility to revolutionary change abroad. Education is presented as a
way out of this cultural bondage:

> Education ... offers one powerful antidote to the long-prevalent core ideas of
> U.S. policy. American values, especially the American conception of liberty,
> do not export as well as we would like to think. It is time Americans ... accepted
> the limits of our power to shape other societies, time we pondered the
> contradiction we have long perpetrated by seeking to impose our conception
> of self-determination and development on peoples with aspirations quite
> different from our own.[44]

2 International relations theory and the decline of American power

(a) *Three perspectives* Notions about America's position in the
world may be located within three perspectives, traditions or paradigms within the study of world politics: realism, interdependence
and structuralism. The first of these, realism, takes the nation-state as
its basic unit of analysis. The international order is inherently anarchic and conflictual, with international co-operation virtually a contradiction in terms. Domestic influences over a nation's foreign policy
are held to have been aggregated at the level of the nation-state, and
thus have little interest to the realist analyst of world affairs. States are
like billiard balls. The job of leaders is 'to judge, by experience and
intuition, the requisite amount of force necessary to move one or
another ball in a preferred direction'.[45] Power is all, and balances of
power the only way to make order out of chaos. The realist tradition

has responded to recent challenge by developing a perspective of 'structural realism', described by one of its exponents, Stephen Krasner, as 'a world of tectonic plates and intermittent earthquakes rather than billiard balls and frequent collisions'.[46]

In their 1977 study *Power and Interdependence*, Keohane and Nye challenged the basic assumptions of realism: its views about the centrality of the nation-state, the use of force and issues of security. They presented a world of complex interdependence, with states maintaining contacts at various levels and in various dimensions.[47] The interdependence paradigm sees inter-state relations as disaggregated, international co-operation as feasible and actual, and the 'national interest' of realist theory as illusory. The line between domestic and foreign issues blurs, with 'intermestic' concerns (such as the price of oil) becoming central. The rise of integrated world markets for capital constitutes another dimension of contemporary interdependence. In the world of the 'soft-shell state',[48] non-state actors – from multinational corporations to the international Red Cross, from the United Nations to international crime cartels – are seen as of increased importance.[49] Most interdependence theorists would still retain some concept of the state as a unit of analysis, although not all.[50] Almost a competing paradigm, rather than an outgrowth of interdependency, is the 'international political economy' approach. It is, perhaps, better regarded as a field of study, however, rather than a competing paradigm or as an aspect of interdependency. As such, it has 'realist' (notably Robert Gilpin), 'interdependency' and 'structuralist' exponents.[51]

Security-oriented realism fits most easily with policies and politics on the right of the political spectrum. Its East-West orientation is replaced by a more genuinely internationalist (including North-South) perspective in interdependence theory. The centre and left of the American political spectrum have an affinity with this perspective; although it should be remembered that economic, free market liberals, taking the individual rather than the state as their basic unit of analysis, have also been attracted to it.[52] Structuralism, while there are realist and interdependency variants on the concept, tends to be articulated within the Marxist tradition – or, more properly, given the unorthodoxy of many of these thinkers, the Marxian tradition. International relations are discussed in terms of the relations between the core and periphery of the international capitalist system. Here, the units of analysis are neither nation-states nor the disaggregated agents of interdependency. Rather, the basic analytical unit is the capitalist world system itself. The Marxian structuralist approach is concerned with the spatial and structural characteristics of capitalist accumulation on a world scale. Wallerstein's world systems theory and the (originally, Latin American-oriented) 'dependency' school are its best known facets.[53]

(b) *Indicators of decline* Of these three approaches, realism is clearly most concerned with fluctuations in the power of particular nation-states. Within these terms, and according to conventional indicators, there is no question about the decline of American power, especially compared with the period 1945–65. On 21 August 1989, the Tokyo-based Economic Planning Agency announced that the US was no longer the world's richest country. Japanese assets had risen from 28.3 trillion dollars in 1986 to 43.7 trillion in 1987; American assets had increased from 34 to 36.2 trillion over the same period.[54] In 1985, the United States became a debtor nation, rapidly assuming the status of the world's largest. Gore Vidal composed an address, 'The day the American empire ran out of gas', and announced the death of imperial America.[55] The October 1987 crash on Wall Street appeared to indicate that dominance had given way to interdependence, and that bad times for all were just around the corner. Alongside the apparent facts of decline, and probably equally important, was the perception of decline. The editor of *Foreign Policy* bemoaned in 1989:

In 1960 the United States was responsible for nearly one-half of the gross national product of the world's market economies. Today it is responsible for only about one-third. For a period after World War II the United States enjoyed a nuclear monopoly. Today the USSR enjoys a position of nuclear parity with the United States; U.S. influence in the Western Hemisphere – so enormous in the 1950's that Washington could overthrow a left-leaning Guatamalan government with a minimal covert effort – had so diminished by the late 1980's that the Reagan administration was unable to force out of office a minor-league dictator in Panama.

The editor, C. W. Maynes, traced the roots of decline to the Nixon Presidency: the period of final surrender of nuclear superiority, loss of control of the world's energy industry, and abandonment of the Bretton Woods system of fixed exchanges based on the dollar standard.[56] In this perspective, it appears that American foreign policy since the Vietnam war has been little more than a series of doomed attempts to restore declining world leadership.[57]

By the mid-1970s, some British observers were referring to the end of the relatively brief span of America's imperial age.[58] The implication was that the short American century was over and that the United States would have to turn its attention to finding ways of managing its decline, just as had Great Britain. The USA had acted as guarantor of the post-1945 world settlement. Under its protection, and indeed partly as a result of the success of American reconstruction policies, new challengers emerged to threaten the international order.[59] In the teeth of these changes, the United States is frequently accused of retaining stubbornly the attitudes of a hegemonic leader and a creditor nation. The assumption is that, both for its own and the globe's sake, it needs to adjust.[60] The spectacle in the early 1980s of President Reagan stoking up US military strength with loans from Japan added weight to this line of argument. Part of David Calleo's thesis, in his widely-read *Beyond American Hegemony*, is that the gravest threat to international stability may be a great power that fails to adapt to changed circumstances.[61] The American public debate in the late 1980s resounded to Spenglerian and Toynbeean themes of imperial overextension and the rise and fall of great empires.[62]

(c) *Military decline?* Alongside, and intertwined with, the perception of economic decline is the theme of military-strategic decline. The United States is seen to have lost both its former nuclear superiority *vis-à-vis* the Soviet Union, and its ability to sustain its current military commitments. Calleo argues that, in post-hegemonic conditions, the US has no option but to step back from the NATO (North Atlantic Treaty Organisation) alliance, and to devolve its security responsibilities. The relaxation of East-West tension in the late 1980s may also be seen as offering new opportunities not only for international stability, but for relatively painless US adjustment to a multipolar world.[63]

A number of observations may be made about this thesis of military-strategic decline. Firstly, there is no doubt that, by the late 1960s, the era of unquestioned US nuclear superiority was over. By 1967 (at the very latest), the doctrine of assured destruction for a Soviet Union indulging in a nuclear strike had to be modified into one of *mutual* assured destruction (MAD). By late 1969, the USSR had achieved a marginal quantitative lead in intercontinental ballistic missiles.[64] As Henry Kissinger later noted,[65] the recognition of nuclear parity necessitated a radical shift in American assumptions.

Secondly, there is the question of the relationship between parity, overkill and technological development. At one level, nuclear parity might be thought to be inherently stable, at least in terms of super-power relations. As Admiral Arleigh Burke remarked in 1960: 'You very seldom see a cowboy, even in the movies, wearing three guns. Two is enough.'[66] Why should any nation seek a 'useless' superiority? As long as the United States retains the capacity to destroy the planet, how can there by any possibility of 'decline?' In fact, the achievement of parity has not operated to rule out the push for superiority. The desire to accumulate bargaining chips, or to encourage the opposing power to undertake economically damaging matching spending pro-grammes, may operate against the supposed stability of strategic deterrence.[67] There is also the compelling bureaucratic logic of 'modernisation'. Official US policy seeks to compensate for America's 'quantitative disadvantage' in military power by maintaining 'the lead in critical military technologies'.[68] The prospect of 'winnable' nuclear war, engendered by technological development and more accurate weapons, has not been abandoned. It was implicit in the 'counterforce' ('controlled use') doctrine propounded by the Carter Administration in 1980. It was central to the nuclear strategy of the Reagan Administration in the early 1980s, and made explicit in the arguments of 'nuclear utilisation theorists' (the famous NUTs *v.* MADs debate).[69] Michael Sheehan pointed out in 1988 that, in a sense, strategic deterrence and arms control were not mutually rein-forcing, but tended to pull apart:

To date neither superpower has fully accepted the major constraints implied in deterrence theory: that is, that neither should pursue wholly effective defences or a disarming first-strike capability. At the same time the alleged requirements for effective deterrence have been steadily refined, driven by the belief that if a threat is conceivable it must be assumed to exist and be catered for.[70]

This, however, leads on to our third point: while parity and stra-tegic deterrence theory do not necessarily cancel the drive towards superiority, there is no real question of the Soviets having achieved either 'superiority' or even 'equivalence'. The history of attempts to break out of the condition of strategic parity has, to date, been a history of expensive futility.[71] Ultimately, Arleigh Burke's point about overkill *is* correct, however seductive the promises of absolute security or winnable nuclear wars. The notion that the Soviet Union had achieved the ability in the late 1970s to undertake a successful first-strike was proclaimed loudly by the Committee on the Present Danger, and became an important issue in the domestic politics of the period. It was always, however, highly questionable, with anything like a completely disarming attack on US strategic missiles being virtually unimaginable.[72] It should also be remembered that many of America's nuclear dilemmas derive not from the desire to defend the continental United States, but from the concept of 'extended deterrence': the American nuclear guarantee to Europe.[73] In the last resort, as Admiral W. Crowe noted in 1984, narrowly balanced military capabilities are not easily subject to exact arithmetic: 'We're not General Motors; we don't have a profit and loss column every month. The only way we can tell whether we're doing a good job is to go to war and see if you win or lose'.[74]

Any idea of Soviet military 'superiority', at least in any overarching form, has never made much sense; nor, indeed, has the idea of a more general US – Soviet 'equivalence'. As many observers of the Gorbachev reforms have argued, defence spending in the USSR is not sustained by anything comparable to the American economic base. In 1983, the US spent 6½ per cent of its gross national product on defence; the Soviet Union spent 11½ per cent. This means that simply to keep in step with the US, the Soviet Union has to take nearly twice as many steps. More than America, Soviet superpower status rests on its military base. In a sense, as Z. K. Brzezinski described it in 1983, the USSR is a 'one-dimensional world power'.[75]

The final two observations about American military-strategic decline may be disposed of more briefly. Calleo probably is correct to argue the logic of an American pullback from current commitments. However, the case that the US simply cannot sustain such commitments is, at least from a narrow economic viewpoint, not proven.[76] Maintaining commitments might require difficult choices, such as tax increases, and might (as Calleo suggests) foster instability. Yet it is difficult to argue that, in the last resort, it could not be done. Lastly, it should be noted that the perception of military decline rests perhaps not so much on East-West relations as on the succession of American humiliations in the Third World: Vietnam, Angola, Iran, the Lebanon, even Nicaragua. The Colombian drug cartel may be the latest force to contribute to America's image as a crippled giant.[77]

(d) *Enduring hegemony?* The spectacular growth of the international arms trade has exacerbated many of the United States's problems in the Third World. Nuclear proliferation and the diffusion of conventional arms are indicative of the complex multipolarity of the 1970s and 1980s.[78] Yet the growth of complex international interdependence should not be entirely seen as a facet of, and contributor to, American decline. It tends rather to make the phenomenon of decline itself appear complex, problematic and patchy. The abandonment of the Bretton Woods fixed exchange system thus led to a more complex exercise of American power, rather than any radical decline.[79] Part of the problem here, according to Susan Strange, relates to the narrow territoriality of the indications of supposed decline. What really matters is the share of world output 'under the direction of U.S. companies'. Strange points to the strength of companies like IBM, Genentech and Cray Research, all producing extensively outside the US, as examples of the new 'nonterritorial empire'.[80] The United States has crucial resources in, and control over, four major global power structures: military security, production, finance, and information.[81] The US may now be more vulnerable to global economic crises; yet it is, arguably, still able to set the organisational framework for international trade and business, and to alter the international division of labour.[82] Realist versions of the thesis of decline have a tendency towards rather uncritical reliance upon inappropriate analogies with other great powers in decline, notably Great Britain.[83] They also tend, as Stephen Gill argues, to ignore: 'the quantitative and qualitative aspects of America's unique structural-dominance: the sheer size and weight of the U.S. within the international system substantially affects the psychological, cultural, economic and political conditions under which others must operate, not just their policy responses'.[84] 'Hegemony' thus has cultural, as well as security and economic dimensions.[85]

Of course, the whole idea of 'decline' rests on how exactly 'the United States' is to be defined. Critics of the realist-oriented literature of decline have tended to retain the nation-state as a unit of analysis, but in a 'soft shell' sense: the United States as an empire sprawling out beyond its territorial boundaries a still dominant cultural and structural force. A radical interdependency viewpoint might go farther, eliminating the entity, 'the United States', from discussion altogether. Similarly, within the Marxian structuralist perspective, realist accounts of the decline of great powers seem, at best, valid only at one level: at worst, ideological (in the Marxist sense) and misleading. For example, in his 1984 piece, 'The political economy of late-imperial

America', Mike Davis agrees that the US is in decline by conventional measures. He also describes the shifts in the US economy towards the Pacific, towards service industries, away from 'Fordist' mass production patterns. Such changes clearly have been accompanied by the 'relative shrinkage of the domestically generated US share of the world industrial production' and by trade deficits. But it is not clear that apparent economic decline is more significant than the gradual equalisation of production and consumption in the 'three heartlands of advanced capitalism' (the US, Japan and Western Europe). Indices of 'decline', such as the trade deficit are not incompatible with continued US dominance over 'the general conditions for capitalism'. (These would include 'its strategic nuclear arsenals, price of money capital, supplies of oil and wheat, generation of new technology, and so on'). American hegemony involves not primarily the ascendancy of one nation-state; rather it is 'a historically specific form of adequation between the capitalist state system and the world economy'.[86] In Davis's view, therefore, US 'decline' represents, above all, a re-structuring of the core of world capitalism.

(e) *Hegemonic stability* Many liberal political economists have approached the question of American decline from the perspective of hegemonic stability theory. According to this, stability and success within the international capitalist system are related to, even functions of, hegemonic leadership. A stable system requires a hegemon to absorb exports and to provide a currency for international transactions: 'for the world economy to be stabilised, there has to be a stabiliser, one stabiliser'.[87] Keohane sees hegemony as deriving from control over raw materials, capital and markets, combined with a competitive advantage in the production of valued goods.[88] Hegemony, however, tends to be inherently unstable, even self-destructive. The strains of acting as the system's guarantor rebound upon the hegemon's domestic economy. Its capital exports, though temporarily stabilising, ultimately allow 'free riding' small states to become competitors. US decline has been frequently examined in these terms. Various ways of mitigating the effects of American hegemonic decline have been suggested. A new Japanese-American hegemonic alliance is one such possibility (the idea that the US would become primarily a Pacific power was a common subject of speculation in the late 1980s).[89] Keohane regards it as possible that international regimes may, in a spirit of enlightened self-interest, take on the work of the hegemon.[90] Gilpin sees increased protectionism as virtually inevitable, but with elements of an open 'multinational' international political economy surviving.[91] Ultimately, however, hegemonic stability theorists are faced with the worst-case possibility: atomised protectionism, trade (and actual) wars, an anarchic disorder which harms all.

Returning to our three paradigms of international relations theory, it can be seen that hegemonic stability theory sits most comfortably astride certain realist and interdependency positions. The realist would stress the security dimension of hegemony, and the self-interest of the hegemon. The hegemon alone has the capacity 'to entice or compel others to accept an open trading structure'.[92] The interdependency-oriented hegemonic stability theorist would emphasise the universal benefits, 'collective goods', aspect of hegemony; and also argue that the hegemonic function need not necessarily be performed by a single nation-state. The realist version of hegemonic stability at least seeks to avoid the Panglossian view that a liberal world order is to everyone's ultimate benefit. Hegemonic stability theory has, in fact, been subjected to devastating criticism. It has been criticised as ahistorical, and as a kind of self-fulfilling prophecy which simply serves to disguise poor planning decisions by American leaders.[93] It tends to ignore the political and ideological (in the non-Marxist sense) dimensions of American foreign policy.[94] It rests uneasily with the actual pattern of American decline, which is patchy and subject to apparent reversals.[95] Hegemonic stability theory has been challenged not least from within the literature of public choice and 'collective goods' theory. It has been argued, for example, that hegemonic stability theory is wrong in assuming, under all conditions, a hegemonic preference for free trade.[96] The establishment of new patterns of relations between the hegemon and other nations ('asymmetrical interdependence') also may not automatically presage instability and a decline in hegemonic leaderships.[97] For the Marxist, hegemonic stability theory is simply the rationalisation of exploiter interest. From a developing nation viewpoint, also, the theory fails to impress, at least outside the newly industrialising countries of South East Asia. The idea of a benevolent, liberal, hegemonic world order, in which free trade brings advantages to all, must appear laughable in the 'underdeveloped' Third World. Above all, even in its more realist incarnations, hegemonic stability theory has a tendency towards ferocious ethnocentrism, assuming that 'other nations merely play a passive or disruptive role in the international system, exploiting the benevolence of the US'.[98]

(f) *Summary* It may be useful briefly to summarise the conclusions of this section. The United States today stands in a very different relationship to the rest of the world than it did in the period 1945–65. Its foreign policy needs to recognise, and also, in a sense to 'manage' this decline from the hegemony of that period. Any policy which fails to incorporate an awareness of the limits to American power and the interdependence of the world economy is misconceived. However, the thesis of decline has been over-dramatised, especially in the US public debate of the late 1980s. In the military sphere, the United States is the world's foremost power, albeit one with an interest in negotiating a reduction in commitments. In economic matters, much depends upon the extent to which multinational corporations may be treated as a facet of American power. Nonetheless, there is no question that American-based corporations have maintained, albeit amongst fierce competition, their ability to generate technological innovation.[99] As leader of the liberal economic world order, the US has had, and will have, to come to terms with the rise of Japan and other economic power blocs. Yet, if we define 'hegemony' in qualitative as well as quantitative terms, American hegemony, though receding, may still be said to exist.

3 Interpreting American foreign policy: national mission, realism, revisionism and theories of American imperialism

(a) *National mission* Invocation of the concept of 'national character' immediately invites charges of romanticism and reification. Christopher Hill (the British historian of the seventeenth century) declared in his 1989 Conway memorial lecture: 'To resort to national character as an explanation means that you have no explanation: national character changes with history.'[100]

The centrality of ideas of national mission and exceptionalism, however, to the dominant liberal foreign policy ideology has already been noted. The modern debate about 'Americanism and the national character' cannot easily be separated from the politics of Cold War consensus. Nonetheless, 'Americanism' would include, for example, an optimism about human behaviour and a pragmatic belief in the solubility of the world's problems.[101] It also appears to embody a notion of deliverance from evil: the idea that justice and liberty may be achieved if only the correct dragon is slain.[102] Such attitudes have had an effect on US foreign policy, as has the American public ethos of commitment to capitalism and democracy.[103] Such cultural forces are not reducible to economic interest and form an important part of liberal ideology. (Indeed, as Krasner argues, very powerful nations share with very weak ones the luxury of being able to pursue 'ideological', non-economic goals.)[104]

Most defenders of American foreign policy tend to see it as driven by an 'enlightened selfishness'.[105] Few are prepared to go along with Samuel Flagg Bemis's famous address, *American Foreign Policy and the Blessings of Liberty*.[106] (For Bemis, US foreign policy – at least until the 1890s – embodied a sure-footed and consistent benevolence.) Nonetheless, both Bemis and other, more circumspect, defenders of the tradition stand in the shadow of Thomas Jefferson, who argued for the identity of 'interests' and 'morality'.[107]

For many American policy-makers, of course, the Cold War represented a precise embodiment of the identity of 'interests' and 'morality': capitalism and the spreading of liberty. Problems arise, of course, when the two appear no longer to be mutually supportive. At one level, there is the perennial problem of selectivity.[108] On what grounds may a foreign policy predicated upon the identity of 'interests' and 'morality' stand back from the whole-hearted promotion of liberty? From this dilemma arises an ultimately unsustainable commitment to universality and globalism. At another level, there is the problem of the identity between 'interests' and 'morality' itself. During the Vietnam war, a host of critics, including George Kennan, Walter Lippmann, Senator Fulbright and various military experts, argued that the balance between 'interests' and 'ideals' had become distorted. National interests (including domestic peace) were being sacrificed to 'morality'.[109]

(b) *Realism* Norman Graebner later offered the following realist analysis of a foreign policy based on a national mission to disseminate liberty: 'The United States would use force, more indeed than any country in history, but always in pursuit of a peaceful international order in which force would have no role.'[110] The American realist tradition, as exemplified in Reinhold Niebuhr's writings, takes issue with Thomas Jefferson's view that there is an identity of 'interests' and 'morality', and that individual and collective 'morality' are essentially the same.[111] Nations must protect their integrity and their interests, and will do whatever is necessary so to do. This view was made explicit in National Security Council document 68 of 1950 (NSC-68, largely composed by Paul Nitze). According to NSC-68:

> Our free society, confronted by a threat to its basic values, naturally will take such action, including the use of military force, as may be required to protect those values. The integrity of our system will not be jeopardized by any measures, covert or overt, violent or non-violent, which serve the purposes of frustrating the Kremlin design.[112]

American realism always has the tendency to be overtaken and absorbed by moralistic, messianic liberal internationalism. This is apparent in the text of NSC-68, which combines a tough-minded realism with a denunciation of 'evil men' in Moscow. George Kennan, the author of the 1946 'long telegram' and 1947 'X' article in *Foreign Affairs*, considered Stalin to be deranged, but nonetheless traced the roots of Soviet aggression to Russia's expansionist, geopolitically driven traditions. Again, however, Kennan's realism, with its implicit acceptance of 'spheres of influence', became the servant of a universalist, moralistic theory of containment.[113]

Geopolitics may be regarded as the hard edge of realism. Henry Kissinger has consistently used a geopolitical vocabulary to advocate American adoption of a consistent 'continental', rather than an 'island', foreign policy orientation.[114] As a foreign policy-maker, Kissinger was concerned to erect regional balances of power in a kind of 'discriminate globalism'.[115] Geopolitical imperatives for the United States are generally held to include containing Soviet expansion, maintaining access to raw materials (notably oil in the area of the Persian Gulf) and safeguarding US naval superiority in the Atlantic, Pacific and Indian Oceans.[116]

Some of the difficulties with geopolitics become apparent if one considers a contemporary geopolitical text like C. S. Gray's *The Geopolitics of Superpower*.[117] It simply fails to convince as a work of disinterested science, transcending moralism. Following Halford Mackinder, Gray argues that the Soviet Union has to be prevented from dominating the resources of the European-Asian landmass (the 'world island'). The US must mobilise the 'rimlands' to offset Soviet control of the 'heartland'. The book succeeds in being both grandiloquently trivial and hair-raising. Its explanatory structure is also static and ahistorical. Almost by definition, for example, the geopolitician can have little of interest to say about the process of liberalisation in Eastern Europe.

(c) *Revisionism and theories of imperialism*   Historians who focus on 'national mission' would see the motor force of American foreign policy as the desire to spread liberty. Geopolitical realists would interpret it in terms of protecting interests and filling power vacuums. A third school would urge the explanatory claims of imperialism and the wish (or need) to secure overseas outlets for 'surplus' American production. In the context of most major foreign policy debates, this perspective would be labelled 'revisionist'. It should be noted, however, that 'revisionism' refers simply to a challenging of received orthodoxy and has no essential left or Marxian inclination. In the case of the Vietnam war, for example, 'revisionism' refers to the work of those like Richard Nixon who challenge the view that the war was immoral and unjustifiable.[118]

'Revisionist' *versus* 'orthodox' debates have been waged over, for example, interpretations of the Spanish-American war (1898) and of US entry into the two world wars. The dispute over the origins of the Cold War (*c.*1945–48), however, has become one of the great set-pieces of modern historiography. 'Orthodox' histories tended to portray Soviet behaviour as aggressive and expansionist and to stress the idealistic, indeed philanthropic, orientation of US policy. 'Revisionists' described a Soviet foreign policy which was essentially defensive, with American policy-makers concerned to promote a new economic and political hegemony. It was argued that leading American figures looked above all to the securing of open markets for US exports, thus avoiding any possibility of the post-war domestic economy sliding back into depression. Contemporary accounts of these matters draw on archival sources unavailable to protagonists of this earlier debate. So-called 'post-revisionists' see American policy-makers as reacting to Soviet provocation and as being 'invited in' by Western European governments fearful of Russian aggression. They allow that the United States may in the process have constructed its own empire, but portray it as essentially a defensive one. On the other hand, 'neo-revisionists' have revived earlier criticisms of the 'ortho-dox' position. They point, for example, to intelligence reports within the Truman Administration which portrayed Soviet ambitions as confined largely to Eastern Europe.[119]

The inspiration for much modern revisionism and for many New

Left historians of US foreign policy is the work of W.A. Williams. For
Williams, the 'essence of American foreign relations' was 'the evolution of one fragile settlement' planted on the 'perimeter of a vast and
unexplored continent into a global Empire'.[120] The search for
markets abroad, especially after the closing of the frontier, through
Open Door policies was the engine of expansion. Williams combined
a commitment to the primacy of economics, a radical American
populism and an account of expansion derived from the frontier thesis
of F.J. Turner. Such eclecticism left Williams open to charges of
ambiguity and theoretical naivety. It is not entirely clear, for example,
whether Williams saw the history of American foreign relations as
driven unavoidably, deterministically, by the search for markets; or,
whether Williams was calling upon US leaders to change course.[121]
Was American idealistic liberalism itself an empty expression of
economic interest? Or had it simply become perverted by greedy
capitalists and was thus capable of being redeemed from them?

Williams was no crude conspiracy theorist. Yet he did not resolve
the problem of reconciling a commitment to the primacy of
economics with a belief in the independent force of ideas: the problem
formulated by Marxist structuralists in terms of 'relative autonomy'.
One way out of Williams's dilemma, of course, was to write more
orthodox Marxist history, with a commitment to revolutionism over
reformism. The work of Gabriel Kolko indicates that such an
approach need not automatically lead to arid reductionism.[122]
(Another alternative was the unabashed radical populism of Noam
Chomsky.) [123] What Williams and his New Left followers did do,
however, was to reinvigorate diplomatic history by turning it once
again away from a paralysing concentration upon 'high politics'.
Reviving the approach of writers like Charles Tansill and Charles
Beard, a generation of New Left historians 'muckraked' the history of
American foreign relations, indicating the persistence – often very
near the surface – of the economic motive.[124] This approach is always
open to accusations of narrow determinism, disingenuousness, con-
spiratorialism and a blindness to the political (diplomatic) dimension.[125] Such charges, however, injure only the weaker examples.

Among contemporary historians, Williams's influence is felt in the
work of the 'corporatist' school. Within this perspective, government
and business elites are seen as combining (non-conspiratorially) to set
a predictable, ordered pattern of foreign relations conducive to profit.
Such collaboration is rooted in liberal notions of a 'middle way'

between unfettered business and socialistic solutions. Herbert Hoover's idea of the 'associative state' and President Eisenhower's attraction towards the 'corporate commonwealth' are examples of this 'middle way'.[126] The corporatist school has been criticised for failing adequately to define the central concept of 'corporatism', and also for being more successful in treating periods of foreign policy consensus than in accounting for consensus breakdown.[127] Nonetheless, this approach does represent a coherent attempt to transcend the 'economics' *versus* 'politics' debate, while retaining the critical thrust of the 'old' New Left histories.[128] The concept of 'political economy' is useful for students of diplomatic history, as it is for students of contemporary international relations.

For W. A. Williams, the Open Door *was* imperialism. This view echoes the older historical debate over the putative imperialism of free trade.[129] Clearly, the desire to protect markets may encompass political and military action which give rise to a more easily recognisable form of imperialism. However, to regard a free trade relationship *per se* as imperialistic does raise difficulties. What seems to be required is a quantitative demonstration that the terms of trade are structured so as to replicate and reinforce inequality. (In the Marxist tradition, the work of Arghiri Emmanuel on 'unequal exchange' attempts to provide such a demonstration.)[130]

The term 'imperialism' is a slippery one, with strong polemical and emotional accretions. K. N. Waltz has correctly ridiculed the use of the term to describe virtually any relationship between unequal partners.[131] Certainly, in the legal-formal sense, the United States is an imperial power only to a very limited degree. Since the Philippines became independent in 1946, the US may be said to have maintained a quasi-imperial relationship (in the legal-formal sense) with Puerto Rico, Guam, the Panama Canal Zone, American Samoa, the Virgin Islands and parts of the Territory of the Pacific Islands.[132] The United States was born from colonial rebellion. It has strong anti-imperialist, as well as imperialist traditions. Walt Whitman celebrated and predicted 'The New Empire' in 1860: 'I chart the new empire, grander than any before.' In 1899, Henry Blake Fuller, anti-imperialist and supporter of William Jennings Bryan, replied:

G is for Guns
That McKinley has sent,
To teach Filipinos
What Jesus Christ meant.[133]

However, to restrict the use of the word 'imperialism' to its legal-formal sense is overly fastidious. American determination to prevent unwanted (leftist) political change in Latin America, and indeed much more generally in connection with postwar containment policies, at least approaches the status of imperialism.[134] To extend the term beyond its legal-formal dimension is not frivolous. It raises fearsomely tricky questions about the relationship between power, influence and control. Yet it does try to take seriously the conventional definition of 'imperialism' as a condition where key decisions are made by 'persons, processes and institutions foreign to the colony'.[135] As was implicit in the discussion in the preceding section, 'hegemony' is generally a more satisfactory term than 'imperialism'. From a Third World perspective, however, the two do not seem very different. Imperialism, like hegemony, is seen, for example, to have a cultural dimension. Gill and Law point out that Latin American radicals have depicted Mickey Mouse as an instrument of American imperialism: a symbol of the individualistic North American way, as well as a trademark of the powerful, transnational Disney corporation.[136] (One presumes that a similar point was intended in the closing sequences of Stanley Kubrick's Vietnam war film, *Full Metal Jacket*.)

Some realist (or 'neo-mercantilist') theories of American power would endorse the notion of economic power as an engine of imperialism. (See the discussion in Chapter 8, section one.) However, it is to Marxism that we look for the most developed theories of economic imperialism. An indicated above, the national origins of imperial economic power are here of diminished importance. Early twentieth century Marxist thought was concerned with the phenomenon of inter-capitalist warfare. Lenin regarded such wars as the inevitable outcome of imperialism: an interpretation challenged by Karl Kautsky in his notion of 'ultra-imperialism' or capitalist collaboration. (The Lenin-Kautsky debate finds echoes in contemporary ideas about the future of US – Japanese relations). However, the focus of Marxist thought is on the structure of capital itself, certainly in its historically specific forms, but not primarily as linked to the power of a particular nation-state. (So, the question raised earlier, and to be taken up in Chapter 8, of the degree to which multinational corporations operate as facets of 'American' power, also becomes secondary.) For Lenin imperial expansion was driven by the need to export capital and to ameliorate problems of domestic overproduction-underconsumption. Imperialism would stimulate industrialisation in the colonies, eventually giving rise to revolutionary proletariats.[137]

The stubborn underdevelopment of colonial areas led to a questioning of Lenin's assumptions. The Communist International after 1928 came to see progress as blocked by colonial ties which tended to perpetuate pre-capitalist, feudal or 'Asiatic' economic forms in the colonies. By the 1960s, various Marxisant writers (primarily Latin American 'dependency' theorists and the North American *Monthly Review* group) were arguing that capitalist integration itself was the problem. 'Underdevelopment' was not a backward condition preceding capitalism, but a specific instance of capitalism in areas which had been 'capitalist' for centuries. A.G. Frank argued that capital found its way from the periphery to the core of the international capitalist system, not – as in Lenin's formulation – the other way around. Others, notably Harry Magdoff, inclined to describe such periphery-core relations as characteristic of only the most recent, 'monopoly' stage of world capitalist development.[138]

Recent Marxist writing on imperialism has tended to incorporate either a refinement or a critique of the 'dependency' perspective. It has been concerned with the dynamics of capitalist accumulation on a world scale, with a greater prioritisation of class analysis than was found, for example, in the earlier work of Frank. Painting with an extremely broad brush, dependency theory offered little in the way of policy advice for developing areas. Liberal critics like Robert Gilpin have been quick to point to the experience of the newly industrialising nations of South Asia as destructive of the 'dependency' view.[139]

The anti-Leninist, 'development of underdevelopment' approach now appears (like its characterisation of Third World development) something of a dead end. The same is not true, however, of the entire Marxian structuralist view of international relations. Realist perspectives have been undermined by the rise of interdependence. The interdependency paradigm itself, especially in its 'international political economy' mode, is extremely valuable; yet it does have a tendency to become absorbed into rather uncritical notions of benevolent liberal world order. The Marxian tradition assaults such assumptions and reminds us of the links between interdependency and inequality.

Notes

1 T. A. Bailey, *A Diplomatic History of the American People*, New York, 1945, pp. 806–7.
2 A. M. Schlesinger, *The Cycles of American History*, London, 1987, p. 67. See also C. V. Crabb, *American Diplomacy and the Pragmatic Tradition*, Baton Rouge, 1988.
3 See G. Duncan, 'Understanding ideology', *Political Studies*, 35, 1987, pp. 649–59, p. 649.
4 *Ibid.*, p. 650.
5 M. Howard, 'Ideology and international relations', *Review of International Studies*, 15, 1989, pp. 1–10, p. 1.
6 L. Hartz, *The Liberal Tradition in America*, New York, 1955. See also J. A. Hall, *Liberalism*, London, 1987, pp. 166–7; D. McLellan, *Ideology*, Milton Keynes, 1986, ch. 5.
7 See *Two Treatises on Government*, ed. P. Laslett, Cambridge, 1960; J. Dunn, *Western Political Theory in the Face of the Future*, Cambridge, 1979, ch. 2.
8 See E. Weisband, *The Ideology of American Foreign Policy*, Beverly Hills, 1973. On the links between liberalism and capitalism, see A. Arblaster, *The Rise and Decline of Western Liberalism*, Oxford, 1984. See also R. Masters, 'The Lockeian tradition in American foreign policy', *Journal of International Affairs*, 21, 1967, pp. 253–77; H.M. Roelofs, *Ideology and Myth in American Politics*, Boston, 1976; K. Krankau, 'American foreign relations: a national style?' *Diplomatic History*, 8, 1984, pp. 253–272; A.K. Henrikson, 'Ordering the world', *Reviews in American History*, 12, 1984, pp. 606–611.
9 C. E. Adams, ed., *The Works of John Adams*, 8, Boston, 1853, p. 178.
10 See D. Green, *Shaping Political Consciousness*, Ithaca (New York), 1987, pp. 120, 135–138.
11 On the ambiguities of containment, see T.L. Deibel and J.L. Gaddis, eds., *Containing the Soviet Union*, London, 1981.
12 See R.E. Osgood, *Ideals and Self Interest in America's Foreign Relations*, Chicago, 1953; H. Jones, *The Course of American Diplomacy*, Chicago, 1988.
13 *International Affairs*, 64, 1987–88, p. 160.
14 New York, 1942, p. 18.
15 See R. Dallek, *The Style of American Foreign Policy*, New York, 1983, p. 258 (on President Nixon and Henry Kissinger); see also W. D. Anderson and S.J. Kernek, 'How "realistic" is Reagan's diplomacy?', *Political Science Quarterly*, 100, 1985, pp. 389–409.
16 See Anderson and Kernek, 'How "realistic" is Reagan's diplomacy?', p. 390.
17 B. Y. Pines, *How Conservative is Reagan's Foreign Policy?*, Washington D.C., 1983, pp. 2, 5, 7.
18 J. J. Kirkpatrick, *Legitimacy and Force*, I, New Brunswick (New Jersey), 1988, p. 26. See also L. J. Medcalf and K.M. Dolbeare, *Neopolitics*, New York, 1985, ch. 8.
19 E. Shewmaker, 'Daniel Webster and American conservatism', in N.A. Graebner, ed., *Traditions and Values: American Diplomacy, 1790–1945*,

Lanham (Maryland), 1985, pp. 129–52, p. 134.

20   N. A. Graebner, ed., *Ideas and Diplomacy*, New York, 1964, p. 287.

21   S. F. Bemis, *A Diplomatic History of the United States*, New York, 1936, pp. 803–4.

22   See R. Radosh, *Prophets on the Right*, New York, 1975; *Congressional Record*, 1951, A4762.

23   Radosh; also O. R. Holsti, 'The study of international politics makes strange bedfellows', *American Political Science Review*, 68, 1974, pp. 217–42.

24   See J. T. Patterson, *Mr. Republican: A Biography of Robert A. Taft*, Boston, 1972, p. 489; G. Matthews, 'Robert A. Taft, the Constitution and American foreign policy', *Journal of Contemporary History*, 17, 1982, pp. 507–22; R. A. Taft, *A Foreign Policy for Americans*, New York, 1951.

25   Green, *Shaping Political Consciousness*, p. 175.

26   For an attempt to locate George Kennan in this tradition, see D. Mayers, *George Kennan and the Dilemmas of U.S. Foreign Policy*, New York, 1988. See also R. Crockatt, 'A New Burke', *The Times Higher Education Supplement*, 25 August 1989.

27   B. Goldwater, *Why Not Victory?*, New York, 1962; D. Reinhard, *The Republican Right since 1945*, Lexington (Kentucky), 1983, p. 215.

28   R. Steel, *Walter Lippmann and the American Century*, Boston, 1980, p. 586.

29   W. LaFeber, *The American Age*, New York, 1989, p. 34.

30   M. Hunt, *Ideology and U.S. Foreign Policy*, New Haven, 1987, p. 209.

31   New York, 1934.

32   Cited in J. Rourke, *Congress and the Presidency in Foreign Policy Making*, Boulder (Colorado), 1983, p. 148

33   C. Bowles, *Tomorrow without Fear*, New York, 1946. See also W. H. Chafe, *Unfinished Journey*, New York, 1986, p. 80.

34   For various interpretations, see C. Jonsson, 'The ideology of foreign policy', in C. W. Kegley and P. McGowan, eds., *Foreign Policy USA/USSR*, Beverly Hills, 1982, pp. 91–110; S. Adler, *The Isolationist Impulse*, New York, 1957; J. D. Doenicke, *Not to the Swift*, London, 1979; T. G. Paterson, *Meeting the Communist Threat*, New York, 1988, pp. 211–21.

35   See G. Smith, *Morality, Reason and Power*, New York, 1986, pp. 12–18; also S. Brown, *On the Front Burner: Issues in American Foreign Policy*, Boston, 1984, pp. 10–14.

36   LaFeber, *The American Age*, p. 254; T.J. McCormick, 'Drift or mastery? A corporatist synthesis for American diplomatic history', *Reviews in American History*, 10, 1982, pp. 318–30, pp. 326, 324.

37   See H. Sklar, ed., *Trilateralism*, Boston, 1980; J. Pearce, *Under the Eagle*, London, 1982, pp. 103–21.

38   Paterson, *Meeting the Communist Threat*, p. 110.

39   C. W. Kegley and E.R. Wittkopf, *American Foreign Policy: Pattern and Process*, 3rd ed., New York, 1987, p. 71.

40   Paterson, pp. 18–19; see also N. D. Markowitz, *The Rise and Fall of the People's Century*, New York, 1972.

41   See, e.g., E. McCarthy, *Up 'Til Now*, San Diego, 1987, pp. 212–13.

42   J. Witcover, *85 Days: The Last Campaign of Robert Kennedy*, New York,

1988, p. 49.

43 R. D. Hatch and F. E. Watkins, eds., *Reverend Jesse Jackson: Straight from the Heart*, Philadelphia, 1987, p. 225.

44 Hunt, pp. 194, 159, 193.

45 R. L. Rothstein, 'On the costs of realism', *Political Science Quarterly*, 87, 1972. pp. 346–62, p. 351. See also H. J. Morgenthau, *Politics among Nations*, New York, 1985; M. J. Smith, ed., *Realist Thought from Weber to Kissinger*, Baton Rouge (Louisiana), 1986.

46 Krasner, 'Regimes and the limits of realism', in S. Krasner, ed., *International Regimes*, Ithaca (New York), 1983, pp. 355–68, p. 367. See also K. N. Waltz, *Theory of International Politics*, London, 1979 and R. K. Ashley, 'The poverty of neorealism', in R. A. Keohane, ed., *Neorealism and its Critics*, New York, 1986, pp. 255–300. For a recent defence of realism, see A. James, 'The realism of Realism: the state and the study of international relations', *Review of International Studies*, 15, 1989, pp. 215–29.

47 R. O. Keohane and J. S. Nye, *Power and Interdependence*, Boston, 1977.

48 See G. Smith, 'A future for the nation-state?', in L. Tivey, ed., *The Nation-State*, Oxford, 1981, pp. 197–208, p. 201.

49 See H. K. Jacobson, *Networks of Interdependence*, New York, 1984.

50 See Y. H. Ferguson and R. Mansbach, *The State, Conceptual Chaos and the Future of International Relations Theory*, Boulder (Colorado), 1989.

51 See S. Gill and D. Law, *The Global Political Economy*, New York, 1988, pp. 14–15; also R. Tooze, 'I.P.E. – what is it?', in W. G. Olson, ed., *The Theory and Practice of International Relations*, 7th ed., Englewood Cliffs, 1987, pp. 29–35; R. Gilpin, *The Political Economy of International Relations*, Princeton, 1987; R.J.B. Jones, ed., *The Worlds of Political Economy*, London, 1988. See generally S. Smith, 'Paradigm dominance in international relations', in H. C. Dyer and L. Mangasarian, eds., *The Study of International Relations*, New York, 1989, pp. 3–27

52 See Gill and Law, ch. 4.

53 See I. Wallerstein, *The Modern World System*, I and II, New York, 1974 and 1980; I. Wallerstein, *The Politics of the World Economy*, Cambridge, 1984; I. Roxborough, *Theories of Underdevelopment*, London, 1979; A. G. Frank, *Capitalism and Underdevelopment in Latin America*, London, 1969; S. Amin et al., *Dynamics of Global Crisis*, London, 1982.

54 *Guardian*, 22 August 1989. See also M. Feldstein, 'Introduction', in Feldstein, ed., *The United States in the World Economy*, Chicago, 1985, pp. 1–8.

55 G. Vidal, *Armageddon? Essays, 1983–1987*, London, 1989, pp. 115–25.

56 C. W. Maynes, 'Coping with the '90s', *Foreign Policy*, 74, 1989, pp. 42–62, pp. 42–3.

57 See P. Williams, 'The limits of American power: from Nixon to Reagan', *International Affairs*, 63, 1987, pp. 575–87.

58 R. Jenkins, 'Britain's role in America's European commitment, 1945–1975', in D.K. Adams, ed., *Diplomacy, Detente and the Democracies*, Keele, 1976, pp. 18–30, p. 28.

59 See T. Geiger, *The Future of the International System*, London, 1988. See also W. Hanrieder, 'The short American century', *Western Political Quarterly*, 37, 1984, pp. 140–73.

60 See C. Bergsten, 'Economic imbalances and world politics', *Foreign Affairs*, 65, 1987, pp. 770–94; also R. Vernon and D. L. Spar, *Beyond Globalism: Remaking American Foreign Economic Policy*, New York, 1988.

61 D. Calleo, *Beyond American Hegemony*, Brighton, 1987 (e.g. p. 11).

62 P. Kennedy, *The Rise and Fall of the Great Powers*, London, 1988; also S.E. Finer, 'The burden of Tyre', *Government and Opposition*, 23, 1988, pp. 487–95. See also G. Modelski, *Exploring Long Cycles*, Boulder (Colorado), 1987; J. W. Fulbright, *The Price of Empire*, London, 1989.

63 For a discussion of opportunities opened by the new Soviet direction, see G. Flynn, 'Problems in paradigm', *Foreign Policy*, 74, 1989, pp. 63–84.

64 See R. E. Powaski, *March to Armageddon*, New York, 1987, pp. 114. (The US retained clear superiority in delivering systems and warheads.)

65 H. Kissinger, *Years of Upheaval*, London, 1982, p. 258.

66 D. A. Rosenberg, 'The origins of overkill: nuclear weapons and American strategy', in N. A. Graebner, ed., *The National Security*, New York, 1986, pp. 123–95, p. 178.

67 See F. Halliday, *The Making of the Second Cold War*, London, 1983, pp. 48–54.

68 The Joint Staff, *United States Military Posture for FY 1989*, 1988, p. 14.

69 See Kegley and Wittkopf, *American Foreign Policy*, pp. 89–95.

70 M. J. Sheehan, *Arms Control: Theory and Practice*, Oxford, 1988, pp. 153–4.

71 See S. Bialer, 'Lessons of history: Soviet-American relations in the postwar era', in A. L. Hoselick, ed., *U.S.–Soviet Relations: The Next Phase*, New York, 1986, pp. 86–110, p. 95.

72 See Halliday, *The Making of the Second Cold War*, pp. 70–5. Also C. G. Jacobson, 'International Dynamics', in Jacobson, ed., *The Uncertain Course*, Oxford, 1987, pp. 3–18, at p. 7.

73 See L. Freedman, *The Evolution of Nuclear Strategy*, 2nd ed., London, 1989, p. 424; also P. Bobbitt, *Democracy and Deterrence*, London, 1988.

74 P. Hayes *et al.*, *American Lake: Nuclear Peril in the Pacific*, Harmondsworth, 1987 (back cover)

75 Cited in K. W. Ryavec, *United States – Soviet Relations*, New York, 1989, p. 77. See also R. L. Sivard, *World Military and Social Expenditures*, 1986, Washington D.C., 1986, p. 33.

76 See A. L. Friedberg, 'The political economy of American strategy', *World Politics*, 41, 1989, pp. 381–406; also D. Calleo *et al.*, 'The dollar and the defence of the West', *Foreign Affairs*, 66, 1988, pp. 845–80.

77 See J. W. Fulbright, *The Crippled Giant*, New York, 1972. See also, e.g., K. L. Teslik, *America's Ordeal in the Lebanon*, London, 1988; N. C. Livingstone and T. E. Arnold, eds., *Beyond the Iran-Contra Crisis*, Lexington (Massachusetts), 1988.

78 See Gill and Law, *The Global Political Economy*, p. 114; also M. Kaldor, *The Baroque Arsenal*, Harmondsworth, 1981. For an analysis of U. S. decline articulated within an 'interdependency' perspective, see J. S. Nye, 'The multinational corporation in the 1980's', in C. P. Kindleberger and D. B. Audretsch, eds., *The Multinational Corporation in the 1980's*, Cambridge (Massachusetts), 1983, pp. 1–17.

79   See J. A. Hall and G. J. Ikenberry, *The State*, Milton Keynes, 1989, p. 85; J. Gowa, *Closing the Gold Window*, Ithaca (New York), 1983.

80   S. Strange, 'The future of the American empire', *Journal of International Affairs*, 42, 1988, pp. 1–18, pp. 5–6.

81   S. Strange, *States and Markets*, London, 1988.

82   See H. M. Birkenbach *et al.*, 'Transatlantic crisis', in M. Kaldor and R. Falk, eds., *Dealignment: A New Foreign Policy Perspective*, Oxford, 1987, pp. 113–42, p. 118.

83   See, e.g., Strange, 'The future of the American empire', p. 7. For other criticisms of the thesis of decline, see B. Russett, 'The mysterious case of vanishing hegemony', *International Organization*, 39, 1985, pp. 207–31; and S. Strange, 'The persistent myth of lost hegemony', *International Organization*, 41, 1987, pp. 551–74. I am also indebted throughout this section to D. Hunter, 'Cooperation and conflict in United States – European community agricultural relations', paper presented to the annual meeting of the International Studies Association, London, March 1989.

84   S. Gill, 'The rise and decline of great powers: the American case', *Politics*, 8, 1988, pp. 3–9, p. 5.

85   See Gill and Law, *The Global Political Economy*, pp. 76–80. See also E. Augelli and C. Murphy, *America's Quest for Supremacy in the Third World: A Gramscian Analysis*, London, 1988; and R.O. Keohane, *After Hegemony*, Princeton, 1984, p. 45.

86   M. Davis, 'The political economy of late-imperial America', *New Left Review*, 143, 1984, pp. 6–18, pp. 6–7. For the expression of right wing opposition to the thesis of decline, see essays in A. Anderson and D.L. Bark, eds., *Thinking about America*, Stanford, 1988.

87   C. Kindleberger, *The World in Depression*, Berkeley, 1973, p. 305.

88   *After Hegemony*.

89   See, e.g., Z. K. Brzezinski, 'America's new geostrategy', *Foreign Affairs*, 66, 1988, pp. 81–103; T. A. Pugel, ed., *Fragile Interdependence*, Lexington (Massachusetts), 1986.

90   *After Hegemony*.

91   *The Political Economy of International Relations*.

92   S. D. Krasner, 'State power and the structure of international trade', *World Politics*, 28, 1976, pp. 317–47, p. 321.

93   Strange, 'The future of the American empire', pp. 12–13.

94   See Hall, *Liberalism*, p. 225. See also J. A. Hall, 'The decline and fall of the American empire', *Government and Opposition*, 23, 1988, pp. 240–45.

95   For an indication of this, see the articles in *Annals of the American Academy*, 500, 1988.

96   J. Gowa, 'Rational hegemons, excludable goods, and small groups: an epitaph for hegemonic stability theory?', *World Politics*, 41, 1989, pp. 307–24.

97   R. H. Wagner, 'Economic interdependence, bargaining power and political influence', *International Organization*, 42, 1988, pp. 461–83.

98   Hunter, 'Cooperation and conflict', p. 21.

99   See R. Lalkaka, 'Is the United States losing technological influence in the developing countries?', *Annals of the American Academy*, 500, 1988, pp. 33–50.

100   *Guardian*, 29 May 1989.

101   See S. Huntington, *American Politics: The Promise of Disharmony*, Cambridge (Massachusetts), 1982, p. 25; W. J. Field, *American Foreign Policy: Aspirations and Reality*, New York, 1984, p. 109; R. Wilkinson, *The Pursuit of American Character*, New York, 1988.

102   M. Harrington, *The Dream of Deliverance in American Politics*, New York, 1986 (e.g. p. 24).

103   H. McCloskey and J. Zaller, *The American Ethos*, Cambridge (Massachusetts), 1984.

104   S. D. Krasner, *Defending the National Interest*, Princeton, 1978, pp. 340, 345.

105   L. M. Sears, *A History of American Foreign Relations*, London, 1928, p. 584.

106   New Haven, 1962.

107   See A. Wolfers and L. W. Martin, eds., *The Anglo–American Tradition in Foreign Affairs*, New Haven, 1956, p. 156.

108   See C. V. Crabb, *Policy-Makers and Critics*, New York, 1976, p. 70.

109   See, e.g., W. C. Berman, *William Fulbright and the Vietnam War*, Kent (Ohio), 1988; B. Buzzanco, 'The American military's rationale against the Vietnam war', *Political Science Quarterly*, 101, 1986, pp. 559–76.

110   N. A. Graebner, *America as a World Power*, Wilmington (Delaware), 1984, p. xvii.

111   See Wolfers and Martin, eds., *The Anglo-American Tradition*, p. 158; R. Niebuhr, *The Irony of American History*, New York, 1952.

112   Cited in Smith, *Morality, Reason and Power*, p. 21.

113   See J. A. Combs, *American Diplomatic History*, Berkeley, 1983, pp. 236–7.

114   G. D. Cleva, *Henry Kissinger and the American Approach to Foreign Policy*, London, 1988.

115   See G. R. Sloan, *Geopolitics in United States Strategic Policy, 1890–1987*, New York, 1988, p. 202.

116   See S. Brown, *On the Front Burner: Issues in American Foreign Policy*, Boston, 1984, pp. 4–5. The classic geopolitical texts are A. T. Mahan, *The Problem of Asia and its Effects upon International Relations*, Boston, 1900; H. J. MacKinder, 'The geographical pivot of history', *Geographical Journal*, 23, 1904, pp. 421–41; and N. Spykman, *The Geography of the Peace*, New York, 1944. See also E. Plischke, *Foreign Relations*, New York, 1988, p. 228.

117   Lexington (Kentucky), 1988.

118   See J. Dumbrell, 'Introduction', in J. Dumbrell, ed., *Vietnam and the Antiwar Movement: An International Perspective*, Aldershot, 1989, pp. 1–6; R. M. Nixon, *No More Vietnams*, London, 1986.

119   The debate may be followed in: T. G. Paterson, *On Every Front*, New York, 1979; J. L. Gaddis, 'The emergent postrevisionist synthesis on the origins of the Cold War', *Diplomatic History*, 7, 1983, pp. 61–93; M. Leffler, 'The American conception of national security and the beginnings of the Cold War', *American Historical Review*, 89, 1984, pp. 137–71; R. A. Garson, 'The origins of the Cold War in Asia', *Review of International Studies*, 12, 1986, pp. 293–300; J. L. Gormly, *The Collapse of the Grand Alliance 1945–1948*,

Baton Rouge, 1987; B. R. Kuniholm, 'The origins of the first Cold War', in R. Crockatt and S. Smith, eds., *The Cold War: Past and Present*, London, 1987, pp. 37–57; R. J. McMahon, 'United States Cold War strategy in South Asia', *Journal of American History*, 75, 1988, pp. 812–40; and R. Crockatt, *The United States and the Cold War 1941–53*, British Association for American Studies pamphlet, 1989.

120 W. A. Williams, *From Colony to Empire*, New York, 1972, p. 476; see also *The Tragedy of American Diplomacy*, 2nd ed., New York, 1978; *Empire as a Way of Life*, New York, 1980.

121 This point is made in several essays in L. C. Gardner, ed., *Redefining the Past: Essays in Diplomatic History in Honor of William Appleman Williams*, Corvallis (Oregon), 1986. See also J. A. Thompson, 'William Appleman Williams and the "American Empire" ', *Journal of American Studies*, 7, 1973, pp. 91–104, p. 98; M. Kraus and D. D. Joyce, *The Writing of American History*, Norman (Oklahoma), 1985, pp. 337–46; B. Perkins, 'The tragedy of American diplomacy: twenty-five years after', *Reviews in American History*, 12, 1984, pp. 1–18.

122 See G. Kolko, *The Roots of American Foreign Policy*, Boston, 1969; *Vietnam: Anatomy of a War*, London, 1986.

123 E.g. N. Chomsky, *Towards a New Cold War*, London, 1982.

124 Among the best such studies are: W. LaFeber, *The New Empire*, Ithaca (New York), 1963 and L. C. Gardner, *Architects of Illusion*, Chicago, 1970. See also Combs, *American Diplomatic History*, chs. 18–21.

125 See W. H. Becker and S.F. Wells, eds., *Economics and World Power*, New York, 1984.

126 E. W. Hawley, 'Herbert Hoover, the Commerce Secretariat, and the vision of an "associative state" ', *Journal of American History*, 61, 1974, pp. 116–40; R. Griffith, 'Dwight D. Eisenhower and the corporate commonwealth', *American Historical Review*, 87, 1982, pp. 87–122.

127 J. L. Gaddis, 'The corporatist synthesis: a skeptical view', *Diplomatic History*, 10, 1986, pp. 357–62.

128 See McCormick, 'Drift or mastery?'; M. J. Hogan, 'The search for a synthesis: economic diplomacy in the Cold War', *Reviews in American History*, 15, 1987, pp. 493–8 and *The Marshall Plan*, Cambridge, 1987; D. S. Painter, *Oil and the American Century*, Baltimore, 1986.

129 See Thompson, 'William Appleman Williams', pp. 102–3.

130 A. Emmanuel, *Unequal Exchange: A Study of the Imperialism of Trade*, London, 1972; also A. Brewer, *Marxist Theories of Imperialism*, London, 1980, ch. 9.

131 *Theory of International Relations*, Reading (Massachusetts), 1979, p. 33.

132 Residents of Guam, Puerto Rico, the Virgin Islands and the Northern Marianas are US citizens; Samoans are US 'nationals'. Panama will take over control of the Canal Zone in 2000 (by 1978 treaty). Puerto Rico is a 'free commonwealth associated' with the US.

133 Cited in LaFeber, *The American Age*, pp. 130, 211.

134 See C. Reynolds, *Modes of Imperialism*, Oxford, 1981, p. 48; S. Hoffman, *Primacy or World Order*, New York, 1978; G. Liska, *Career of*

Empire, Baltimore, 1978.

135   R. W. Sterling, *Macropolitics*, New York, 1974, p. 204.

136   *The Global Political Economy*, p. 155.

137   V. I. Lenin, 'Imperialism: the highest stage of capitalism' (1917), in *Selected Works of Lenin*, Moscow, 1971, pp. 169–263; Brewer, *Marxist Theories*, ch. 5.

138   Frank, *Capitalism and Underdevelopment*; Samir Amin, *Imperialism and Unequal Development*, Brighton, 1977; H. Cardoso and E. Falletto, *Dependency and Development in Latin America*, Berkeley, 1971; H. Magdoff, *The Age of Imperialism*, New York, 1969. See also A. Szymanski, *The Logic of Imperialism*, New York, 1981; R. Munck, *Politics and Dependency in the Third World*, London, 1984; D. Seers, ed., *Dependency Theory*, London, 1983.

139   See C. A. Barone, *Marxist Thought on Imperialism*, London 1985 (especially ch. 7); Gilpin, *The Political Economy of International Relations*.

Theories of foreign policy-making

1 Rationality and its limits

Varying perspectives on the making of foreign policy emerge from the general orientations on problems of international relations outlined in the first chapter. As Steve Smith has argued, 'all perspectives on the subject of international relations contain statements about foreign policy'.[1] Thus, a realist would tend to see foreign policy as structured around a more or less rational pursuit of national interest. A proponent of interdependence would see it much more as the product of intra- and extra-state mutual adjustment and disaggregation.

Notions of rationality in decision-making have, of course, been subjected to violent attack in recent years, and not only in the context of criticisms of the realist tradition in the study of international relations. Writing in 1978, D. R. Kinder and J. A. Weiss declared that for a generation social science literature on decision-making had 'been divided into two camps: work premised on rational models of choice and work designed to discredit such models'. The relevant vocabulary now included 'such concepts as "satisficing", "bounded rationality", "muddling through", "bureaucratic politics", "heuristics", and so forth'.[2] According to Herbert Simon, whose name is associated with the concepts of 'satisficing' behaviour and 'bounded rationality', decision-makers operate in a world where choices are made on the basis of picking the least unsatisfactory option: the course of action which exhibits minimally satisfactory standards of acceptability as a basis upon which to proceed.[3] Robert Jervis has written of decisions invariably being pitched at the level of the 'suboptimal' and taken amidst behavioural inconsistency.[4]

Much of the history of modern social science can indeed be written in terms of debates about rational decision-making and the 'rational actor' model. Since the 1960s, the 'rational actor' model of decision-making has tended to be appropriated by public choice theorists, many (although by no means all) of whom have come to espouse the normative views of American neo-conservatism in particular and the New Right in general. Building on neo-classical market economics and mathematical games theories, they see the 'rational actor' as the logically indispensable starting point for political analysis.[5] Outside the tradition of public choice theory, formulations of the 'rational actor' model of foreign policy-making have often been undertaken merely as a prelude to mounting an attack upon the model. The more successful formulations, however, involve not simply the erection of a figure of straw, to be blown over by subsequent argument, but have allowed the 'rational actor' model its due grant of explanatory power. The most celebrated of such formulations is Graham Allison's 'Model I', in his 1971 discussion of the Cuban missile crisis. Allison saw rational choice as consisting of 'selecting that alternative whose consequences rank highest in the decision-makers' payoff function' (a rationally conceived hierarchy of goals and objectives).[6] Phil Williams has put forward a model of 'strategic rationality' in the context of foreign policy crisis management. This model presupposes some 'controlling intelligence' and a set of decision-makers who take national interests seriously, consider the likely responses of international rivals to various policy options, and (at least in a situation of crisis) do not allow domestic pressures unduly to influence rational policy.[7]

The sheer complexity of human motivation, along with the apparent intractability and contingency of international politics, can scarcely help but put us on our guard against easy acceptance of the 'rational actor' model. As Michael Clarke writes: 'any study of a state's foreign policy over a given period quickly reveals that rather than a series of clear decisions, there is a continuing and confusing "flow of action", made up of a mixture of political decisions, non-political decisions, bureaucratic procedures, continuations of previous policy, and sheer accident.'[8]

The various 'middle level' theories[9] to be discussed below – psychological approaches, 'groupthink' and misperception, cybernetics and information processing, organisational perspectives and 'bureaucratic politics', roles, implementation and crisis theory – all constitute, to varying degrees, limits on rationality and counterpoints to the 'rational actor' model. However, at least three comments may be made upon the 'rational actor' model before moving on.

Firstly, as volumes of diplomatic and international history will attest, the 'rational actor' model can, albeit supplemented by other approaches, provide valuable explanations and insights. It can act as a kind of Occam's razor, cutting back the explanatory undergrowth. As public choice theorists point out, 'parsimony' in explanation is worth encouraging.[10] Secondly, the fact that rationality may be 'bounded' does not, in itself, mean that rational frameworks for considering decision-making need be abandoned altogether. As Allison wrote, rationality 'refers to consistent, value-maximizing choice *within specified constraints*'.[11] Thirdly, at the level of prescription, the unattainability of perfect rationality similarly does not preclude or negate efforts to promote more rational decision-taking. J. D. Steinbruner's 'analytic paradigm' is relevant here: 'A given process of decision is analytic if upon examination one can find evidence that there was at least limited value integration, that alternative outcomes were analyzed and evaluated, and that new information regarding central variables of the problem did produce plausibly appropriate subjective adjustments.'[12]

Here is a practical yardstick, broadly within the 'rational actor' framework, by which to judge actual decisions. Awareness of the limits to rationality does not present progress towards – indeed almost certainly enhances – closer approximations to the 'analytic paradigm'.

2 Overarching theory and comparative foreign policy

J. N. Rosenau's 'pre-theory' article of 1966[13] set the agenda for a 'normal scientific', quantitatively-based and behaviourally oriented study of foreign policy. The hope engendered by the article was that such a project would lead to an explanatory general theory of foreign policy behaviour. The 'pre-theory' described foreign policy behaviour as a dependent variable, contrasted with independent variables involving the developmental and geotypical status of the countries under examination. Foreign policy behaviour and the independent variables are putatively linked by five 'source' variables: the international (systemic) environment, the type of social context, the relevant governmental context, the individual characteristics of policy-makers, and factors relating to the roles performed by decision-makers.

Rosenau's 'source' variables offer a convenient framework within which to examine complex issues.[14] More importantly, the 'pre-theory' occasioned an explosion (critics might say an implosion) of behaviourist work on comparative foreign policy: attempts, for example under the auspices of the Inter University Comparative Foreign Policy Project of the 1960s and 1970s, to move from 'pre-theory' to general theory. Although faltering in its latter years, this approach produced a vast body of research, with the Comparative Research on the Events of Nations (CREON) project possibly extending itself into the 1990s.[15]

In general, however, as Rosenau himself acknowledged,[16] results have been disappointing. In a volume significantly entitled *New Directions in the Study of Foreign Policy*, C. F. Hermann and G. Peacock point to fundamental difficulties emanating from the two modes of scientific inquiry typical of comparative foreign policy: neo-positivist induction and Kuhnian normal science. The accumulation of data has simply not led by a process of induction to general theory. Again, there is no commonly shared paradigm directing the work of researchers in this field.[17] Any theory which seeks to balance internal factors (the decision-making environment, 'national attributes', electoral pressures, and so on) with external determinants (such as the constraints of a bi-polar or multi-polar international structure) faces massive obstacles. It has to transcend the formidable 'levels of analysis' problem in international relations theory. Construction of an explanatory general theory of foreign policy raised especially acute epistemological difficulties,[18] even in the period before what Rosenau calls 'cascading interdependence'.[19] The relationship between 'foreign policy', as a discrete field of study, and 'international politics', has always been rather problematic.[20] The rise of interdependence has made it doubly so. It is hard conceptually to separate 'foreign policy' not only from international, but also from domestic politics.[21] In modern conditions, simply *defining* the term 'foreign policy' raises enormous hurdles. The whole comparative foreign policy project, indeed, has had the greatest difficulty in even leaving the starting stalls of definitional, threshold questions.[22]

The rise of behaviourist, quantitative approaches to the study of foreign policy in the 1960s and 1970s pointed up the different traditions and perspectives of British and American scholars, and drew attention to the divergent status of social science in the two countries.[23] To many British students of foreign policy, the American approach seemed little more than empty, arrogant neologising. The cry, familiar among opponents of quantifying behaviourism, was raised: see how so much misdirected energy leads to such trivial conclusions![24] Even Steve Smith, no traditionalist in these matters, wrote of the 1982 CREON volume that it was 'open to the criticism that after 366 pages one has found out very little more about what foreign policy behaviour is than one knew at the start'.[25] To less sympathetic observers than Smith, the whole enterprise appeared little more than a muddled attempt to provide an apology for post-1945 US forign policy.[26]

The study of foreign policy does have room for different approaches, and pleas for intellectual tolerance should be heeded.[27] Nonetheless, it cannot be pretended that overarching theory of the sort advocated by Rosenau in 1966 has emerged in any persuasive form.

3 'Middle level' perspectives

These theories occupy a position between overarching theory and empirical, single country description. They tend to focus upon subjective factors – the perceptions and cognitions of leading actors – and also upon the degree to which the process of decision-making determines its substance. These perspectives also tend to call into question the common tendency to concentrate upon key, 'strategic', turning-point decisions in foreign policy.[28] Decisions may be incremental, embedded in process. They need also to be set against the record of their own implementation.

(a) *Psychological approaches* The study of perception, cognition, memory and belief systems as they apply to the making of foreign policy is most commonly undertaken in connection with individuals, especially Presidents. Concentration upon individual personality types – 'crusaders' and 'pragmatists', hawks and doves, introverts and extroverts, authoritarians and anti-authoritarians[29] – tends to imply that individuals have a determining influence upon policy. Reflection, of course, tells us that the impact that individuals have on policy will vary according to circumstance. (Kegley and Wittkopf suggest that individual impact is enhanced by individual self-confidence, personal involvement, and by 'recent or dramatic ... assumption of power'. Complex issues, with little information available to illuminate them, may also encourage the substantive impact of highly placed individuals.)[30] However, psychological and belief system approaches do not have to be limited to individuals. A considerable amount of work has been done on the belief systems of foreign policy elites, and also on the shifting belief structures of the public at large.

The most successful discussion of the relationship between Presidential character and performance is contained in the work of James David Barber. He defines and describes Presidents in terms of their energy and commitment (active/passive) and in terms of the emotional satisfaction they derive from the office (positive/negative). The most successful Presidents tend to be active-positives, of whom the archetype must be Franklin D. Roosevelt. Active-positives 'want most to achieve results. Active-negatives aim to get and keep power. Passive-positives are after love. Passive-negatives emphasize their civic virtue.'[31] Among recent Presidents, Reagan is seen as passive-positive, Johnson (at least after 1965) and Nixon as active-negative, and Eisenhower as passive-negative. Each type has its dangers, with active-negatives being the most dangerous. But active-positives, with their passion for results, may also court failure.

Barber's approach, not only concerning Nixon, but also Carter and Reagan,[32] has been both stimulating and impressive in its predictive qualities. Numerous psychobiographies of individual Presidents come to mind, not least Garry Wills's evocation of Ronald Reagan's place amidst American myth: a psychohistory which pushed the Reagan Administration into 'the major leagues of pretending'.33 Beyond the Presidency, one may cite analogous treatments of leading foreign policy actors, especially Secretaries of State.[34]

Contemporary psychological approaches tend to invoke the concept of the 'belief system'. This is a broadly defined concept which tends to blend at some point into 'ideology'. It includes both instrumental beliefs (concerning how an individual seeks to achieve goals) and fundamental judgements about politics.[35] Defined in this broad fashion, the notion of 'belief system' also embraces 'operational code' and 'cognitive map' approaches to the study of international relations. 'Operational coding' involves, typically, the examination of a leading foreign policy actor's published work for indications as to his operational beliefs. How does he conceptualise conflict? What role is ascribed to chance in human affairs? Stephen Walker, for example, see Henry Kissinger's 'operational code' as present both in his academic work, and in his negotiating strategy during the Vietnam peace talks: a relatively consistent, predictable, 'metagame' code.[36] The 'cognitive map' is a yet more sophisticated concept: the literal mapping of an individual's belief system in terms of concepts and causal beliefs.[37]

Drawing together elements traditionally subsumed under cognition and ideology, the 'belief system' approach raises formidable operational and philosophical problems. In *describing* beliefs and their impact, are we really *explaining* anything? What is the impact of the observer's own belief system? In what sense are these things 'knowable'? What is the relationship between individual and group beliefs?[38] Despite such difficulties, it remains the case that empirical study of foreign policy does well to pay attention to individuals' key beliefs about themselves and their environment, and to how these beliefs relate to each other. Applying the 'belief system' approach to Presidents Carter and Reagan, Spear and Williams point out the value of paying attention, in particular, to five Presidential belief 'clusters': beliefs about the nature and structure of the international system, about the Soviet Union and about the United States, about the use of (especially military) power, and about the role of the President.[39]

(b) *'Groupthink' and misperception* 'Belief systems' also apply at the group level, where special dynamics may operate to keep them in place.

In *Victims of Groupthink* (1972), his original and influential formulation of the concept, Irving Janis characterised 'groupthink' as something that 'people engage in when they are deeply involved in a cohesive in-group, when the members striving for unanimity override their motivation to realistically appraise alternative courses of action'. Janis analysed the Kennedy inner circle thinking prior to the 1961 Bay of Pigs invasion of Cuba in these terms. Many of their false assumptions – for example, that it would be possible to disguise US responsibility for the invasion, and that it would spark off domestic insurrections in Cuba – were traced to the group's 'concurrence-seeking tendency' and the need for members to maintain a sense of group identity. The situation was worsened by Kennedy's demand, at the crucial 4 April meeting at the State Department, that 'each person, in turn, state his overall judgement, especially after having just heard an outsider' – Senator Fulbright – 'oppose the group's consensus'. Janis examined the autumn 1950 decision to escalate the Korean war, the unpreparedness leading to the Pearl Harbor attack in 1941, and the 1965 escalation of the war in Vietnam, in similar terms. The Cuban missile crisis of 1962 and the genesis of the Marshall Plan in 1947, however, were seen as cases where 'groupthink' had been avoided. In the former case, the very same people who erred over the Bay of Pigs invasion performed better, because of the 'magnitude of the obvious threat of nuclear war' and 'improved decision-making procedures used by the Executive Committee' which made the crucial decisions. The Executive Committee had no formal agenda and frequently broke into sub-groups (often with Kennedy absent). Members were also encouraged to 'function as sceptical generalists'. The Marshall Plan decision-makers also had a 'multiple-group structure'.[40]

Robert Jervis's *The Logic of Images in International Relations*[41] called attention to the importance, especially in the nuclear age,[42] of how different sets of decision-makers in different countries perceive each other; he analysed the repertoire of signals and deception which could be used to influence perception. Building on this work, Jervis's *Perception and Misperception in International Politics* (1976) argued: 'actors are more apt to err on the side of being too wedded to an established view and too quick to reject discrepant information than to make the opposite error of too quickly altering their theories. People often undergo premature cognitive closure.'

Belief structures tend towards consistency and balance. Decision-makers are 'consistency seekers'. The phenomenon of 'cognitive dissonance' also involves the holding of incompatible beliefs under a false or irrational framework of consistency. Jervis also drew attention to the way in which immediate concerns ('evoked sets') may distort the rational processing of information. Decision-makers also tend to overestimate their own importance, to ascribe to opponents a degree of centralised calculation which is unrealistic, and to engage in either 'wishful' or 'unwishful' (over-pessimistic) thinking. Jervis urged that decision-makers be aware of the existence of these common modes of misperception and argued that policy-makers should try to specify in advance what evidence would be needed to destroy or damage a particular hypothesis. This might help prevent the erection of beliefs which are effectively impervious to revision on the basis of observed fact.[43]

Students of post-1945 US foreign policy will have no difficulty in applying notions of 'groupthink' and misperception, at least *prima facie*. Hamilton Jordan's account of the 1980 Iran hostage crisis reads almost like a textbook example of 'groupthink' dynamics. Jordan, President Carter's chief of staff, recorded group resentments of Secretary of State Cyrus Vance's caution about the ill-fated hostage rescue mission. Vance transgressed the dominant 'groupthink', and was excluded from crucial meetings.[44] The history of the Cold War, in fact, bristles with apparent examples of 'groupthink', and of misperception of the sort described by Jervis. E.R. May's work on the use of historical analogy is relevant here. According to May, policy-makers use history badly. They tend to use historical analogies inappropriately and without adequate reflection upon their precise relevance. Thus were appeasement analogies from the 1930s allowed to affect policy in the early Cold War years. Memories of conflicts in the Philippines and Malaysia, as well as the 'loss' of China in 1949, were also allowed to distort US policy in Vietnam.[45] President Kennedy's acceptance of the CIA's invocation, in connection with the Bay of Pigs invasion, of parallels with the 1954 covert operation in Guatemala also springs to mind.[46] May and Neustadt's *Thinking in Time*[47] attempts to provide practical advice to decision-makers on how best to use history. Issues should be traced historically, with key questions constantly in mind: what is known/unclear/presumed? What facts would cause presumptions to be changed? What are the precise likenesses/ differences between the analogy and contemporary problems?

Perhaps the most impressive attempt to discuss US foreign policy in terms of perception is D. Michael Shafer's *Deadly Paradigms*. Directly discussing the role of cognition, Shafer examines a long record of unquestioned assumptions: 'a pervasive, compelling, but distorted vision of the Third World state as beleaguered moderniser and the United States as manager of modernisation'. Examining US policy in Greece (1947–50), the Philippines (1946–53) and Vietnam (pre-1965), Shafer argues that approaches based on 'rational actor' and 'bureaucratic politics' assumptions can tell only an incomplete story. By defining Greece, the Philippines and Vietnam in terms of US-led-modernisation, in the context of a test of wills between the superpowers, policy-makers underwent premature, and distorting, cognitive closure. Such a position was reinforced by 'defensive avoidance', the tendency of policy-makers to discount information which challenges cherished and prevailing beliefs.[48]

'Groupthink' and misperception are both useful tools of analysis. The very seductiveness and apparent applicability of the concepts can, however, lead to difficulties. Paradoxically, they themselves can be used simply to 'shut off' explanation and effect premature cognitive closure. David Barrett has elsewhere provided a convincing description of this process at work in connection with the 1965 escalation of

the war in Vietnam.[49] It should also be remembered that
'groupthink', of itself, is not automatically harmful. After all, the
dominant group-view may be 'correct'. Seen like this, 'groupthink' is
simply part of the necessary social process of decision-making. The
problem, however, is that 'groupthink' exacerbates conditions which
lead to distortion, and tends to eliminate opportunities for constructive criticism. (A. Stein has similarly argued that misperception is
by no means automatically harmful.)[50]

As with the other 'middle-level' perspectives, it should be remembered that psychological approaches occupy only one dimension of
analysis, and do not produce explanations that suit every purpose. For
example, it might reasonably be questioned whether 'cognitive dissonance' is really the appropriate way of describing the policy of
combining support for pro-American Third World dictators with
advocacy of the ideals of liberty. Might 'hypocrisy' not be better?

(c) *Cybernetics, heuristics and discourse analysis* If these various
approaches offer only partial explanations, then attempts at synthesis
are to be welcomed. 'Cybernetics' represents a conscious and
impressive attempt to build a bridge between cognitive and
'bureaucratic politics' approaches to foreign policy analysis.

Building on Karl Deutsch's *The Nerves of Government*,[51] J. D.
Steinbruner presents the following 'cybernetic paradigm' to set
against the 'analytic paradigm' quoted earlier: 'a process in which
decisions are fragmented into small segments and the segments
treated sequentially. The process is dominated by established procedure.'[52] Both analytic and cybernetic paradigms need to be
modified according to cognitive theory, especially regarding the
human mind's tendency to generalise without duly confronting
complexity. The convergence of this cognitive tendency to over-sim-
plify with the fragmentation of problems, and their 'resolution'
according to established bureaucratic procedure, leads to distortion.
'Grooved thinking', the narrow and over-simple treatment of issues,
may be one outcome. 'Uncommitted thinking', the random selection
of completing over-simplifications, and 'theoretical thinking' (stable,
unexamined assumptions) may be others.[53]

Steinbruner draws attention to the extent to which the processing
of information takes place beyond conscious direction. As Dwain
Mefford argues: 'this preliminary structuring of the imagination or
effort to manage the "structural" uncertainty of the decision problem'

may be of 'greater importance when compared to subsequent steps in the decision activity involving the application of optimal or satisficing decision rules'.[54] Unexamined information processing procedures may operate both for individuals and within and across bureaucratic structures. Studies of cognition and heuristics – the working hypotheses used to aid problem-solving – may be applied at both the individual and trans-governmental level.[55] Again, at both levels, unexamined 'simple intuitive heuristics'[56] tend to predominate. A 1986 study of the Carter and Reagan Administration policies towards Southern Africa argues that contrasting heuristic procedures contributed to actual policy differences.[57] This 'information processing' perspective may prove fruitful; nonetheless it is hard to distinguish the effects of heuristic rituals (conscious or unconscious) from more obvious factors, such as the obviously contrasting Cold War philosophies of the Carter and Reagan Administrations.

The ascendency within the discipline of international relations of empirico-descriptive approaches and (opposing them) behaviourist-positivist approaches has rendered the discipline somewhat resistant to the application of a body of theory, which has revolutionised thought elsewhere: postmodern and poststructuralist theory. These theories are various: for example, the deconstructionism of Jacques Derrida, the power relations theory of Michel Foucault, feminist psychoanalytic theory, theories of intertextuality. Yet they all share an opposition to 'common sense' rationalism and positivism. Concentrating on the operation, coding and conventions of language itself, these approaches offer radical insights into the social construction of meaning. Especially relevant to the study of international politics and foreign policy is the analysis of 'discourses of power': the way in which apparently objective – neutral language privileges certain groups and assumptions. M. L. Shapiro, for example, draws attention to this process as it relates to talking and writing about 'security'. 'Security talk' is 'a kind of discourse that represents structures of authority and control'. Attention needs to be directed to 'the processes wherein the idea of "security" came to be a dominant reading strategy for spatializing the world' and for 'locating the United States as a knowing subject within such a world'.[58]

(d) *Organisational perspectives and 'bureaucratic politics'* The organisational perspective on foreign policy-making begins with the assertion that organisation matters. As Allison and Szanton have put it, organisation 'creates capabilities, it vests and weights certain interests and perspectives, and it helps assure the legitimacy of decisions taken'.[59] Modern accounts of bureaucracy tend to stress the boundaries which it imposes upon rationality. We should not forget, however, that, as in the Weberian tradition, politically controlled bureaucracies may be a focus for rationality: developing policy alternatives, identifying problems, making decisions with efficiency. Nonetheless, organisations manifestly have 'counter-rational' dimensions too: institutional rivalries, decisions as the result of 'pulling and hauling' between vested interests, stubborn resistance to all but incremental change, fractionated standard procedures, and so on. The ethos is one of 'muddling through' (scientifically or otherwise) rather than purposeful rationality.[60]

It may be useful here to distinguish between the general organisational perspective on foreign policy-making, and the narrower 'bureaucratic politics' model. Allison, although he found the distinction difficult to sustain,[61] did originally distinguish 'organisational process' from 'bureaucratic politics'. The former characterises government as a 'conglomerate of semi-feudal, loosely allied organisations, each with a substantial life of its own'.[62] 'Long-range planning tends to become institutionalised ... and then disregarded.'[63] Problems become fragmented and 'solved' according to short-term needs.

Allison's 'Model III', on the other hand, invoked 'players who make government decisions not by a single, rational choice but by the pulling and hauling that is politics'.[64] Policy outcomes depend on the skills, strategy and positions of the bureaucratic players. Halperin's study of the 1967 US decision to deploy an anti-Chinese anti-ballistic missile system concluded:

most governmental actions, which look to the casual outside observer as if they resulted from specific presidential decisions, are more often an amalgam of a number of coincidental occurrences: actions brought about by presidential decisions (not always those intended), actions that are really manoeuvres to influence presidential decisions, actions resulting from decisions in unrelated areas, and actions taken at lower levels by junior participants without informing their superiors or the President.[65]

As these quotations from Allison and Halperin demonstrate, these organisational-bureaucratic perspectives were developed largely in opposition to the 'rational actor' model, and particularly against the implicit view that foreign policy may be satisfactorily explained solely in terms of Presidential leadership. Attacking notions of comprehensive rationality, the 'bureaucratic politics' tradition tended to develop similar universalist pretensions. Many subsequent critics have pointed out, not unreasonably, that bureaucratic explanations, by their very nature, cannot tell the whole story. For one thing, they barely mention Congress, much less extra-governmental forces. They tell us little of the power of private business or the operation of the 'military-industrial complex'. When it purports to be anything like a comprehensive account of decision-making, the 'bureaucratic politics' model reflects a naive view of the nature of power and the system of domination within organisations. As Jenkins and Gray have put it, a focus upon intra-bureaucratic bargaining reveals 'little about how relative advantages of players have emerged or how bias has developed in the system', with the decision-making agenda being constricted within 'safe' parameters.[66] Robert Art concluded as early as 1973 that 'too many constraints of a non-bureaucratic nature must be set before the paradigm works, and more often than not, once we set the constraints, the paradigm will account for very little'.[67]

Allison himself appealed for 'additional paradigms'[68] and candidates were not slow in presenting themselves.[69] In particular, it is clear that the 'bureaucratic politics' paradigm severely understates the power of the President. Of course, as Halperin argued, it is naive to see policy as the rational calculation of the dominant leader. Yet, especially in crisis situations, and certainly during the Cuban missile crisis,[70] it is not simply naive romanticism to point out that the buck really does stop at the Oval Office. The White House also has the ability severely to limit and short-circuit bureaucratic decision-making across a variety of issue areas. J. N. Rosati has compared the American involvement in strategic arms limitation talks (SALT I) under Presidents Johnson and Nixon. Under Johnson, who was rarely actively involved in SALT proposals, the bureaucratic model was clearly applicable. The State Department and the Arms Control and Disarmament Agency (tending to favour restrictions in strategic weaponry) indulged in a prolonged process of 'pulling and hauling' with the more hawkish Pentagon and CIA. Under Nixon, however, the change in Presidential focus and prioritisation led to apparent White House domination of events.[71] (This is not, of course, to deny that bureaucratic 'pulling and hauling' may not occur within the White House. Nonetheless, the crucial distinguishing feature of the variations in SALT policy-making does seem to be the attitude of the principal bureaucratic actor: the President.) While it certainly is appropriate to regard foreign policy decision-making as a 'social process',[72] the decision environment is not an unregulated jungle of 'pulling and hauling'. It is regulated by 'decision rules' (the established procedures of cybernetic theory); but also by the ability of Presidents to alter the agenda, to confront bureaucratic sabotage, and to act as final court of appeal.

(e) *Roles theory* A sub-field of the 'bureaucratic politics' approach, roles theory, at the level of national policy-making starts with the bureaucratic maxim, 'where you stand depends upon where you sit'. (Roles theory may also be applied on an international basis, referring to how different sets of policy-makers see their international positions and functions.)[73]

The notion of people fitting into predetermined role-patterns is, in fact, a common and common-sensical one. As President Reagan approached his second term in office, numerous commentators spoke of the old Cold Warrior being impelled to assume the role of peacemaker. The Secretary of Defence is regularly depicted as having a difference in perspective to the Secretary of State, with their different clienteles pressing for different policies.[74] In practice, it may be very difficult to unscramble role requirements, psychological variables, individual preferences and 'belief systems'. Margaret Hermann sees the following traits as impacting upon policy: 'nationalism, belief in one's own ability to control events, need for power, need for affiliation, conceptual complexity, and distrust of others'.[75] Such qualities have obscure and sinuous origins, and role theory, again, can only offer a partial explanation. Nonetheless, the roles perspective can have impressive explanatory power, especially when it addresses this interface between role requirements and personality. In effect, it represents a salutary modification of the rather narrow, mechanistic 'bureaucratic politics' model: a reassertion of the centrality of the link between individuality and position in the decision-making network.[76]

(f) *Implementation* The relative lack of interest shown by students of decision-making in the actual implementation of decisions has often been remarked upon. Louis Fisher, writing about the US budgetary process, urged researchers to turn from spending decisions to a study of the actual spending itself: 'It is as though we visited the race track, watched the horses parade back and forth in front of the stands, saw them line up in the starting gate, and then went home just as the bell sounded. The outcome of the race does not interest us. We do not see the budget cycle to its completion.'[77]

Those areas of foreign policy, such as foreign aid, with a notoriously high degree of 'slippage' between intention and result, have traditionally provoked attention to the actual 'outcome of the race'.[78] Nonetheless, there is no question that this is an undertilled field. The gap between formulation and implementation of decisions was, of course, an important part of the case advanced by 'bureaucratic politics' theorists. Allison and Halperin pointed out that the actual behaviour of the US troops in the Dominican Republic during the invasion of 1965 had only a slight logical relationship to the original invasion decision.[79] Organisational structures, geared to short-term solutions, tend not to be concerned with techniques of evaluating faithful implementation. According to Halperin: 'What is done will be heavily influenced by the standard operating procedures and interests of the implementers.'[80] From this perspective, implementation appears as a kind of bureaucratic 'fail safe': a final assertion of the vested interests of the implementing agencies.

Clarke and Smith offer three examples of the way in which implementation relates to policy-making. Firstly and most obviously, there is 'slippage': the fiasco of Carter's 1980 Iran hostage rescue mission, or the propensity of 'CIA assets' in the Third World to indulge in drug dealing and other activities which lose them Congressional and public support in the US. Secondly, Clarke and Smith cite 'routine complexity', where policy implementation – exchange rate policy is a good example – is bound, due to the complexity and unpredictability of the implementing environment, to bear only a generalised resemblance to decisions made in Washington. Thirdly, there is 'self-implementation': policies which subsist at the level of rhetoric, position-taking, or promises.[81] (A related concept might be 'implementation by others': for example, President Bush's thinly disguised calls in May 1989 upon the Panamanian military to stage a coup against General Noriega.)

Concentration upon implementation raises not only questions about control of bureaucratic sabotage, but also necessitates making distinctions between domestic and foreign policy. Much research on domestic policy implementation[82] needs to be modified for foreign policy. For example, Chris Hood's 'horse-shoe-nail' problem[83] – the problem of incomplete bureaucratic planning – is likely to loom even larger in the uncertain foreign policy environment. On the other hand, Pressman and Wildavsky's multiple 'clearance points'[84] – the inter-agency agreements and co-operation that facilitate implementation – may be less of a problem in foreign policy.

The implementation perspective is, in many policy areas, indispensable. Understanding of, for example, President Kennedy's Alliance for Progress (in Latin America)[85] or US human rights policy, [86] is impossible without it. Moreover, the implementation perspective has the virtue of shifting attention away from abstract (and often misleadingly conceptualised) decisions, to a study of the whole process, including concrete, observable events.[87]

(g) *Crisis decision-making*   Academic studies of crisis decision-making have tended to concentrate upon problems of crisis definition, the manageability of crisis, why some situations lead to conflict and some do not, and the relationship of international crisis to developments in military technology.

At first inspection, crisis decision-making might seem the mode of policy-making at furthest remove from rationality. The effects of stress would seem to point towards irrationality. In fact, it is not easy to establish such a link; stress may actually have a stimulative effect. Richard Nixon's almost mystical evocation of crisis as an emotional and intellectual high[88] may illuminate the Nixon psyche more than it informs us about crisis-induced stress. Nonetheless, it is at least arguable than creative problem-solving is enhanced by certain types of stress. There may be an 'optimum' stress level, beyond which any beneficial effects are rapidly put into reverse.[89]

Regarding the 'bureaucratic politics' model, it may confidently be asserted that it tends to decrease in applicability during periods of apparent crisis when core values seem threatened. Certainly, organisational processes and established procedures still impact on decisions, but are more likely to be short-circuited by Presidential initiative and discretion. Rather than allowing insufficient time for adequate information processing, crises may mitigate heuristic distortions and encourage rapid passage of information through the bureaucracy.[90] 'Groupthink' and misperception, of course, may thrive under crisis conditions, with decision-makers feeling beleaguered and defensive. A combination of information overload and the consequent likelihood of premature cognitive closure may induce erratic behaviour or actual paralysis of the decision structure.[91] Nonetheless, it is at least arguable that, paradoxically, and in some limited senses, crisis may actually stimulate rationality.[92] Such an argument does, however, contain an important unexamined assumption: the equation of rational efficiency with elite domination and the minimisation of democratic controls.

4 Foreign policy-making and theories of state power

(a) *Pluralist approaches* Virtually all the literature considered thus far in this chapter may be most easily located within either a pluralist or an 'elite-managerial' tradition of studying policy-making and state power. For American pluralists of the 1950s and 1960s, US capitalism was a modernising force, bringing representative institutions, extended opportunities for citizen participation and democratic freedoms. The American political process more or less represented a 'polyarchy', with policy being seen as the outcome of the free play of group pressures. For pluralists, state power was 'a consequence of democracy, normally not a threat to it'.[93]

The golden age of American pluralism rested primarily upon studies of domestic and community politics, rather than foreign policy. Foreign policy, with its more obviously elitist decisional environment and with less clearly organised competing pressure groups, always fitted into pluralist frameworks less comfortably. It is noticeable, for example, that *The Process of Government*, D.B. Truman's classic exposition of pluralist group theory, had virtually nothing to say about foreign policy.[94] Nonetheless, for traditional pluralists, American foreign policy was the result of multiple pressures – electoral, international, economic, ethnic, and so on. (The overarching theories of Rosenau and his associates may be seen as an attempt to delineate an authoritative taxonomy of such pressures.) It was, and is, for example, a strong part of the pluralist case that business interests in the United States are not monolithic, but rather exert contradictory pulls upon foreign policy-makers.

By the early 1970s, pluralism of the sort espoused by Dahl in *A Preface to Democratic Theory* (1956) had obtained a reputation for Panglossian complacency. Its favourite methodological tool, behaviourism, had also been subjected to severe challenges. Quentin Skinner wrote in 1973 that Dahl's ascription of the term 'democracy' to the type of political system he described amounted to 'an act of political conservatism', serving to 'commend the recently prevailing

values and practices of the contemporary U.S.A.'.[95] The crisis of pluralism provoked defections to right and left. Some formerly optimistic pluralists began to develop new emphases, especially concerning the power of large business corporations, which implicitly admitted the inadequacy of earlier formulations.[96]

In a sense, the plethora of investigation into the elite politics of decision-making during the 1970s represented a retreat from the now less reassuring world of societal pluralism into the apparently hard-headed environment of bureaucratic warfare. Concern for the psychological and organisational orientations of decision-makers is not, of course, incompatible with pluralism, nor indeed with any approach which allows a measure of state autonomy in these matters. (Among non-Marxist formulations, only the corporatist perspective with its failure to draw distinct lines between state and society[97] would seem to leave little room for state autonomy in the traditional sense.) It was always part of the pluralist case that government, like business, was not monolithic, and that competition extended within high policy-making circles.[98] However, the approach adopted by writers like George, Jervis, Allison and Halperin may also be fitted within an 'elite-managerial' focus, which allows a greater degree of free play to intra-governmental forces than would traditional pluralism. Such a focus was characteristic of the shift in attention in the late 1970s and 1980s to problems of bureaucratic control, 'technology' and the professional state.[99]

(b) *Ruling elite and Marxist theories*   Since most of this chapter has been concerned implicitly with pluralist and 'elite-managerial' approaches, it is now the intention to move on to consider more radical perspectives. These link up with the imperialist interpretations of US foreign policy discussed in the first chapter. Firstly, there are ruling elite models, which, in the American context, are most characteristically articulated within the radical populist tradition, and, secondly, various formulations within Marxism. In his book, *Democracy for the Few*, Michael Parenti denies that the United States is ruled by a monolithic elite. There are:

severe differences in tactics, differences in how best to mute class conflict and maintain the existing system at home and abroad. Differences can arise between moderately conservative and extremely conservative capitalists, between large and not-so-large investor interests, and between domestic and international corporations. ... When push comes to shove, what holds them

together is their common interest in preserving a system that assures their continued accumulation of wealth and enjoyment of social privilege.[100]

Ruling elite theorists, like Parenti, C. Wright Mills and G.W. Domhoff,[101] tend to identify the ruling group by reference to common and interlocking social, educational and occupational backgrounds. (Within Marxism, this approach is known as 'instrumentalism' or the 'power structure' perspective. It is best represented by Ralph Miliband, who, in *The State in Capitalist Society*, pointed to the social provenance of political and administrative elites, to the screening of candidates for state offices, and to the 'revolving door' between top jobs in government and in the private sector.[102])

Marxist theory regarding foreign policy-making may be approached from two directions: class conflict defined either internationally or domestically.[103] The first, global, orientation leads to the theories of imperialism and capitalist world order discussed in Chapter 1; the second, national, approach, to the various formulations discussed here. Broadly speaking, Marxists would define foreign policy in this sense as 'the external pursuit of the policies of a given ruling class'.[104]

For present purposes, the most convenient typology of Marxist viewpoints will be one based on differing degrees of state autonomy (in other words, the extent to which foreign policy-makers are seen to be operating independently of dominant class interests). At one extreme, there is the famous definition in *The Communist Manifesto* of 'the executive of the modern state as but a committee for managing the common affairs of the whole bourgeoisie'.[105] As in state-monopoly-capitalism theories,[106] which postulate a fusion between governmental and monopoly capital interests, there is little room here for the state policy-making process itself impacting upon substantive policy. The 'state' becomes little more than an inert epiphenomenon of class politics. The convoluted, multi-faceted, multi-accessional nature of the American political process makes it difficult to apply this analysis to the United States (although, again, the multi-dimensional, decentralised characteristics of the domestic policy-making environment are far less prevalent in the realm of foreign policy). Despite the difficulties with this analysis, O'Connor has argued that a 'class-conscious political directorate' may emerge when dominant class interests are directly threatened. He gives the example of the War Industry Board during the First World War.[107] In more unorthodox fashion, Alan Wolfe attempted to deal with this problem in his notion of the 'dual state'. Emerging from the international policy needs of postwar American capitalism, the 'dual state' presented two faces: one, 'democratic and popular', geared to elections and to public and Congressional discussion of foreign policy, was concerned to win public support; the other was 'liberal (in the classic sense), responsible for the accumulation of capital and for the protection of the agencies doing the accumulating'. The Vietnam war appeared as both the apogee, and, in its failure to effect counter-revolution, the undoing of this second face of the 'dual state'.[108]

Especially influential have been the theories of relative autonomy developed by Nicos Poulantzas. Building on the structural Marxism of Louis Althusser, Poulantzas maintained in the early 1970s that structural causation was the key to understanding the capitalist state. Following Marx's line in *The Eighteenth Brumaire of Louis Bonaparte*, rather than in *The Communist Manifesto*, structural Marxists came to concede a relative autonomy to the state, and to deny any necessity for the capitalist state to be staffed by personnel with direct links to the dominant class. This analysis put structuralists at odds with the 'instrumentalist' tradition represented by Ralph Miliband. The deep structure of the state sets limits for policy-makers and determines (although not in an absolute sense) where, within the state apparatus, decisions are made.[109] The structuralist approach, although it raised familiar problems of falsifiability, offered a vocabulary within which to consider the continuity-within-change so characteristic of the foreign policies of capitalist countries.[110]

The Marxist position on state autonomy furthest away from *The Communist Manifesto* may be seen in the work of Claus Offe, together with writers, like Fred Block, influenced by him. For Offe, the state occupies a quasi-independent position, flanked by the disorganised ranks of capital and labour. The policies pursued by state managers are nonetheless shaped by the managers' dependence on revenue generated by capitalist activity. A functionally 'successful' state structure depends upon the degree to which policy-making practices satisfy both the independent needs of state managers and those of capital.[111] This 'extreme state autonomy' variant of Marxism, in fact, sails close to the non-Marxist position of a writer like Stephen Krasner,[112] and, indeed, raises questions about the distinction between 'Marxist' and 'non-Marxist' positions in this area.

5 Concluding remarks

In this concluding section, it is the intention to enter two pleas. The first is against static and ahistorical explanations. Modes of foreign policy-making vary both across different policy areas,[113] and over time. Cyclical theorists like Schlesinger and Huntington implicitly accept that different historical eras produce correspondingly different styles of policy-making.[114] Linear studies of capitalist development – for example, of the shifts in American capitalism which took place in the late 1970s and 1980s[115] – also do well to embrace the notion of dynamic change in policy-making as well as in policy.

The second plea is for more concern for democracy and accountability. What is striking about so much of the literature considered in this chapter is the virtual silence about Congressional, much less public, roles in foreign policy. The silence is, of course, attributable to a variety of attitudes: for example, a resolute determination to eschew the normative dimension of explanation; an implicit embrace of elite-based, secretive decision-making; or, indeed, a metaphysical despair about prospects for improvement. Nonetheless, it is worth emphasising that efficiency and democracy are not mutually exclusive. Secretiveness and elitism encourage abuses of power, the perpetuation of misperceptions, and the artificial constriction of policy agendas.

This chapter has considered various theoretical approaches to the politics of foreign policy-making, thus complementing the 'international politics' approach of Chapter 1. Overarching theory of the type advocated by Rosenau has proved disappointing.[116] 'Middle level' theory, relating to individual decision-makers and governmental structures, has provided valuable insights and opened new avenues. As with overarching behaviourist-positivist theory, however, 'middle level' theories have their own provenance and limitations. In particular, it should be recognised that much of the theory considered in this chapter clearly bears the imprint of its Cold War context, together with the rather uncritical and ahistorical acceptance of American hegemony.[117] Similarly, the American debate between pluralist and ruling elite theorists of state power was largely defined by Cold War concerns and priorities. The test of this whole body of theory lies in its ability to survive in post-Cold War, post-hegemonic conditions.

Notes

1   S. Smith, 'Theories of foreign policy: an historical overview', *Review of International Studies*, 12, 1986, pp. 13–29, p. 13.

2   D. R. Kinder and J.A. Weiss, 'In lieu of rationality: psychological perspectives on foreign policy decision-making', *Journal of Conflict Resolution*, 22, 1978, pp. 707–36, p. 707.

3   H. A. Simon, *Administrative Behaviour*, New York, 1959.

4   R. Jervis, 'Rational deterrence: theory and evidence', *World Politics*, 41, 1989, pp. 183–207, p. 204.

5   See I. McLean, *Public Choice: An Introduction*, Oxford, 1987; B. Hindess, *Choice, Rationality and Social Theory*, London, 1988; P. Dunleavy and B. O'Leary, *Theories of the State: The Politics of Liberal Democracy*, London, 1987, pp. 75, 91, 93.

6   G.T. Allison, *Essence of Decision: Explaining the Cuban Missile Crisis*, Boston, 1971, pp. 29–30.

7   P. Williams, *Crisis Management: Confrontation and Diplomacy in the Nuclear Age*, London, 1976, p. 63.

8   M. Clarke, 'The foreign policy system: a framework for analysis', in M. Clarke and B. White, eds., *Understanding Foreign Policy: The Foreign Policy Systems Approach*, Aldershot, 1989, pp. 27–59.

9   Smith, 'Theories of foreign policy', p.19.

10   Dunleavy and O'Leary, *Theories of the State*, p. 88. See also L. Jensen, *Explaining Foreign Policy*, Englewood Cliffs, 1982, p. 6.

11   *Essence of Decision*, p. 30 (my emphasis).

12   J. D. Steinbruner, *The Cybernetic Theory of Decision*, Princeton, 1974, p. 45.

13   J. N. Rosenau, 'Pre-theories and theories of foreign policy', in R. B. Farrell, ed., *Approaches to Comparative and International Politics*, Evanston, 1966, pp. 27–92. See also Smith, 'Theories of foreign policy', p. 18.

14   For example, it provides the organising structure for C.W. Kegley and E.R. Wittkopf, *American Foreign Policy: Pattern and Process*, 3rd ed., New York, 1987.

15   See P. Callahan *et al.*, eds., *Describing Foreign Policy Behaviour*, Beverly Hills, 1982; M. A. East *et al.*, eds., *Why Nations Act*, Beverly Hills, 1978; and G.F. Hermann and G. Peacock, 'The evolution and future of research in the comparative study of foreign policy', in C. F. Hermann *et al.*, eds., *New Directions in the Study of Foreign Policy*, Boston, 1987, pp. 13–32, at p. 28. See also J. Wilkenfield *et al.*, *Foreign Policy Behaviour*, Beverly Hills, 1980 (Interstate Behaviour Analysis project).

16   J. N. Rosenau, *The Scientific Study of Foreign Policy* 2nd ed., London, 1980, pp. 231–9. See also C. W. Kegley, *The Comparative Study of Foreign Policy: Paradigm Lost?*, Columbia (South Carolina), 1980.

17   Hermann and Peacock, 'The evolution and future of research', pp. 18–21. See also R. J. Bernstein, *The Restructuring of Social and Political Theory*, Philadelphia, 1978; T. S. Kuhn, *The Structure of Scientific Revolution*, Chicago, 1970; and C. Reynolds, *Theory and Explanation in International Politics*, London, 1973.

18 See Smith, 'Theories of foreign policy', pp. 22–5.

19 J. N. Rosenau, 'A pre-theory revisited: world politics in an era of cascading interdependence', *International Studies Quarterly*, 28, 1984, pp. 245–305.

20 See, e.g. K. N. Waltz, *Theory of International Politics*, Reading (Massachusetts), 1979, p. 122.

21 See M. Clarke, 'Foreign policy and comparative politics: a strange divide', *Politics*, 6, 1986, pp. 3–8; see also, C. Tempest, 'Clarke and comparative politics', *Politics*, 7, 1987, pp. 48–50.

22 See East, *et al.*, eds., *Why Nations Act*, at p. 20; also P. Callahan *et al.*, eds., *Describing Foreign Policy Behaviour* (especially C. F. Hermann, 'Foreword', pp. 7–10).

23 See S. Smith, ed., *International Relations: British and American Perspectives*, Oxford, 1985.

24 The debate may be traced in S. Smith, 'Foreign policy analysis: British and American orientations and methodologies', *Political Studies*, 31, 1983, pp. 556–65; J. Palmer, 'The study of British foreign policy: a reply to Brian White', *British Journal of International Studies*, 4, 1978, pp. 266–9; and F.S. Northedge, 'Transnationalism: the American illusion', *Millenium*, 5, 1976, pp. 21–39; S. Grader, 'The English school of international relations', *Review of International Studies*, 14, 1988, pp. 29–44.

25 S. Smith, 'Describing and explaining foreign policy behaviour', *Polity*, 17, 1985, pp. 595–607, p. 602.

26 See G. Berridge, 'The political theory and institutional history of state-systems', *British Journal of International Studies*, 6, 1980, pp. 82–92, at p. 82.

27 Rosenau, *The Scientific Study of Foreign Policy*, p. 14. See also J. C. Garnett, *Commonsense and the Theory of International Politics*, London, 1984, pp. 22–3.

28 See Clarke, 'The foreign policy system', p. 42.

29 See J. G. Stoessinger, *Crusaders and Pragmatists: Movers of Modern American Foreign Policy*, New York, 1985; R.C. Snyder and P. Diesing, *Conflict Among Nations*, Princeton, 1977, p. 308; L.S. Etheredge, 'Personality effects on American foreign policy' *American Political Science Review*, 72, 1978, pp. 434–51; and W. P. Kreml, *The Anti-Authoritarian Personality*, Oxford, 1977.

30 Kegley and Wittkopf, *American Foreign Policy*, pp. 535–6.

31 J. D. Barber, *The Presidential Character*, 3rd ed., Englewood Cliffs, 1985, p. 10. See also J. D. Barber, *Politics by Humans*, Durham (North Carolina), 1988.

32 See *The Presidential Character*, 1st ed., 1972, and J. D. Barber, 'President Reagan's character' (1980), in C.W. Kegley and E.R. Wittkopf, eds., *Perspectives on American Foreign Policy*, New York, 1983, pp. 494–500.

33 G. Wills, *Reagan's America: Innocents at Home*, London, 1988, p. 404. See also N.N. Holland, 'The L-shaped mind of Ronald Reagan', in A. McIntyre, ed., *Aging and Political Leadership*, Oxford, 1988, pp. 243–59.

34 See, e.g. D. Caldwell, ed., *Henry Kissinger, his Personality and Policies*, Durham, 1983.

35 See S. Smith, 'Belief Systems and the Study of International Relations', in S. Smith and R. Little, eds., *Belief Systems and International Relations*, Oxford, 1989, pp. 11–36, p. 21.

36 S. G. Walker, 'The interface between beliefs and behaviour', *Journal of Conflict Resolution*, 21, 1977, pp. 129–68. 'If his opponent chooses an absolute gain policy, then Kissinger counters with a relative loss manoeuvre. He continues this response pattern until he converts his opponent to a relative gain solution' (p. 158).

37 See Smith, 'Belief Systems', pp. 23–4.

38 *Ibid.*, pp. 27–35. See also G. Hopple, ed., *Biopolitics, Political Psychology and International Politics*, New York, 1982, p. 99; W. Carlsnaes, *Ideology and Foreign Policy*, London, 1986, pp. 98–9; J. Vogler, 'Perspectives on the foreign policy system: psychological approaches', in Clarke and White, eds., *Understanding Foreign Policy*, pp. 135–62, pp. 141–2; R. Mandel, 'Psychological approaches to international relations', in M. G. Hermann, ed., *Political Psychology*, San Francisco, 1986, pp. 251–78.

39 J. Spear and P. Williams, 'Belief Systems and Foreign Policy', in Little and Smith, eds., *Belief Systems*, pp. 190–208, pp. 193–4.

40 I. L. Janis, *Victims of Groupthink*, Boston, 1972, pp. 8, 48, 35–48, 44, 165, 147, 180. See also I. L. Janis, *Groupthink*, 2nd ed., Boston, 1982; and I.L. Janis and L. Mann, *Decision-Making*, New York, 1977, p. 132.

41 Princeton, 1970.

42 See R. Jervis, *The Illogic of American Nuclear Strategy*, Ithaca, 1984, p. 38.

43 R. Jervis, *Perception and Misperception in International Politics*, Princeton, 1976, pp. 187, 117, 382, 203, 343, 319, 356–66, 414–16.

44 See H. Jordan, *Crisis: The Last Year of the Carter Presidency*, London, 1982, at p. 264. See also S. Smith, 'Groupthink and the Hostage Rescue Mission', *British Journal of Political Science*, 15, 1984, pp. 117–26.

45 E. R. May, *Lessons of the Past: The Use and Misuse of History in American Foreign Policy*, New York, 1973.

46 See T. Higgins, *The Perfect Failure: Kennedy, Eisenhower and the CIA at the Bay of Pigs*, London, 1988.

47 R. E. Neustadt and E.R. May, *Thinking in Time*, New York, 1986.

48 D. M. Shafer, *Deadly Paradigms: The Failure of U.S. Counterinsurgency Policy*, Princeton, 1988, pp. 6, 166, 203, 178. For a 'misperception' analysis of the Cold War, see R. J. Barnet, 'An absence of trust', in C. W. Kegley and E. R. Wittkopf, eds., *The Global Agenda*, 2nd. ed., New York, 1988, pp. 127–37. See also C. A. Kupchan, 'American globalism in the Middle East, *Political Science Quarterly*, 103, 1988–89, pp. 585–612, p. 603.

49 D. M. Barrett, 'The mythology surrounding Lyndon Johnson, his advisers, and the 1965 decision to escalate the Vietnam war', *Political Science Quarterly*, 103, 1988–89, pp. 637–4.

50 A. A. Stein, 'When misperception matters', *World Politics*, 34, 1982, pp. 505–26.

51 New York, 1966.

52 Steinbruner, *The Cybernetic Theory of Decision*, pp. 86–7.

53 *Ibid.*, pp. 153–326.

54 D. Mefford, 'Analogical reasoning and the definition of the situation', in Hermann, Kegley and Rosenau, eds., *New Directions in the Study of Foreign Policy*, pp. 221–47, p. 240.

55 On cognition, see A.L. George, *Presidential Decision-Making in Foreign Policy*, Boulder (Colorado), 1980, pp. 145–9; M. L. Cottam, *Foreign Policy Decision Making*, Boulder, 1986; D. A. Sylvan and S. Chan, eds., *Foreign Policy Decision Making*, New York, 1984.

56 C. A. Powell *et al.*, 'Opening the "black box" ', in Hermann *et al.*, eds., *New Directions*, pp. 203–20, p. 210.

57 H. E. Purkitt and J. W. Dyson, 'The role of cognition in U.S. foreign policy towards Southern Africa', *Political Psychology*, 6, 1986, pp. 71–96.

58 M. J. Shapiro, 'Textualizing global politics', in J. Der Derian and M. J. Shapiro, eds., *International/Intertextual Relations*, Lexington (Massachusetts), 1989, pp. 11–22, p. 17.

59 G. T. Allison and P. Szanton, *Remaking Foreign Policy: The Organizational Connection*, New York, 1976, pp. 20–1.

60 The following may be cited from the enormous literature: C. E. Lindblom, 'The science of muddling through', *Public Administration Review*, 19, 1959, pp. 79–88; M. H. Halperin, 'Why bureaucrats play games', *Foreign Policy*, 2, 1971, pp. 70–90; M. H. Halperin, *Bureaucratic Politics and Foreign Policy*, Washington D.C., 1974; D. Caldwell, 'Bureaucratic foreign policy making', *American Behavioural Scientist*, 21, 1977, pp. 87–110; C. F. Hermann, 'Bureaucratic constraints on innovation in American foreign policy', in Kegley and Wittkopf, eds., *Perspectives on American Foreign Policy*, pp. 390–409; and R. Hilsman, *The Politics of Policy Making in Defense and Foreign Affairs*, New York, 1987.

61 G. T. Allison and M.H. Halperin, 'Bureaucratic politics: a paradigm and some policy implications', *World Politics*, 24, 1972, pp. 40–79.

62 *Essence of Decision*, p. 67.

63 *Ibid.*, p. 92.

64 *Ibid.*, p. 144.

65 Halperin, *Bureaucratic Politics and Foreign Policy*, p. 293.

66 B. Jenkins and A. Gray, 'Bureaucratic politics and power', *Political Studies*, 31, 1983, pp. 177–93, p. 188; see also L. Freedman, 'Logic, politics and foreign policy processes', *International Affairs*, 52, 1976, pp. 434–49; E. E. Schattsneider, *The Semi-Sovereign People*, New York, 1960; S. Lukes, *Power: A Radical View*, London, 1974; and C. Ham and M. Hill, *The Policy Process in the Modern Capitalist State*, Brighton, 1984, pp. 64–71.

67 R. J. Art, 'Bureaucratic politics and American foreign policy: a critique', *Policy Sciences*, 4, 1973, pp. 467–90, p. 486.

68 *Essence of Decision*, p. 277.

69 See, e.g. B. Kellerman, 'Allison redux: three more decision-making models', *Polity*, 15, 1983, pp. 351–67.

70 See S. Smith, 'Perspectives on the foreign policy system: bureaucratic politics approaches', in Clarke and White, eds., *Understanding Foreign Policy*, pp. 109–34, pp. 116–17. See also T. C. Sorensen, *Decision Making in the White House*, New York, 1969, p. 12.

71 J. N. Rosati, 'Developing a systematic decision-making framework:

bureaucratic politics in perspective', *World Politics*, 34, 1982, pp. 418–36.

72 See P. A. Anderson, 'What do decision makers do when they make a foreign policy decision?', in Hermann et al, eds., *New Directions*, pp. 285–308, p. 288.

73 See K. J. Holsti, 'National role conceptions in the study of foreign policy', *International Studies Quarterly*, 14, 1970, pp. 233–309.

74 On Reagan (and Nixon's 1972 trip to China), see J. N. Rosenau, 'Roles and role scenarios in foreign policy', in S. G. Walker, ed., *Role Theory and Foreign Policy Analysis*, Durham, 1987, pp. 44–65, at p. 47. See also R. W. Cottam, *Foreign Policy Motivation*, Pittsburgh, 1977, pp. 321–2.

75 M. G. Hermann, 'Foreign policy role orientations and the quality of foreign policy decisions', in Walker, ed., *Role Theory*, pp. 123–40, at p. 123.

76 Rosenau, 'Roles and role scenarios', p. 45. See also M. Hollis and S. Smith, 'Roles and reasons in foreign policy decision making', *British Journal of Political Science*, 16, 1986, pp. 269–86, p. 285; and J. M. Roberts, *Decision-Making during International Crises*, London, 1988, pp. 165–6.

77 L. Fisher, *Presidential Spending Power*, Princeton, 1975, pp. 3–4.

78 See G. M. Guess, *The Politics of United States Foreign Aid*, London, 1987, pp. 52–78.

79 Allison and Halperin, 'Bureaucratic politics', p. 46.

80 Halperin, *Bureaucratic Politics and Foreign Policy*, p. 313.

81 M. Clarke and S. Smith, 'Perspectives on the foreign policy system: implementation approaches', in Clarke and White, eds., *Understanding Foreign Policy*, pp. 163–84, pp. 165–72.

82 See B. G. Peters, *American Public Policy*, 2nd ed., Chatham (New Jersey), 1986, pp. 84–100.

83 C. Hood, *The Limits of Administration*, New York, 1976, pp. 192–97.

84 J. L. Pressman and A. Wildavsky, *Implementation*, Berkeley, 1973, p. xxii.

85 See A. F. Lowenthal, 'United States policy towards Latin America: "liberal", "radical" and "bureaucratic" perspectives', *Latin American Research Review*, 8, 1973, pp. 3–26.

86 See E. S. Maynard, 'The bureaucracy and implementation of U.S. human rights policy', *Human Rights Quarterly*, 11, 1989, pp. 175–248.

87 S. Smith and M. Clarke, eds., *Foreign Policy Implementation*, London, 1985, p. 3.

88 R. M. Nixon, *Six Crises*, New York, 1962, p. xiv.

89 J. M. Roberts, *Decision-Making during International Crises*, pp. 218–26; also O. R. Holsti, *Crisis, Escalation, War*, London, 1972, p. 12.

90 See Williams, *Crisis Management*, p. 67.

91 See R. N. Lebow, *Nuclear Crisis Management*, Ithaca (New York), 1987, p. 85; R. N. Lebow, *Between Peace and War*, Baltimore, 1981, p. 119. See also R. McNamara, *Blundering into Disaster*, London, 1987.

92 See J. R. Oneal, 'The rationality of decision making during international crises', *Polity*, 20, 1988, pp. 598–627.

93 R. R. Alford and R. Friedland, *Powers of Theory: Capitalism, the State and Democracy*, Cambridge, 1985, p. 134. See also R. Dahl, *A Preface to Democratic Theory*, Chicago, 1956.

94 New York, 1951.

95 Q. Skinner, 'The empirical theorists of democracy and their critics', *Political Theory*, 1, 1973, pp. 287–306. See also Dunleavy and O'Leary, *Theories of the State*, p. 22.

96 C. Lindblom, *Politics and Markets*, New York, 1977; and R. Dahl, *A Preface to an Economic Theory of Democracy*, London, 1985.

97 See Dunleavy and O'Leary, *Theories of the State*, p. 193.

98 See D. H. Blake and R.S. Walters, *The Politics of Global Economic Relations*, 3rd ed., Englewood Cliffs, 1987, pp. 215–18.

99 Dunleavy and O'Leary, ch. 6. See also E. Nordlinger, *The Autonomy of the Democratic State*, Cambridge (Massachusetts), 1981.

100 M. J. Parenti, *Democracy for the Few*, 5th ed., New York, 1988, pp. 299–300.

101 C. W. Mills, *The Power Elite*, New York, 1956; G. W. Domhoff, *Who Rules America?*, Englewood Cliffs, 1967, and *The Powers that Be*, New York, 1978.

102 London, 1973, pp. 111–13. For an attempt to synthesise various radical theories of state power, see J. Hoffman, *State, Power and Democracy*, New York, 1988.

103 See V. Kubalkova and A. A. Cruickshank, *Marxism and International Relations*, Oxford, 1985, p. 20.

104 G. Therborn, *What does the Ruling Class do when it Rules?*, London, 1978, p. 97.

105 K. Marx and F. Engels, *Collected Works*, 6, London, 1976, p. 486.

106 See B. Jessop, *The Capitalist State*, Oxford, 1982, ch. 2.

107 J. O'Connor, *The Fiscal Crisis of the State*, New York, 1973, pp. 67–68.

108 A. Wolfe, *The Limits of Legitimacy*, New York, 1977, pp. 1780, 202, 213.

109 N. Poulantzas, *Political Power and Social Classes*, London, 1973; R. Miliband, 'Poulantzas and the capitalist state', *New Left Review*, 82, 1973, pp. 83–92; N. Poulantzas, 'The capitalist state: a reply to Miliband and Laclau', *New Left Review*, 95, 1976, pp. 63–83. On the mechanisms of structural causation in foreign policy-making, see P. McGowan and S. G. Walker, 'Radical and conventional models of U.S. foreign and economic policy making', *World Politics*, 33, 1981, pp. 346–82, pp. 359–65. See also H. Ward, 'Structural power – a contradiction in terms?', *Political Studies*, 35, 1987, pp. 593–610; and A. Vincent, *Theories of the State*, Oxford, 1987, pp. 171–5.

110 See N. Poulantzas, *State, Power, Socialism*, London, 1979, for his later 'class struggle' orientation. See also M. Carnoy, *The State and Political Theory*, Princeton, 1984, pp. 220–35.

111 Jessop, pp. 110–11; C. Offe, 'The theory of the capitalist state and the problem of policy formation', in L. Lindberg *et al.*, eds., *Stress and Contradiction in Modern Capitalism*, Lexington, 1975, pp. 87–106; C. Offe, *Disorganised Capitalism*, Cambridge, 1985; F. Block, 'Beyond relative autonomy', in R. Miliband and J. Saville, eds., *The Socialist Register 1980*, London, 1980, pp. 227–42; T. Skocpol, 'Political response to capitalist crisis', *Politics and Society*, 10, 1982, pp. 155–70; Carnoy, *The State and Political Theory*, pp. 213–19.

112   S. Krasner, *Defending the National Interest*, Princeton, 1978. See also P. B. Evans *et al.*, *Bringing the State Back In*, Cambridge, 1985 (especially T. Skocpol, 'Bringing the state back in', pp. 3–43); F. Halliday, 'State and society in international relations', in H.C. Dyer and L. Mangasarian, eds., *The Study of International Relations*, New York, 1989, pp. 40–59.

113   See McGowan and Walker, 'Radical and conventional models', pp. 367–69.

114   S. P. Huntington, *American Politics: The Promise of Disharmony*, Cambridge (Massachusetts), 1982; A. M. Schlesinger, *The Cycles of American History*, New York, 1987; also C. Paton, 'Paradigm of U.S. politics', *Politics*, 9, 1989, pp. 36–42, at p. 37.

115   See K. Hoover and R. Plant, *Conservative Capitalism in Britain and the United States*, London, 1989.

116   See articles in *International Studies Quarterly*, 33, 3, September 1989.

117   See E. Krippendorff, 'The dominance of American approaches in international relations', in Dyer and Mangasarian, eds., *The Study*, pp. 28–39.

Presidential foreign policy

1 Introduction: a president chooses between war and peace

In the summer of 1965, the government of the United States faced an either/or choice of monumental proportions: either send hundreds of thousands of soldiers to South Vietnam and try to save the faltering non-communist government of that country, or call it quits to America's military presence in Southeast Asia. For over a decade, the US government had subscribed to the proposition that the 'loss' of South Vietnam to communism would signify another triumph for the Soviet Union and Red China (as Americans then called the People's Republic of China) in their efforts to move the entire world towards communism. As exaggerated as that American fear may seem in retrospect, most Republicans and Democrats in the United States shared that fear.[1]

In July 1965, the chickens had come home to roost. Despite pouring billions of dollars and tens of thousands of advisers and soldiers into Vietnam for years, the United States confronted the near-collapse of its aims there. The National Liberation Front (Viet Cong) guerrillas from South Vietnam itself and troops from North Vietnam were about to achieve the goal enunciated by North Vietnam's Marxist, nationalist leader, Ho Chi Minh – a unified Vietnam, comprising the old North and South Vietnam, free of foreign domination and led by a communist government. Throughout 1965, the Viet Cong and North Vietnamese had been defeating the poorly organised and dispirited South Vietnamese military, its leadership riddled by corruption.

The decision of whether or not to transform America's military presence in Vietnam rested almost entirely with one man, the President of the United States. How had it come to this, that one person – admittedly a powerful one, but still just one person in American government – could decide whether or not American boys would die (and kill) in a little country on the other side of the world? The question demands attention because there is no doubt that the founders of the American republic (the men who wrote its Constitution) had emphatically not wanted decisions of war and peace to be made by a single individual, not even the President.[2]

The President in July 1965 was Lyndon Baines Johnson. The decision was war. The results for the US over the following seven and a half years were disastrous – over fifty thousand soldiers killed and ultimate defeat. But Johnson was neither the first nor the last modern President to send troops to faraway corners of the world. How, indeed, had it come to this?

2 The founders, Presidents and foreign policy

The men who wrote the Constitution of the United States in 1787 were determined that neither a President nor the Congress (and certainly not a military leader) would be empowered to engage America in a war and lead that effort. They separated foreign policy powers, in general, and war powers, in particular. The President would be Commander-in-Chief of the military, ensuring that generals and admirals would answer to a civilian leader. But Congress would hold the powers to declare war and to raise and support an army and navy. There would be no Presidential wars, if the founders had their way.

Alexander Hamilton, one of the advocates of the new Constitution in 1787, provides the most persuasive testimony for this, because he favoured a strong Presidency. He compared the President's war powers to that of the British monarch:

It would amount to nothing more than the supreme command and direction of the military and naval forces, as first general and admiral of the Confederacy; while that of the British king extends to the *declaring* of war and to the *raising* and *regulating* of fleets and armies – all which, by the Constitution under consideration, would appertain to the legislature.[3]

Similarly, James Madison, who perhaps was more responsible than any other figure for the creation of the Constitution, wrote after its adoption of 'the necessity of a rigid adherence to the simple ... fundamental doctrine of the constitution, that the power to declare war, including the power of judging the causes of war, is fully and exclusively vested in the legislature'.[4]

More broadly, in terms of foreign policy, the President would appoint and receive ambassadors and would, with the 'advice and consent' of the Senate, make treaties with other countries. There would be no American foreign policy *embodied* by the President; instead, both Congress and the President would guide America's relations with the world.

Not that there were no disagreements over foreign policy powers. Some feared Congress might be too slow to respond to a sudden attack by a foreign power on the United States. Thus a proposal to empower Congress to *make* war was changed to the power to *declare* war. But, except for such emergency 'protection of the community against foreign attacks', war powers were divided, with Congress, not the President, given the authority to decide for or against such bloody and costly entanglements.[5] For most of the nineteenth century and the early twentieth century, it worked out that way. Presidents played a key role in foreign policy, to be sure, but were mostly deferential to the will of Congress. In 1801, for instance, Tripoli declared war on the United States and attacked its naval vessels in the Bay of Tripoli. President Thomas Jefferson (1801–09) explained to Congress how the Americans under his command responded: 'Unauthorised by the constitution, without the sanction of Congress, to go beyond the line of defence, the vessel, being disabled from committing further hostilities, was liberated with its crew.'[6] It was constitutionally inappropriate and thus impermissible for a President and those under his command to go further, thought Jefferson, without Congressional authorisation.

Mostly, the nineteenth century was a long era of what political science professor (later President) Woodrow Wilson characterised in 1888 as 'Congressional government' – 'the predominant and controlling force, the centre and source of all motive and of all regulative power is Congress'.[7]

3 Theodore Roosevelt, Woodrow Wilson, Franklin Roosevelt and the growth of Presidential power

Towards the end of the nineteenth century, America began to experience changes which slowly transformed the Presidency. A growing capitalist economy accelerated a shift from a mostly agrarian society to a much more industrialised one, with millions of immigrants pouring into the country for jobs and new lives. With

industrialisation came more international trade and relative prosperity, but also complex societal problems – urban slums, overburd-
ened public education systems, and public health dilemmas, to name
but a few. With such problems came the beginnings of what political
scientists call the 'welfare state', and what many ordinary Americans
simply call 'big government'.

Along with this came the belief that the United States had a role to
play in international affairs. Rejecting the advice of President George
Washington in his Farewell Address to 'avoid entangling alliances'
with other countries, Presidents Theodore Roosevelt (1901–09) and
Woodrow Wilson (1913–21) personified the new thinking about
America's role in the world and the Presidency's role in managing
American government and foreign policy. Simple deference to Congress was out. Wilson thought the Presidency uniquely endowed to
represent the democratic values of the American people in world
affairs. He thus threw himself into an exhaustive (albeit failed) mission
to persuade the necessary two-thirds of the Senate to approve
American entry into the League of Nations. Roosevelt was similarly
internationalist and aggressive in asserting presidential power. He
later explained: 'I declined to adopt the view that what was
imperatively necessary for the nation could not be done by the President unless he could find some specific authorisation to do it.'[8]
Therefore, in an era when the United States became involved in the
Spanish-American War and the First World War, a new view of
Presidential power was ascendant.

Nonetheless, the approach of the Second World War made it clear
that Presidents could go only so far in involving the United States in a
military conflict. A strong isolationist sentiment arose in America in
the aftermath of the First World War, in the belief that the US had
wasted the lives of thousands of young men in a war that achieved
nothing for America. President Warren G. Harding (1921–23)
typified this view with his popular pledge to return the country to
'normalcy', a state of affairs distinguished by peace, prosperity, weak
government, and little involvement with European affairs. Controversial as this view was as Europe entered another great conflict in
the late 1930s, Congress was dominated by such isolationist
sentiment.

Passing a Neutrality Act in 1936 with President Franklin
Roosevelt's (1933–45) reluctant agreement, Congress frustrated the
President's efforts to align the United States closely with Britain and

its allies in the fight against Germany's Hitler. Roosevelt had been conspicuously successful in the 1930s in adding to the Presidency's domestic powers, as he fought a deep economic depression. But on questions such as war, his powers were partially restrained. Thus his confidential aide, Harry Hopkins, faced the difficult problem on a mission to Britain of 'explaining our constitutional provision that only Congress can declare war. Churchill understood this – perhaps he had learned it at his (American) mother's knee – but there were others of eminent rank in the British government who couldn't seem to get it through their heads.'[9]

Only an attack by Japan on the United States Pacific Ocean naval base at Pearl Harbor in December 1941 induced Congress to get behind the President and declare war on Japan and Germany. During the war, Roosevelt was very much the leader of America's foreign policy. Left open to question, though, was the future of the Presidency's powers in foreign affairs after the war's end. If events followed the patterns set after the Civil War and the First World War, Congress would then reassert itself.

4 Harry Truman and the modern American Foreign Policy Presidency

Despite constitutional provisions dividing foreign policy powers, and the founders' intent that only Congress should take America to war, events and decisions after the Second World War transformed the Presidency's role to one of long-term dominance in foreign affairs. The events grew out of the Cold War. Faced with what he and most American leaders perceived as Soviet adventurism, President Harry S. Truman (1945–53) responded in a number of important ways. Truman's approach is best illustrated by his response to communist North Korea's invasion of non-communist South Korea in the summer of 1950. Seeing the incursion as part of larger communist designs on world domination, Truman told his Secretary of State, Dean Acheson, 'We've got to stop the sons of bitches, no matter what.' Flying to Washington after receiving news of the invasion, Truman reflected how 'Communism was acting in Korea just as Hitler, Mussolini, and the Japanese had acted ten, fifteen, twenty years earlier.'

Without waiting for authorisation from Congress or the United Nations, Truman ordered troops along with air and naval support to defend South Korea. As Truman hoped, Congress and the UN followed his lead, the latter with a Security Council resolution (passed in the absence of the Soviet Union) calling on UN members to oppose the North Korean invasion. Significantly, Truman declined to ask for a Congressional resolution authorising or approving his war decision, even after the fact. Acheson later explained:

At the moment, troops of the U.S. were engaged in a desperate struggle in and around Pusan (South Korea). Hundreds, thousands of them were being killed ... if, at this time, action was pending before Congress, by which hearings might be held, and long inquiries were being entered into as to whether or not this was the right thing to do, or whether the President had the authority to do it, or whether he needed congressional authority for matters of that sort – we would be doing about the worst thing we could possibly do for the support of our troops and their morale.[10]

However, honourable Truman's and Acheson's motives may have been, their actions represented a new era in the history of Presidential foreign policy power.

Some members of Congress objected to American entry into the Korean War. Senator Robert Taft said Truman had 'simply usurped authority, in violation of the laws and the constitution', while Senator Arthur Watkins complained that 'the United States is at war by order of the President'. In response to such critics, the Truman administration claimed that 'the President, as Commander in Chief of the Armed Forces of the United States, has full control over their use thereof'. It was a sweeping assertion and defence of Presidential dominance in foreign affairs. One constitutional scholar writes that previous American history 'offers no example of a President who plunged the nation into war in order to repel an attack on some foreign nation'.[11]

Truman fully subscribed to the previously described views of Theodore Roosevelt on Presidential power and to a controversial Supreme Court decision written by Justice George Sutherland. The Justice set forth the modern theory of 'inherent' Presidential power over foreign affairs in the *Curtiss-Wright* decision, writing of a 'plenary and exclusive power of the presidency as sole organ of the federal government in international relations'.[12] Though the decision was based on a highly questionable reading of the Constitution, Presidents since the Truman era have often cited Sutherland's opinion.

Significantly, Congress retained its constitutionally mandated power of the purse – the power to fund or not fund any governmental activity – during this period. But as an institution, it deferred to

President Truman's Korean policy and supported it with budgetary outlays, despite the misgivings of some of its members. A new era in Presidential power had begun, the modern era of Presidential 'prerogatives', in which authority is unilaterally asserted in foreign affairs, justified by constitutional construction and interpretation.[13]

The Truman era was significant for another reason in the history of the Presidency and foreign policy – the creation by Congress of a national security bureaucracy in the White House to assist the President in co-ordinating other foreign policy bureaucracies, in gathering information, and in providing expertise and advice on foreign policy. No longer would Presidents have to rely on officials in the State Department, located across town from the White House, for such assistance. The National Security Council staff, working geographically and bureaucratically closer to the President, was yet another enhancement of the executive branch's ability to lead in foreign affairs.[14] The National Security Council itself (created in 1947 and placed in the Executive Office of the President in 1949) had a statutory membership of President, Vice-President and the Secretaries of State and Defence, together with others to be chosen by the President.

Importantly, Truman's assertions of Presidential power in foreign policy and the acquiescence of Congress, some constitutional scholars, and the Supreme Court, itself, did not occur in a political vacuum. They happened in an era when, despite America's creation of the atomic bomb and its rise to a position of supreme political, military, and economic power, there was widespread fear and distrust of the also nuclear-armed Soviet Union. Because they shared Truman's view of America's role in world affairs, most other political actors in Washington and the nation were ready to see the Presidency in a significant new role. Its occupant was not just leader of the United States, but also leader of the 'free world'.

5 Vietnam: a test of the limits of Presidential dominance in foreign affairs

Although there have been exceptions, the broad pattern of foreign policy decision-making in the last four decades has been one of the Presidency as prime mover. For instance, a number of key Republican leaders in Congress supported the so-called Bricker Amendment, which would have significantly limited a President's powers to make agreements with other nations. Although this put its sponsors and (fellow-Republican) President Dwight Eisenhower in an awkward conflict, the President sought and gained a bipartisan coalition in Congress sufficient to reject the Amendment.

A dramatic example of modern Presidential leadership on international matters is the case of America's relations with Vietnam. For over two decades, from the early 1950s until the mid-1970s, Presidents from both the Democratic and Republican parties moved the United States deeper and deeper into a seemingly unshakeable commitment of American resources in southeast Asia.

Despite a traditional American ideal of anti-colonialism, the Truman administration allied itself with France in that country's fight against Ho Chi Minh's movement to kick the French out and establish a unified, Marxist Vietnam, free of foreign domination. Dealing with such problems as the 'fall' of China to communism (with the victory of Mao Tse Tung's revolution), the war in Korea, and the Cold War, Truman started sending aid to the French in 1950. His Administration said:

The extension of communist authority in China represents a grievous political defeat for the U.S.; if southeast Asia also is swept by communism we shall have suffered a major political rout, the repercussion of which will be felt throughout the rest of the world, especially in the middle east and in a then critically exposed Australia.[15]

The Eisenhower Administration accepted these premises. In line with Truman's general policy of containment, President Eisenhower enunciated the so-called 'domino theory'. This was the idea that the fall of South Vietnam (an entity created at the 1954 Geneva Conference after the French defeat) would represent the beginning of a 'crumbling process' that would spread to the rest of Asia and beyond. By 1958, the Eisenhower Administration was sending South Vietnam more military aid than it was to any other nation. Eisenhower, as is often stated, kept America out of war, but he kept many Americans in Vietnam. He did so with the support of Congress, which had few dissenters.[16]

The Kennedy era (1961–63) saw a heightening of the Cold War. President Kennedy saw and refined plans for the Bay of Pigs invasion, with virtually no consultation with Congress.[17] The invasion led to the confrontation of 1962 over missiles in Cuba – a confrontation again managed with a minimum of Congressional involvement. The Soviet Union continued to enunciate a policy of supporting Third

World guerrilla wars of 'national liberation' against despotic or colonial-style governments allied with the United States. Not surprisingly, Kennedy's Administration announced the objective of preventing 'communist domination of South Vietnam'. But this became increasingly hard to achieve, as Viet Cong guerrillas and North Vietnamese soldiers continued to defeat the South Vietnamese army.

Meanwhile, various sectors of the South Vietnamese society became disenchanted with the autocratic President Diem. Just weeks before his own death, President Kennedy approved a plan for South Vietnamese military leaders to stage a coup to overthrow Diem. Kennedy and his advisers hoped that a non-violent coup might be possible, and would lead to a more stable and popular government of South Vietnam. Instead, President Diem was assassinated by the coup's leaders (who had worked closely with the CIA and other American government officials in planning the coup). Thus, an American President, again with virtually no consultation with Congress, had drawn the United States deeper into the Vietnam quagmire. When Kennedy was murdered three weeks after Diem's death, there were 16,000 American advisers in Vietnam.

Unfortunately for the American government and its new President, Lyndon Johnson (1963–69), the removal of Diem did not lead to stability in South Vietnam. Instead, governments were coming and going about every other month in 1964, prompting President Johnson's private remarks, 'I'm tired of all this coup shit.' After Kennedy's assassination, Johnson had pledged to support the late President's policies 'from Berlin to South Vietnam'. But the deterioration of the South Vietnamese government and military continued.

In August 1964, North Vietnamese torpedo boats attacked a US destroyer in the Gulf of Tonkin. The destroyer was vastly superior in firepower to what Johnson himself called 'three little PT boats', and damage to the American ship was slight, but the event caused a political firestorm in Washington. When, two nights later, commanders of another American ship reported what they believed to be another attack, Johnson consulted his advisers and authorised a retaliatory aid raid against North Vietnam.[18]

More importantly, Johnson asked for and received from Congress a mandate to take whatever actions he believed necessary 'to repel any armed attack against the forces of the United States and to prevent further aggression'. Senator J. William Fulbright was floor manager for this so-called Gulf of Tonkin Resolution in Senate debate. One wavering Senator asked Fulbright, 'looking ahead, if the President decided that it was necessary to use such force as could lead into war, will we give that authority by this resolution?' Fulbright answered, 'That is the way I would interpret it.'[19] The Resolution passed unanimously in the House of Representatives and with only two opposing votes in the Senate. It was yet another dramatic expansion of the Presidency's war powers.

In the first half of 1965, the South Vietnamese military lost more and more battles with the Viet Cong and North Vietnamese. Johnson faced in reality a prospect that three previous Presidents had faced more in the abstract – the fall of America's Vietnamese ally. Eisenhower and Kennedy especially had been able to stave off such a defeat with aid and advisers. But most of Lyndon Johnson's foreign policy advisers warned him in early 1965 that he needed either to engage the US military in a fully-fledged combat effort, involving hundreds of thousands of American soldiers, or to pull out what forces were there and accept defeat at the hands of Ho Chi Minh.

While Johnson gave serious attention to those advisers urging American withdrawal, most of his counsellors favoured a major military commitment.[20] On 28 July, Johnson (without a Congressional declaration of war, but with the Tonkin Resolution on the books) announced on live television: 'I have asked the commanding general, General Westmoreland, what more he needs to meet this mounting aggression. He had told me. We will meet his needs ... I do not find it easy to send the flower of our youth, our finest young men, into battle.'[21]

Johnson hoped that sending troops would force the communists to agree to a peace treaty that would save South Vietnam, but the Viet Cong and North Vietnamese met the Americanisation of the war with stubborn resistance. American soldiers began dying by the thousands, with no victory in sight. Increasingly, some members of Congress and the general public started questioning Johnson's constitutional right to have entered the war. Feeling trapped, unable either to win or pull out, Johnson did not seek re-election in 1968. Not only anti-war demonstrators on college campuses, but a majority of all Americans had lost their faith in Johnson as a war leader.[22]

Though much has been written about certain Congressional dissenters against the war, the more important fact about Congress is that, as a body, it supported the war policies of Vietnam-era Presidents up right to 1973. This point will be developed further in

Chapter 5. Many in Congress denounced aspects of Johnson's or Nixon's war policies, such as the bombing of North Vietnam, but only a few voted against funding the war. One of these was Senator Wayne Morse, who had also opposed the Gulf of Tonkin Resolution in 1964. In 1967, he lamented: 'So many of my colleagues tell me in the cloakroom and elsewhere, that they disagree with that policy, yet they come on the floor and vote to carry on that policy.'[23]

By the war's end, however, Vietnam had divided American society and weakened Presidential primacy in war powers. The 1973 War Powers Resolution was an explicit effort to 'fulfil the intent of the framers of the Constitution' in this area.[24] Further discussion of the Resolution's provisions and limitations is undertaken in Chapter 5 of this book. It may briefly be noted at this stage, however, that none of the Presidents who have taken office since 1973 have given their full support to the War Powers Resolution. Additionally, while the Resolution does place some limits on Presidential power, it also recognises considerable Presidential discretion, especially in the first sixty days of a military operation.[25] In the years since 1973, what one scholar calls the Constitution's 'invitation to struggle' over foreign policy has continued between Presidents and Congress.[26]

6   Decision-making styles and choices of modern Presidents

Each President must make important choices about how to structure the foreign policy advisory system which serves him. One key choice is whether or not to centre most foreign policy decision-making in the White House and thus become a 'hands on' manager of day-to-day problems in foreign affairs. The alternative is to place much of the responsibility on the Secretary of State, leaving the President free to deal with a limited number of prioritised problems.

A remarkable example of a White House-centred foreign policy decision-making system comes from the Nixon Administration. After his election in 1968, Richard Nixon met with Harvard professor Henry Kissinger to discuss the latter's possible appointment as National Security Adviser. In his memoirs, Kissinger writes that Nixon spoke of a 'massive organisational problem'. The President-elect 'had very little confidence in the State Department. Its personnel had no loyalty to him ... he was determined to run foreign policy from the White House.'[27] So he did, with Kissinger's help, and with Secretary of State William Rogers's frequent ignorance.

On issues ranging from opening relations with China to negotiating the Vietnam peace treaty, President Nixon purposely kept his own Secretary of State in the dark, while Kissinger travelled the world on secret diplomatic missions. Decisions and important deliberations took place at the White House, not the State Department. Kissinger recalls, for example, that Nixon excluded Rogers from the first meeting with Soviet Ambassador Dobrynin: 'Throughout his term, when a state visitor was received in the Oval Office by Nixon for a lengthy discussion, I was the only other American present.'[28] Similarly, Nixon offered key American ambassadors the permission and technical means to communicate with the President (by way of Kissinger), avoiding the normal procedure of ambassadors communicating with Washington by sending cables to the Secretary of State.[29]

Most modern Presidents have chosen to centre much of the foreign policy-making action in the Oval Office and in the nearby office of the National Security Adviser, though none have taken the practice to the extremes that Nixon did. Like him, they have felt frustrated or suspicious about the willingness and capability of the State Department bureaucracy to carry out their orders or those of the Secretary of State. John Kennedy respected his Secretary, Dean Rusk, but as President, Kennedy wanted to be (in effect) his own Secretary of State. So, with the assistance of his National Security Adviser, McGeorge Bundy, and the advice of persons scattered throughout his administration, Kennedy kept a close eye on foreign relations.

In two recent Administrations, Presidents Carter and Reagan allowed their National Security Advisers to rival the influence of their Secretaries of State. This does not mean that men such as Cyrus Vance (in the Carter Administration) and George Shultz (in the Reagan Administration) had no important influence on foreign policy. Quite the contrary. Still, the writings and testimony of Vance and Shultz make clear the continual struggles they faced in trying to be their respective Presidents' top foreign policy official.

Another choice Presidents must make is how they wish advice on foreign policy to be presented to them. Will many advisers have direct access to the President on foreign policy, or shall he have most information and advice routed through one or a few key advisers? John F. Kennedy and Lyndon Johnson were highly informal in their interactions with advisers. Kennedy was known to call up lower-level bureaucrats in the State Department or elsewhere in the government, bypassing normal channels to seek advice. Though Johnson met regularly with a small group of top advisers, known as the Tuesday Lunch Cabinet, on Vietnam War matters, he also talked with a diverse assortment of longtime political friends and advisers who lacked official standing.[30] Such an approach to advisers is sometimes referred to as a 'hub in the wheel' style, since a number of different advisers have direct access to the person at the centre of government, the President. Often these advisers have no idea who else the President is consulting.

Presidents Truman, Eisenhower and Nixon preferred more formal systems of receiving advice. These men employed so-called 'pyramid' advisory structures, which place the President at the top of the decision-making system and allow very few persons to transmit the advice of others to the chief executive. Presidents Truman and Eisenhower placed their Secretaries of State just below them at the top of their advisory systems. Therefore much of the advice these Presidents received was routed to them by their Secretaries. Eisenhower also relied heavily on formal meetings of the National Security Council to present him with alternatives in addressing problems on the international scene. Richard Nixon relied heavily on Henry Kissinger as the prime collector and conveyor of foreign policy alternatives.

Still, the extent to which Presidents have confined their advisory interactions to the 'hub in the wheel' or 'pyramid' models should not be exaggerated. Recent research suggests that Presidents Eisenhower and Johnson, for example, sought more diverse types of advice than had been previously thought.[31] No political scientist or historian can ever know with certainty all of the people to whom a President spoke and which conversations were most crucial.

Ultimately, an adviser is anyone chosen by a President to counsel him (or her, in the future) on a problem. Sometimes this is one with little or no official standing. A good example comes from the brief Presidency of Gerald Ford (1974–77) when Cambodian forces seized the American ship, the *Mayaguez*, and its men off the shores of Cambodia in 1975, Ford met with top advisers to consider an American response. Beyond recovering the American hostages, advisers such as then Secretary of State Henry Kissinger leaned toward a 'strong response' – heavy air strikes, as a form of punishment against the Cambodia government. In a room full of foreign policy heavyweights – the Secretaries of State and Defence, various military leaders, the Vice-President, and the Director of the CIA – the atmosphere was tense. Kissinger became emotional in warning Ford that if the United States failed to respond to the challenge, it would be a serious blow to American prestige around the world. Suddenly, as Ford recounts in his memoirs:

from the back of the room, a new voice spoke up. It was (White House official photographer David) Kennerly, who had been taking pictures of us for the past hour or so ... 'Has anyone considered', he asked, 'that this might be the act of a local Cambodian commander who has just taken it into his own hands to halt any ship that comes by? ... you can blow the whole place away and it's not gonna make any difference.'[32]

Ford recalls that there was a moment of silence in the Cabinet room before discussion resumed. When decision time came, Ford decided that 'what Kennerly had said made a lot of sense. Massive air strikes would constitute overkill.' Instead, the President directed that a rescue attempt proceed as planned, accompanied by only limited air strikes against a few military targets. This was neither the first nor the last time that a crucial 'adviser' to a President would be a friend, a family member, or some other person not listed on an administration's official personnel chart.

Some political scientists have extolled the benefits of a 'multiple advocacy system' serving the President.[33] Such an advisory system brings the President diverse points of view on foreign policy issues, with key members of his Administration (or others from outside the Administration) debating their differences in front of the President. While one can hardly argue against the ideal of a President confronting wide-ranging, in-depth presentations of competing policy alternatives, there are certain prices to be paid for employing such systems.

Presidents as diverse as the outgoing Lyndon Johnson, the formalistic Dwight Eisenhower, and the almost reclusive Richard Nixon have often found large meetings unwieldy, because irrelevant advice and discussions take up valuable time.[34] A stronger Presidential concern is over leaks. It is a fact of modern American political history that all Presidents, Democrats and Republicans, liberals and conservatives, have been driven to extreme frustration by leaks to the press about debates and differences among top policy-makers in the Administration. Even more upsetting to Presidents have been leaks about imminent Presidential decisions – sometimes disgruntled Administration figures leak a tentative Presidential decision to the press, in hopes that a negative reaction from Congress or other quarters might force the President to change his mind and not announce the decision.

No matter that Presidents themselves often leak information to the press – they see this as a Presidential prerogative – they are infuriated when others do it. President Ronald Reagan's response to leaks was to sign a directive requiring all top office-holders to take polygraph examinations (so-called 'lie detector' tests). But Reagan's Secretary of State, George Shultz, refused to submit to such examinations. While sympathetic to Reagan's frustration over leaks, Shultz went public with his criticism of such tests. He told reporters, 'The minute in this government I am told that I'm not trusted is the day I leave.'[35] Shultz offered his resignation to Reagan over the matter, but the President refused to accept it, withdrawing the lie-detector policy instead.

Rejecting such spectacular solutions as the Reagan polygraph plan, previous Presidents have often restricted the most important discussions of crucial foreign policy issues to relatively small groups of trusted advisers. While Presidents have been accused of tilting too strongly against multiple advocacy approaches to decision-making, they understand the costs associated with meetings of large groups of people to discuss key issues. Yet the alternative, that of a President seeing only a small number of advisers, has obvious problems – he may be cut off from important opinions in the American political environment. He may not understand, for example, how strong a protest may come from Congress in response to a particular action, unless there are advisers to warn him.

More importantly, if a President relies on the counsel of only a few advisers, he may choose an unwise course of action. Certainly, John Kennedy came to believe that a wider pattern of advisory interactions might have turned him against the Bay of Pigs fiasco. And Ronald Reagan might have avoided the Iran-Contra scandal had he directed his National Security Council to present him with more acceptable solutions to the problem of American hostages being held in Lebanon than selling arms to Iran in hopes of freeing the hostages.

7 Presidential leadership on foreign policy issues: recent Presidents, from Nixon to Bush

(a) *The Nixon Administration*   Despite the disgrace brought about by his concealment of evidence in the Watergate scandal and his unprecedented resignation from the Presidency, Richard Nixon led an Administration of unusual importance in foreign affairs. The great crowning achievement of the Nixon era was opening relations with the People's Republic of China, which had been estranged from the United States for over two decades. Since the Marxist government headed by Mao Tse Tung took power in 1949, the United States had clung to the fiction that the government of the little island nation of Taiwan was the *real* government of China. This was justified on the basis that the one-time leader of all of China, Chiang Kai Shek, had taken his government-in-exile to Taiwan after being overthrown in the Revolution. For years afterwards, conservative Republicans in the United States charged loudly that President Truman's administration had 'lost' China. To most policy-makers in Washington, it was unthinkable that the United States should even talk to leaders from Red China.

But Richard Nixon brought unique credentials to the Presidency which allowed and led him to travel to China for discussions with its leaders. First, Nixon had an undeniable reputation as an anti-communist, dating back to his days as an influential Congressman in the 1940s and 1950s who searched out communists in the American government. That reputation gave Nixon more freedom than a liberal, Democratic president would have had in reaching out to China without being politically damaged by the predictable conservative charges of 'selling out' the people of China.

Second, Nixon understood quite well that China had long since dropped its alliance with its giant communist neighbour, the Soviet Union. He knew that the opportunity existed to play the 'China card', that is to pressure the Soviet Union to accept continuance of American global leadership by showing the Russians that the US could ally itself more closely with the world's only other communist superpower. By pursuing better diplomatic relations with both China and the USSR, each of the mutually hostile communist countries was kept on guard about American relations with the other.[36]

Nixon pursued a policy of detente with the Soviet Union. After two decades of an often tense Cold War, both Nixon and the Soviet leadership recognised the need for dispassionate negotiations leading to a more stable management of the rivalry of the world's two most powerful nations. Detente did not mean friendship, exactly. (That word would only start being used in reference to the Soviet government in the late 1980s by President Bush.) But it did mean at least limited co-operation between governments, and talks about such crucial problems as a burgeoning nuclear arms race and serious differences on issues such as human rights and revolutions in Third

World countries. One product of these negotiations was the first SALT Treaty, which placed limits on the growth of strategic nuclear arms stockpiles.

Ironically, while Nixon might criticise the USSR in negotiations about certain human rights abuses, he apparently cared little about such abuses by American allies. Not that preceding American Presidents had shown overwhelming concern about the issue, of course, but pressure was building in American society and the Congress for a more honest and humane recognition that the rights of human beings were violated in capitalist countries, not just communist ones. Since most American allies were capitalistic, the presumption of these critics was that the United States could and should do something about allies who routinely violated the rights of their citizens.

Nor did the Nixon Administration care very much about Third World countries, unless they showed signs of moving towards friendlier relations with the Soviet Union. Then, the Administration would show a good deal of attention. In Chile, the Central Intelligence Agency played a role in the overthrow of the democratically elected Socialist President Salvador Allende in 1973. Still a virulent anti-communist when it came to Latin America, Nixon seemed to accept at face value the warning of a businessman friend who told him: 'If Allende should win, and with Castro in Cuba, you will have in Latin America a red sandwich. And, eventually, it will all be red.'[37] Nixon took Allende's election as almost a personal affront, signifying the 'loss' of Chile under Nixon's watch.

In non-crisis times, however, Kissinger and Nixon treated countries of Africa, Latin America, and other parts of the Third World with benign neglect. This attitude was forcefully demonstrated by Kissinger, when he became irritated at a foreign minister of a Latin American country who had dared to 'lecture' President Nixon about international affairs. Kissinger told the minister: 'You come here speaking of Latin America, but this is not important. Nothing important can come from the South. History has never been produced in the South. The axis of history starts in Moscow, goes to Bonn, crosses over to Washington, and then goes to Tokyo. What happens in the South is of no importance.'[38]

Granted that Kissinger was speaking in a moment of anger, his remarks nonetheless reflected the *Realpolitik* philosophy of international affairs which Nixon and Kissinger shared, emphasising the importance of power as the main determinant in international relations. Since Third World countries were not powerful themselves, they counted for little.

Finally, for the Nixon administration (and the Ford Administration, which completed Nixon's term of office), there was the problem of Vietnam. Nixon was in the unenviable position of taking over a war he had not started, one which had already polarised and dispirited the American people, and one with little prospect for a successful conclusion. Nixon rejected the idea of a quick American withdrawal from Vietnam, but he did start 'Vietnamisation' – slowly withdrawing American troops, while turning over their combat duties to soldiers of the government of South Vietnam.

In retrospect, Nixon's Vietnam policies (like those of the Democratic and Republican Presidents who preceded him) have to be considered a failure. The recognition that the United States was fighting not just communism, but a very strong brand of Vietnamese nationalism, never took hold in his or preceding Administrations. Therefore, Nixon and Kissinger wasted tens of thousands of lives and billions of dollars on a venture which ended only in 1975, with the creation of a unified communist Vietnam.

(b)   *The Carter Administration*   Jimmy Carter (1977–81) was elected President during an era of American citizens' revulsion over the apparent lies of preceding administrations about Vietnam and Watergate. Recalling the idealistic approach to international affairs of Woodrow Wilson, Carter asserted as a Presidential candidate that American idealism should be at the heart of foreign policy-making. In his 1976 campaign autobiography, Carter wrote that in 'such areas as Pakistan, Chile, Cambodia, and Vietnam, our government's foreign policy has not exemplified any commitment to moral principles.'[39] President Carter, therefore, made concern for human rights a top priority during his four years of office. While he enjoyed some success in at least putting human rights on the agenda during international negotiations and in America's own policy deliberations, he also met some embarrassing setbacks.

Carter's approach is best understood in contrast to the Nixon-Kissinger-Ford foreign policy era. While Congress pushed increasingly hard during the Nixon era for human rights criteria to be employed in dealing with America's allies, such efforts were largely resisted by the Administration. The usual response was that 'quiet diplomacy' was more effective in prodding other countries to treat their citizens humanely than would be a 'sledgehammer' approach of threatening to cut off American foreign aid or publicly labelling such countries serious violators of human rights. A major shift occurred under Carter, with the President's frequent rhetoric about human rights supported by institutionalisation (in the State Department bureaucracy) of that concern. Each year the State Department issued a 'report card' assessing how well or poorly countries around the world performed in respecting human rights.

As the case-study in Chapter 9 will show, the human rights campaign had most impact in Latin America, with beneficial effects in Argentina and Guatemala. In the case of the Dominican Republic, pressure from the Carter Administration stopped that country's military leadership from aborting the election of a liberal candidate for President.[40] Critics point out, however, that Carter was inconsistent in applying human rights standards. They charge that he was willing to overlook the abuses by despotic governments which were useful to America's military position in the world, such as that of the Shah of Iran and Ferdinand Marcos of the Philippines. For instance, Carter complimented the Shah on his government's progress as an 'island of stability' because of the 'love which your people give to you'.[41] Soon thereafter, the Shah was forced to leave Iran due to a popular revolution against his rule.

Also, many Western Europeans such as West German Chancellor Helmut Schmidt were irritated by Carter's alleged inconsistencies in applying human rights standards. Certainly, the leadership of the Soviet Union found Carter hard to understand. When all is said and done, however, Carter's emphasis on human rights struck a responsive chord with millions of people in the United States and around the world. It also set precedents which subsequent Presidents have not been able to ignore entirely.

The most spectacular success of the Carter Administration was the Camp David Accords, which brought about peace between Israel and Egypt. As the largest Arab nation in the Middle East, Egypt had fought wars with Israel in 1967 and 1973. Carter himself could take much personal credit for the peace agreement, as he personally negotiated between Israel's Menachem Begin and Egypt's Anwar Sadat, who personally disliked each other. By inviting Sadat and Begin to the Presidential retreat at Camp David and trying to forge a peace agreement between two countries which were longtime enemies,

Carter took a big gamble. Certainly, there were moments during the thirteen days of negotiations when collapse appeared imminent. At one point, Sadat was so exasperated with Begin that he packed his bags and was standing outside waiting for a helicopter to take him away, when Carter walked over to dissuade him from leaving. Carter recalled:

We walked into the cabin, we sat down, and we looked at each other. I didn't say anything for quite a while because I didn't know what to say. I don't think I've ever been so grave or so serious about anything that I have said in my life. I then said to him, 'I understand you're leaving.' He said, 'Yes.' I said to him, 'Have you really thought about what this means?' He said, 'Yes.' 'Then let me tell you. It will mean first of all an end to the relationship between the United States and Egypt. There is no way we can explain this to our people ... last but not least, it will mean the end of something that is very precious to me: my friendship with you.'[42]

After further talk and reflection, Sadat said simply, 'I will stay.' What followed were historic agreements, which did not solve all of the problems of the Middle East, but were nonetheless unprecedented. Begin and Sadat later were awarded the Nobel Peace Prize, but many thought Carter should have shared in the award for his remarkable venture into personal diplomacy.

Other successes during the Carter years included winning Senate approval of the Panama Canal Treaty, which provided for the eventual return of the Canal to the nation of Panama itself. This was an important step towards disassociating the United States government from its past record and reputation as the imperialist neighbour to the north. Also, the Carter Administration followed the lead set by Nixon in formalising the new relationship with China by extending full diplomatic relations with the People's Republic.

On other matters, Carter appeared inept. When the Iranian revolution occurred, some critics thought Carter was responsible for the downfall of the Shah of Iran. The charge is unfair, as the revolution was going to occur, with or without Carter's opposition. The President's problems were compounded when Iranian radicals raided the American embassy in Teheran and seized sixty-three Americans as hostages in November 1979. It was a remarkable incident violating longstanding traditions of international law, but the kidnapping won the blessings of Iran's new leader, the Ayatollah Khomeini. Carter reacted sharply, imposing economic and military sanctions on the Iranian government, and for a while the American people rallied around their President. But frustration mounted, especially after an American attempt at rescuing the hostages failed in the spring of 1980.

Another shock also dominated the news in the last year of the Carter presidency – the invasion of Afghanistan by the Soviet Union. The USSR sent over 80,000 troops into Afghanistan to show its displeasure with the government in power. Ultimately, a new leader took office, supported by the Soviets, but most of the governments of the world condemned the invasion. Carter's early public reaction was that his 'opinion' of the Soviet leadership changed 'drastically' because of the incursion.[43] In part, Carter's remark reflected his frustration with the uneven progress of the preceding two and a half years in improving relations with the Soviet Union. At a time when the agonising process of negotiating a second Strategic Arms Limitation Treaty (SALT) with the Soviet Union had been completed, it was clear that Afghanistan would destroy the Treaty's chances for ratification by the United States Senate. Still, Carter's comments sounded naive to many. Soon, however, he responded forcefully: an embargo on American grain being sold to the Soviet Union, limitation of high-technology sales to the Soviets, and a request (ultimately honoured) that American athletes not participate in the 1980 Olympics, which were to be hosted by the Soviet government.[44]

Nonetheless, these reverses in foreign policy, plus high energy costs and interest rates (caused in large part by policies of OPEC, the Organisation of Petroleum Exporting Countries) ruined Carter's image with many voters. So did the quite obvious splits among his top foreign policy advisers over how tough the United States should be in dealing with other countries. Carter's National Security Adviser, Zbigniew Brzezinski, frequently went public with his hawkish views, particularly on dealing with the Soviet Union; meanwhile, Carter's Secretary of State Cyrus Vance emphasised diplomacy over military pressure and threats in his public statements and private advice for the President. If other things had been going well for Carter, this incoherence among his advisers might not have mattered to voters. But, given persistent rumours of Carter's alleged incompetence, the Brzezinski-Vance split added to Carter's bad image.

The first anniversary of the taking of the hostages in Iran coincided with the 1980 presidential election. This seems to have contributed to Carter's big loss to Republican challenger Ronald Reagan. In the long run, however, Carter may come to be seen as a President who dealt successfully with many of the extremely difficult foreign policy dilemmas facing the United States.

(c)　*The Reagan Administration*　Ronald Reagan (1981–89) assumed the Presidency insisting that the Soviet Union was to blame for many of the world problems. Indeed, he said, the USSR's provocative foreign policies were behind 'all the unrest that is going on. If they weren't engaged in this game of dominoes, there wouldn't be any hot spots in the world.'[45] For this reason, Reagan opposed previous arms control agreements which Republican and Democratic Presidents had made with the Soviets. The SALT II Treaty, for instance, was 'fatally flawed', he said. In Central America, Reagan saw a battleground between the free world and Soviet-Cuban adventurism. El Salvador's civil war was, in the new President's words, 'a textbook case of indirect armed aggression by Communist powers', while the socialist government of Nicaragua was labelled a Soviet satellite and a threat to democracy in the rest of Latin America.[46]

In the early years of his Administration, Reagan usually succeeded in persuading both the public and Congress to follow his militant anti-communist lead in foreign policy. Defence spending, already on the rise in the latter part of the Carter Administration, was sharply escalated to pay for an expansion of American military power. In 1981, defence spending was approximately $160 billion; five years later, it was almost double that amount.[47]

When President Reagan heard of an idea of creating a 'nuclear shield' which would protect the United States from incoming nuclear missiles in the event of nuclear war, he quickly made it his own. Soon, despite the scepticism of most of the scientific community, the President convinced Congress to begin spending tens of millions of dollars on the Strategic Defense Initiative (SDI), which many others simply called 'Star Wars'.

Following through a pledge by the Carter Administration and its NATO partners, the Reagan Administration oversaw the deployment of intermediate-range nuclear missiles, despite demonstrations by hundreds of thousands of western Europeans and warnings of the Soviet Union. For a while, top level meetings between Soviet and American diplomats ceased.

In Reagan's second term, however, there was a dramatic change in the American stance towards the Soviet Union, undoubtedly brought about by the new policies and appealing image of Mikhail Gorbachev.

The Soviet leader met Reagan in Iceland, in the Soviet Union, and in the United States. A new treaty emerged between the US and the Soviets, mandating the removal of the very same Soviet and NATO intermediate-range missiles which had been the subject of such contention earlier in the decade. More importantly, there were dramatically new perceptions of the Soviet Union in the United States. These perceptions were shared by the public, the Congress, and Reagan himself. Walking in Red Square in Moscow with Gorbachev, a reporter called out a question to Reagan, asking about his description in earlier years of the USSR as 'an evil empire'. The President paused a moment, then told the reporter that those comments were from 'another time, another era'.[48] Ronald Reagan had travelled an odyssey in his thinking about the Soviet Union to rival the odyssey of Richard Nixon in his attitude towards China.

Even as relations with the Soviets began to improve from 1985 onwards, Reagan and his advisers continued to see Central America in Cold War terms. When Congress stopped funding the Nicaraguan *contra* rebels, figures in the Reagan Administration devised an ingenious but illegal plan to get funds to the rebels. These Reaganites, including Colonel Oliver North of the National Security Council, decided to deal with two foreign policy problems at once – in order to secure the release of Americans held hostage by Lebanese radicals who were loyal to Iran, the administration would sell arms to the Iranians. The 'profits' from these sales would then be sent to the *contras*, without the knowledge of Congress. When word leaked to the press of this Iran-Contra operation, Reagan entered a period of relative unpopularity with the public and a new low standing with Congress.

The President himself was inconsistent in his comments on the affair – denying at the time that arms had been traded in return for the hoped-for release of hostages. Reagan also showed difficulty in remembering just how much he had known of the Iran-Contra decisions made in his White House. However, perhaps remembering that Richard Nixon's 'stonewalling' during the Watergate scandal ultimately got him nowhere, Reagan gave measured co-operation with those who wished to investigate the Iran-Contra affair. For starters, Reagan appointed a special Presidential commission, known as the Tower Commission, to investigate what happened. With the President's blessing, the Commission interviewed chief actors in the Reagan foreign policy system, including the President himself. The public report the Commission produced was not flattering to Reagan. For instance, the Commission's report noted matter-of-factly that the President had admitted that 'he had not been advised at any time ... how the plan would be implemented'.[49] The picture emerging from the Tower Commission Report and other sources was of a President with a remarkable 'hands off' style of management, leaving major decisions and implementation of those decisions to others. While finding no evidence that Reagan knew of the illegal plans to divert the arms profits to the *contras*, the Commission found Reagan's usage of the NSC largely to blame for allowing his subordinates to attempt a swap of arms for hostages. The Commission noted that the advisory system of the National Security Council 'will not work unless the President makes it work ... By his actions, by his leadership, the President therefore determines the quality of its performance.'[50]

While Reagan himself emerged from the scandal without any evidence that he broke the law, some Iran-Contra figures faced criminal legal actions late in his Administration and in the early days of the Bush Administration. Meanwhile, the Nicaraguan government continued in power while the *contras* largely faded from the scene, and nine Americans were still held hostage in Lebanon. When the Iran-Contra affair began, there were only seven such hostages.[51]

More than in the Carter Presidency, Reagan's foreign policy-making was subject to chronic bureaucratic politics.[52] As discussed in Chapter 2, theorists of bureaucratic politics assert that policies do not emerge simply as the result of rationally devised *Presidential* decisions; rather they emerge from the *competition* of the various top policy-makers in the President's Administration. But the usefulness of this theoretical framework varies – to the extent that a President is a 'hands on' type manager, bureaucratic politics will be relatively limited and a President can, if not stop competition among his advisers, at least control major decisions. To the extent that a President is a 'hands off' manager, bureaucratic politics can run wild in an Administration, and policies often really aren't so much *Presidential* decisions as they are *resultants* of competition in the Administration. In the words of Reagan's Secretary of State George Shultz, there was such severe competition and infighting among Reagan's foreign policy advisers that it was like 'guerrilla warfare'.[53]

Unlike the Carter Administration, there was no dramatic breakthrough in the Middle East during the Reagan years. Nor was Reagan able to respond effectively to provocations of the corrupt dictator,

Manuel Noriega of Panama. But there had been enough indications of American 'toughness' during the Reagan years – an American invasion of Grenada in 1983 to overthrow an unfriendly government, and bombings of Colonel Qaddafi's Libya in 1986 – to match Reagan's campaign pledges that America would 'stand tall' during his Presidency. Ironically, it is not those hawkish incidents which are most likely to secure Reagan an honourable place in American history. To the extent that new, friendly relations with the Soviet Union continue through the 1990s, perhaps with a genuine end to the decades old Cold War, Reagan will be credited with responding positively towards opportunities to build a newer, more peaceful international system.

(d) *The Bush Presidency* Taking the Presidency in January 1989, George Bush had an impressive list of credentials to his credit – Vice-President in the Reagan administration, former Director of the Central Intelligence Agency, former American representative to China (this was before the US had full diplomatic relations with China), a former Congressman, and one-time Chairman of the Republican Party. Therefore whatever problems Bush may encounter in the Presidency or foreign policy, it will not be because of inexperience.

Still, it often takes a few years for a President to establish his style of management and to make choices about which initiatives (if any) he will take in foreign policy. In his first year as President, the most positive development of the Bush foreign policy Presidency has been the continuing decline in animosity between the United States and the Soviet Union. Bush was not solely responsible for this development – Mikhail Gorbachev has seized the initiative in improving relations during the Reagan and Bush Administrations. But, as it takes two to tango, Bush showed by the end of his first year that he was clearly ready to deal with Gorbachev in improving relations and perhaps ultimately ending the Cold War.

Not all Americans were entirely hopeful about developments in the Soviet Union. Former Reagan Administration Secretary of Defence Caspar Weinberger wrote in autumn 1989: 'All these welcome changes we are seeing in the Warsaw Pact countries are neither irreversible nor cause for concluding that the West and NATO can reduce their military strength now.'[54] During his campaign for President and early in his Administration, Bush himself expressed similar scepticism about rushing into new agreements with Gorbachev. But when the two leaders met in ships off the island of Malta for a 'mini-summit' in December 1989, the chemistry between the two men was good and the prospects for future treaty agreements were positive. A small but illustrative example came from a joint Bush-Gorbachev press conference after their talks. Upset that Nicaragua (a Soviet ally) had apparently sent Soviet-made arms to leftist guerrillas in El Salvador, Bush raised the topic with Gorbachev in their private talks. The Soviet President denied any Soviet involvement in such shipments. Therefore, when the press asked the two men about the subject, Bush made it clear he believed Gorbachev. He said the Nicaraguans must have shipped the weapons to El Salvador and then lied about their activities 'to our Soviet friends'.[55] A treaty to limit long-range strategic arms and conventional forces in Europe was likely to emerge from a formal summit meeting planned for June 1990.

Beyond constructing a new relationship with the Soviet Union, a related challenge facing Bush was how to deal with the quickly changing conditions in Eastern European countries. As the previously docile allies of the Soviet Union moved towards democratisation and away from communist systems of government, the unanswered question facing Bush was what, if anything, should the United States do about the process? How would events in Eastern Europe affect America's relations with Western Europe? The President and his Secretary of State, James Baker, were struggling at the end of his first year in office to formulate coherent short- and long-range policies to deal with the fast paced events in Europe.

Bush also faced a dilemma in dealing with the People's Republic of China in 1989. When the Chinese government cracked down on students and others demonstrating for greater democratisation of China's political system, the American President was restrained in his criticism of the Chinese political leadership. This displeased many Democrats and even some Republicans, who noted that the Chinese students in Tiananmen Square raised a statue they called the 'Goddess of Liberty', which was modelled after the Statue of Liberty in the United States. When Bush sent his National Security Adviser and Deputy Secretary of State to meet Chinese leaders in Beijing in late 1989, many in Congress accused Bush of 'selling out' to pressure from the Chinese government. Democratic Senator George Mitchell, the majority leader of the Senate, condemned the visit as 'embarrassing kowtowing to the Chinese government'. But Bush defended his decision, noting 'I don't want to see that China remains totally isolated.'[56]

Perhaps the toughest foreign policy problem in Bush's first year in office concerned Panama's military dictator, Manuel Noriega, widely considered to be implicated in drug trafficking. Early in the Administration, Bush publicly called on Panamanians to rise against Noriega. When a group of military officers tried to do just that in October 1989, they found an American government unready or unwilling to assist them. Apparently feeling it better to be criticised for sins of commission rather than omission, two months later Bush ordered the invasion which culminated in Noriega's arrest. The Panamanian invasion was the single largest US military operation since the Vietnam War and clearly represented a new high point of Presidential foreign policy.

8 Conclusion

Despite the Constitution's 'invitation to struggle' over the making of US foreign policy, American presidents since the Truman era have had a decidedly upper hand in guiding that policy. Indeed, Congress, the Supreme Court, and the American public *expect* modern Presidents to lead the way in foreign affairs, subject of course to occasional complaints from various quarters. Such critiques should not obscure, however, the deeply rooted bipartisan expectation that the President will set the agenda for America in international affairs. Not even the trauma of Vietnam in the 1960s and 1970s, much less the strains produced by the Iranian hostage affair or the Iran-Contra scandal of the 1980s, could eliminate that expectation. As long as Presidents have appeared to be managing foreign policy with at least moderate competence and success, the public has rallied behind Presidents.[57] Only with long drawn-out evidence of Presidential incapacity to deal with a foreign policy crisis have voters turned against a President's international stewardship. Such was the case with Lyndon Johnson and Vietnam and Jimmy Carter's hostage crisis. If they can avoid such 'endless' crises, Presidents have a good deal of power and freedom of manoeuvre in foreign policy.

This Presidential primacy across the past four decades was created in part by a broad acceptance in America of the President's role as 'leader of the free world'. To the extent that the Cold War diminishes in the 1990s, that unofficial title and role may become less appropriate. Still, there is nothing on the horizon to suggest any desire (much less capacity) for Congress to try to reacquire the full partnership it once insisted on having with Presidents in guiding foreign policy.

Nor, despite the Iran-Contra scandal, is there evidence of any important sentiment to diminish the significant foreign policy bureaucracy that attends to the president at the White House. The authors of the Tower Commission Report (two out of three of them former members of the US Senate) went out of their way to endorse the legitimacy and future necessity of the National Security Council system, despite its illegal misadventures during the Reagan era. Emphasising that 'the President is responsible for the national security policy of the United States', the Commission added:

Our review validates the current N.S.C. system. That system has been utilised by different Presidents in very different ways, in accordance with their individual work habits and philosophical predilections ... The problems we examined in the case of Iran/Contra caused us a deep concern. But their solution does not lie in revamping the N.S.C. system.[58]

In describing the Presidency as the 'sole organ of the federal government in the field of international relations' in the *Curtiss-Wright* case, Justice Sutherland and the Supreme Court gave a skewed interpretation of the Constitution. But as a prediction of the future, their opinion was, for better or worse, only a modest overstatement.

Notes

1   See L. Gelb and R. Betts, *The Irony of Vietnam: The System Worked*, Washington D.C., 1979.

2   The best treatment of this theme is in R. Berger, *Executive Privilege*, New York, 1975.

3   Hamilton, *The Federalist*, 69, quoted in H. Bailey and J. Shafritz, eds., *The American Presidency*, Chicago, 1988, p. 21. Emphasis in original.

4   Madison, *Letters of Helvidius*, quoted in Berger, p. 77.

5   Hamilton, *The Federalist*, 70, in Bailey and Shafritz, eds., *The American Presidency*, p. 25; Berger, *Executive Privilege*, ch. 4. A counter-argument may be found in K.M. Holland, 'The war powers resolution', in R. G. Hoxie, ed., *The Presidency and National Security Policy*, New York, 1984, pp. 378–400.

6   Cited in Berger, *Executive Privilege*, pp. 87–88. See also E. S. Corwin, *The President: Office and Powers, 1787–1957*, New York, 1957, p. 19.

7   Corwin, *The President*, p. 26. The great exception of the nineteenth century was the Presidency of Abraham Lincoln (1861–65), who dominated decision processes during the Civil War. But that was a national emergency of the highest order, uncharacteristic of the rest of the century.

8 Quoted in Bailey and Shafritz, eds., *The American Presidency*, p. 35.

9 R. Sherwood, *Roosevelt and Hopkins*, New York, 1948, pp. 262–3.

10 H. S. Truman, *Memoirs*, Vol. 2, New York, 1956, p. 333; M. Miller, *Plain Speaking: An Oral Biography of Harry Truman*, New York, 1974, pp. 273, 280–4.

11 T. Eagleton, *War and Presidential Power*, New York, 1974, p. 71; Berger, *Executive Privilege*, pp. 84, 92.

12 Quoted in H. Levine and J. Smith, eds., *The Conduct of American Foreign Policy Debated*, New York, 1990, p. 19. Though the decision was written in 1936, its influence grew in the Korean and Vietnam War eras.

13 R. Pious, *The American Presidency*, New York, 1979, pp. 16, 394–5.

14 See A. D. Sandler, *A Staff for the President*, Westport (Connecticut), 1989, chs. 8, 9, 11.

15 Gelb and Betts, *The Irony of Vietnam*, p. 67.

16 See *ibid.*, pp. 68–74.

17 Thus Senator Richard Russell (Democrat, Georgia), who headed the Armed Services Committee and was, effectively, *the* Senator in charge of intelligence oversight, reminded JFK in a private conversation, 'with the exception of the Cuban situation, we have known what was going on in the CIA': transcripts of a telephone conversation between Russell and Kennedy, 9 November 1961, Russell Library, University of Georgia, Athens, Georgia.

18 Some analysts think Johnson and/or his Secretary of Defence, Robert McNamara, lied about the second attack in order to persuade Congress to vote Johnson a wide grant of war-making powers. Others write that the commanders in Vietnam and the decision-makers in Washington *thought* there had been a second attack at the time. See Gelb and Betts, *The Irony of Vietnam*, pp. 100–5; G. M. Kahin, *Intervention*, New York, 1986, pp. 219–25; G. Kolko, *Anatomy of a War*, New York, 1986, pp. 122–25.

19 *Congressional Record*, 6 August 1964, p. 18409; 7 August 1964, p. 18471.

20 See D. M. Barrett, 'The mythology surrounding Lyndon Johnson, his advisers, and the 1965 decision to escalate the Vietnam war', *Political Science Quarterly*, 103, 1988–89, pp. 637–64.

21 L. B. Johnson, *The Vantage Point*, New York, 1971, p. 153.

22 *The Gallup Opinion Index*, April 1968, shows that in late March 1968 only 26 per cent of Americans polled approved of Johnson's 'handling of the situation in Vietnam', while 63 per cent disapproved. (But see also the discussion in Chapter 5 below.)

23 *Congressional Record*, 20 March 1967, p. 7193.

24 See Holland, 'The war powers resolution', p. 378.

25 See Eagleton, *War and Presidential Power*, pp. v–vi.

26 Corwin, *The President*, p. 171; C. V. Crabb and P. M. Holt, *Invitation to Struggle*, Washington D.C., 1984.

27 H. Kissinger, *White House Years*, Boston, 1979, p. 11.

28 *Ibid.*' p. 28.

29 See S. Hersh, *The Price of Power*, New York, 1983, pp. 41–3.

30 See Kahin, *Intervention*, p. 366; E. Redford and R. McCulley, *White House Operations*, Austin (Texas), 1986, pp. 69–75.

31 See P. G. Henderson, *Managing the Presidency*, Boulder (Colorado), 1988, p. 118; Barrett, 'The mythology', pp. 640–57; R.T. Johnson, *Managing the White House*, New York, 1974; S. Hess, *Organizing the Presidency*, 2d ed., Washington D.C., 1988.

32 G. Ford, *A Time for Healing*, New York, 1980, pp. 268–72.

33 A. L. George, *Presidential Decisionmaking in Foreign Policy*, Boulder (Colorado), 1980.

34 Of these Presidents, Eisenhower relied the most on formal NSC meetings, but even he depended on a triumvirate of his Secretaries of State, Defence and Treasury to review important foreign policy plans. See Henderson.

35 J. Mayer and D. McManus, *Landslide*, Boston, 1989, p. 187.

36 See T.G. Paterson, *Meeting the Communist Threat*, New York, 1988, pp. 222–3.

37 R. M. Nixon, *RN: The Memoirs of Richard Nixon*, New York, 1978, p. 490. See also G. Kolko, *Confronting the Third World*, New York, 1988, p. 220.

38 Quoted in Hersh, *The Price*, p. 263.

39 J. E. Carter, *Why Not the Best?*, Nashville (Tennessee), 1975, pp. 140–1.

40 See J. Muravchik, *The Uncertain Crusade*, Lanham (Maryland), 1986, p. 186; Z. Brzezinski, *Power and Principle*, New York, 1983, pp. 124–9.

41 Muravchik, *The Uncertain Crusade*, p. 216.

42 Cited in Brzezinski, *Power and Principle*, p. 272.

43 Quoted in Congressional Quarterly, *President Carter, 1979*, Washington D.C., 1980, p. 41.

44 E. C. Hargrove, *Jimmy Carter as President*, Baton Rouge (Louisiana), 1988, pp. 155, 158.

45 Quoted in Paterson, *Meeting the Communist Threat*, p. 256.

46 *Ibid.*, p. 257.

47 See A. Yoder, *The Conduct of American Foreign Policy since World War II*, New York, 1986, p. 168.

48 Mayer and McManus, *Landslide*, p. 387.

49 *The Tower Commission Report*, New York, 1987, p. 231.

50 *Ibid.*, pp. 71, 79.

51 See Mayer and McManus, *Landslide*, p. 387.

52 See A. Haig, *Caveat*, New York, 1984, ch. 14. A conservative 'insider's' account is that of Constantine Menges, *Inside the National Security Council*, New York, 1988. See also C.V. Crabb and K.V. Mulcahy, *Presidents and Foreign Policy Making*, Baton Rouge, 1986, pp. 296–7, 328 (on 'anarchical' Reagan foreign policy-making system).

53 Shultz testimony before joint Congressional hearings on Iran-Contra, in A. Cigler and B. Loomis, eds., *American Politics: Classic and Contemporary Readings*, Boston, 1989, p. 655.

54 C. Weinberger, 'Too soon to slash defense', *New York Times*, 28 November 1989, p. 27.

55 R. W. Apple, 'Talks convince Bush, Gorbachev that they need each other', *Milwaukee Journal*, 4 December 1989, p. 6A (from *New York Times* news service).

56   E. Sciolino, 'President defends aides' China visit', *New York Times*, 12 December 1989, p. 7.

57   See T. J. Lowi, *The Personal President*, Ithaca (New York), ch. 1.

58   *Tower Report*, pp. 3–4.

4

Executive branch foreign policy

1 National Security Adviser and Secretary of State

The case for locating foreign policy-making firmly in the Secretary and Department of State has been frequently made, and is accorded lip-service even by its most conspicuous bureaucratic opponents. Henry Kissinger, the most powerful of all National Security Advisers, later wrote of his conversion to the view that 'a president should make the secretary of state his principal adviser', with the National Security Adviser (NSA) primarily a senior administrator and coordinator.[1] Zbigniew Brzezinski, Carter's NSA, declared in December 1976: 'I don't envisage my job as a policymaking job. I see my job essentially as heading the operational staff of the president, helping him integrate policy, but above all, helping to facilitate the process of decision-making in which he will consult closely with his principal cabinet members.'[2]

Brzezinski never attained Kissinger's eminence, later writing that he knew that Carter would never countenance this.[3] Nonetheless, his rapid advance to the status of policy-maker and policy advocate is not in doubt.

Such lip-service acknowledges the fact that the Secretary of State is, in formal terms, the leading Cabinet officer. He heads a department with unmatched expertise and potential for taking the long-term perspective on international questions. In a sense, it was the State Department, or at least George Kennan and its Policy Planning staff, who 'invented' the modern world in the early years of the Cold War.

The NSA's organisational origins derive from the National Security Council (NSC) system set up in 1947, and from the need for Presidents to have on their staff a manager and co-ordinator for foreign policy. The emergence of the National Security Adviser (otherwise 'assistant', 'NSC staff director' or 'special assistant') as a potential rival and counterweight to the Secretary of State took place under Presidents Kennedy and Johnson. McGeorge Bundy, JFK's Special Assistant for National Security Affairs, made clear his view that the NSC staff should transcend the clear distinction made in the Eisenhower Administration between 'planning' and 'operations': 'It seems to us best that the NSC staff, which is essentially a Presidential instrument, should be composed of men who can serve equally well in the process of planning and in the operational follow-up.'[4]

In the person of W. W. Rostow, who took over from Bundy in 1966, the NSA became a staunch, and highly public policy advocate.[5]

Since the Johnson years, the NSA and the Secretary of State have generally been perceived as natural adversaries. Communication between NSA Kissinger and Secretary of State William Rogers during the Nixon years was minimal, with Kissinger apparently often directing his staff, 'Don't tell Rogers,'[6] Kissinger himself occupied both posts between 1973 and 1976. President Ford's appointment of Brent Scowcroft (Kissinger's former NSC staff deputy) as NSA in 1976 did not represent a threat to Secretary Kissinger. However, the relationship between NSA Brzezinski and Secretary of State Cyrus Vance during Carter's Presidency was frequently strained. The two clashed publicly over substantive policy: for example, over approaches to the Horn of Africa conflict, and over the extent to which Soviet behaviour in such areas should be linked to the American stance on arms control.[7] Carter's tendency to back Brzezinski's harder line in the period after the Soviet invasion of Afghanistan undoubtedly served to isolate Vance. Reagan's first Secretary of State, Alexander Haig, experienced severe problems of gaining access to the President; he also tended, as a former Kissinger associate, to be distrusted by Reagan insiders. Haig later accused William Clark (Reagan's second NSA) of 'conducting a second foreign policy' in the Lebanon. Conflict with Clark, and more especially with Reagan's White House staff 'troika' (James Baker, Ed Meese and Michael Deaver) precipitated Haig's 1982 resignation.[8] Despite Clark's close friendship with Reagan, none of Reagan's NSAs (Richard Allen, Clark, Robert McFarlane, John Poindexter, Frank Carlucci and Colin Powell) could be regarded as especially powerful figures. It is one of the ironies of the Reagan Presidency that an Administration which became celebrated for the unaccountable irresponsibility of its NSC staff (in the Iran-Contra affair), actually encompassed a substantial downgrading of the NSA post. Allen did not even have direct access to the President. At least before Carlucci's appointment, little effort appeared to be expended upon recruiting competent and experienced personnel. Clark, it seems, was appointed largely as a means of checking Haig (he held the NSA and Undersecretary of State positions simultaneously). He became an influential figure in accelerating the conservative thrust of policy in 1982–83, but soon came into conflict with James Baker over defence spending issues. According to Larry Speakes (the former White House press spokesman), the 'President and his top aides' seemed to hold the NSA in low esteem, paying 'little attention to those who held the post'.[9] The developing situation under Reagan is persuasively summarised by Spanier and Uslaner:

while the secretary of state was not ... given the authority to be Reagan's spokesman and number one policy maker, the president's lack of interest and competence in foreign policy meant that the conflicts that naturally erupt in any administration were usually not resolved. The result was that the secretary of state, secretary of defense, CIA director ... and others were continuously feuding. Instead of a battle between the secretary of state and NSA, the Reagan administration ended up with a confused melee.[10]

Conflicts between Reagan's NSAs and his Secretaries of State – notably between Haig and Allen, Haig and Clark, and between Secretary Shultz and Clark – were frequently made public. An indication of the hostility between the NSC staff and the State Department is provided in a memoir written by a former staffer, Constantine Menges.[11] The book is, in essence, an attack on the integrity and democratic good faith of the State Department. Such conflicts, however, were symptomatic of the deeper confusion within the Administration.

While the desirability of an authoritative role for the Secretary of State is widely acknowledged, at least in theory, the NSA's job description and optimum bureaucratic status is more problematic. The influence and status of the NSA will depend ultimately on the will of the President. As Henry Kissinger's influence within the Nixon Administration waxed, he vacated his former office in the White House basement and occupied a suite near the Presidential Oval Office. Kissinger's position was exceptional. A more familiar situation arises when the President consciously uses his Adviser to promote particular positions within the foreign policy bureaucracy: as a policy advocate in his own right, but one whose terms of reference are closely defined by the President.[12]

The duties of the NSA clearly do involve quasi- 'neutral' managerial tasks. He should, for example, package and co-ordinate the information flowing into the White House Situation Room (or the new crisis management centre in room 208 of the Executive Office building). I. M. Destler describes these managerial functions as including: briefing the President and his foreign policy in-box; managing inter-agency conflicts; and managing Presidential decisional processes. He should communicate decisions and monitor their implementation. His service to the President should include a central role as the presenter and custodian of differing policy options.[13] Information presentation, however, is rarely 'neutral' in anything but name. The NSA and NSC staffers also regularly strengthen their bureaucratic positions by developing their own informational sources and 'back channels'. A common temptation is to highlight these sources at the expense of information emanating from the State Department.

The NSA and the NSC staff clearly represent a potentially vigorous source of policy advocacy. As bureaucratic principals close to the President, they occupy a strong and privileged position. Upon his appointment in 1986, NSA Frank Carlucci acknowledged that his 'first responsibility' was as an 'honest broker'; however, he also asserted that neither constitutional nor statutory authority precluded the Adviser or staff from giving 'independent advice if the president asks for it'.[14] Telegenic and rhetorically skilled Advisers are almost bound to be used as Administration spokesmen and communicators with press, Congress and public. Such an arrangement was not, of course, part of the National Security Council system as originally envisaged or as it emerged under President Eisenhower. Ike's NSA, Robert Cutler, offered this view of his role: 'No speeches, no public appearances, no talking with reporters.'[15] However, since President Kennedy's deinstitutionalisation of the NSC system, the NSA has become a public figure. More controversial is the involvement of the Adviser or the NSC staff in foreign policy operations.

National Security Advisers are used as free-wheeling, high-level diplomats, and, indeed, as actual negotiators. Thus, Carter employed Brzezinski, over Vance's protest, to negotiate the process whereby US relations were normalised with mainland China. In December 1989, Brent Scowcroft (serving his second stint as NSA) was dispatched by President Bush to Beijing to re-open US-Chinese relations after the Tiananmen Square massacres. A clear distinction should be made between this, public, activity and NSC covert operations. The Iran-Contra affair stands as testimony to the folly of such operations. The Tower Commission concluded: 'As a general matter, the NSC Staff should not engage in the implementation of policy or the conduct of operations. This compromises their oversight role and usurps the responsibilities of the departments and agencies.'[16]

There may, of course, be a very fine line between flexibility and irresponsibility. From the President's point of view, NSC operations are inescapably high-risk; failures cannot plausibly be laid at any door other than the Chief Executive's. Ultimately, however, the case against NSC covert operations is a legal one. Congress does not appropriate funds for such operations. If they belong anywhere, their natural bureaucratic lodging is the Central Intelligence Agency.

Why do Presidents tend, despite their apparent original intentions, to turn away from the State Department and towards the National Security Adviser? The answer lies partially in simple proximity. In most Administrations, the Secretary of State – despite his participation in the National Security Council – is not part, nor does he partake of the developing experiential group identity, of the inner White House. In the early stages of Iran-Contra, Secretary Shultz simply could not take on successfully the White House opinion which favoured an Iranian arms deal and secret *contra* aid.[17] As will be seen in the next section, the State Department tends to suffer within Washington generally from negative perceptions. The NSA and NSC staff will, in contrast, tend to be seen as flexible, responsive and relatively free of bureaucratic baggage. (As non-confirmable appointees, they may also be regarded by Presidents as relatively removed from Congressional oversight.) In B. A. Rockman's terms, they are 'irregulars': similar to the 'high-flyers of the British civil service', but without 'the latter's attachment to the civil service system'.[18] It is commonly observed that the most influential of recent Secretaries of State – John Foster Dulles (1953–59) and Kissinger (1973–77) – have also made light of their departmental responsibilities. Any Secretary who attempts scrupulously to derive policy from the various segments of the State Department runs the risk of self-imposed paralysis.

Friction between the NSA and the domestic White House political staff is not uncommon. President Ford's political aides saw Kissinger's public stature as potentially undermining the President's authority; stories were leaked to demonstrate that Ford was capable of overruling Kissinger. Under Reagan, William Clark apparently clashed with James Baker (as White House Chief of Staff) over the political adroitness of the Strategic Defense Initiative. Such friction can be, and during the Reagan Administration certainly was, damaging. Nonetheless, these episodes make it clear that the NSA clearly operates within a world where short-term political expediency is an important consideration. The position of Richard Allen, Clark's predecessor, was virtually destroyed by the hostility to his performance expressed by Baker and his deputy, Michael Deaver.[19] Compared with the State Department, the NSA and the NSC staff are likely to frame their proposals and activity within the context of political expediency. If they do not do so, they will be unlikely to survive. Leslie Gelb puts the point well:

Contrary to endemic Washington cynicism about such matters, my experience has been that the presidents are quite high-minded about the national interest and often are prepared to take political lumps for what is right. But what is right has to be supportable, and presidents soon find that the State Department – with some exceptions from time to time – does a poor job of framing its proposals in terms that will elicit political support, and it does not think about potential costs to the president ... Once a president comes to believe that Foggy Bottom (i.e., the State Department) is not attuned to politics, they are doomed to being ignored. Once he concludes that his staff has political savvy, that staff is on its way to dominating policymaking.[20]

2   The State Department

(a)   *Perceptions of the Department*   A 1989 article in the *Foreign Service Journal* by a former director of the executive development staff of the Foreign Service Institute began: 'The Department of State has qualities of a second-rate organisation: a poorly articulated mission, ill-defined goals, unhappy employees ... and an apparent indifference to developing effective executives.'[21]

A piece in the same edition of the *Journal*, written by a Foreign Service Officer (FSO), elaborated further on another dimension of the department's difficulties:

State ... has been tarred with several negative stereotypes. Some of these, such as the perception that FSO's defend the interests of foreign countries better than those of our own countries, are difficult to avoid. Others, such as the label 'elitist' or 'arrogant', seem unfair and are carried over from another era. The image of a secretive Foreign Service trying to keep a meddling Congress out of our business may be the most difficult stereotype to overcome.[22]

This piece (by Vicki Huddleston) was concerned primarily with State's image on Capitol Hill; it is, however, similarly perceived elsewhere in government. In his memoir, former White House Chief of Staff Don Regan recalled his perception of arrogant State Department career officers delighting in President Reagan's difficulties in supporting President Marcos in the Philippines.[23] Constantine Menges described (especially in connection with the Central American peace process) senior career officials at the State Department having the 'habit' of interpreting Presidential orders 'depending on their own conception of the national interest'.[24]

Why is the Department of State so widely perceived in negative ways? Part of the answer lies in the almost ontological tension between career and political appointees, and also in the self-image of some recent Administrations. As political appointees, the White House staff partake in a political culture which tends to view with suspicion the career orientation of most State Department employees.[25] Even political appointees at State (generally, the Secretary, deputy, under- and assistant under-secretaries) may be seen as likely to be co-opted by the career bureaucracy. Some recent Administrations have also seen themselves as pitted against the perceived institutional ethos of the State Department. President Nixon made no secret of his antipathy towards an organisation which he saw as dominated by East coast Democratic party loyalists. In the early Reagan years, FSO promotions were monitored by the White House political staff, who sought thereby to promote Reaganite ideology in this supposedly hostile environment.[26]

Does the State Department deserve its reputation for elitism, aloofness and arrogance? To some extent, the reputation is an atavistic holdover from the charges made against the department in the McCarthyite period. Although Nixon did, no doubt, have enemies at State, his view of the department was essentially formed in the late 1940s and early 1950s. The reputation for elitism also reflects the distinctive identity of the Foreign Service Officer corps, and the resentment generated among other federal employees. As will be noted in Chapter 7, FSO recruitment patterns have traditionally been narrow. Important changes in this regard have been made since the 1960s. During Vance's tenure at State, affirmative action was taken to increase minority and female FSO representation.[27] Nonetheless, as Barry Rubin suggests, the impact of these changes has not been entirely straightforward: 'The utility of diversifying the recruitment pool is precisely to broaden department culture and introduce people who may be more inclined to question, hold different perspectives, and stress other priorities. Yet these characteristics are often punished rather than valued at State.'

The department has experimented with a 'dissent channel': a means whereby junior opinion may be transmitted direct to the Secretary. Nonetheless, creative dissent is most certainly not regarded as a sure route to promotion. Indeed, as Rubin notes, the very career culture of the department and of diplomacy – emphasising caution, accommodation, compromise, slow progress – to some extent runs counter to America's own national political culture.[28]

(b)   *Organisation and personnel*   The heart of State's organisation is the bureau system. Alongside units dealing with administration, and public and Congressional relations, the bureaux fit into either functional or geographic categories. The functional bureaux include Economic and Business Affairs, Politico-Military Affairs and International Narcotics Matters. The geographic bureaux relate to the five major world regions, along with a Bureau for International Organisation Affairs (pre-eminently the United Nations). Each of the regional bureaux consists of a number of country/area 'desks'. All these units and bureaux are oriented towards the management of diplomacy and foreign policy. Long-range planning is, in theory, concentrated in the Policy Planning staff, located in the Policy Planning Council.

Throughout its recent history, the department has been subjected to virtually constant reorganisation proposals. Despite worries about excessive organisational compartmentalisation at State, these have tended to be directed not so much at the bureau system itself, but rather at reform of the FSO career structure. Many proposals have been concerned to strengthen the career bureaucracy and to answer the familiar complaint that FSO expertise is frequently wasted.[29] Most famously, the Wriston report of 1954 merged the FSO and civil service personnel schemes within the department. It had the effect of clogging the promotions schedule and creating a top-heavy Foreign Service.[30]

The current personnel system is organised around the 'cone' principle, whereby employees operate as political, economic, consular or administrative officers. The system is designed to strike a balance between excessive specialisation and excessive generalisation. The current FSO career structure is also designed to ameliorate the more

drastic consequences of the old 'up or out' system. Before the 1980
Foreign Service Act, failure to secure promotion within a specified
period led automatically to being 'selected out'. The 1980 Act gave
each FSO twenty years to gain promotion – 'the corridor and water
cooler struggle' – to the new Senior Foreign Service. Rapidly a
premium developed upon managerial and generalised experience, at
the expense of specialist (particularly linguistic and regional
economic) expertise.[31]

The extent to which the 1980 Foreign Service Act created an ethos
of simple corridor survival has stimulated yet further reorganisation
plans: notably the Thomas and Bremer reports, both issued in 1989.
Both seek to restructure the 'cone' system and to effect a new balance
between specialisation and generalisation.[32] They reflect major problems of morale among the more than four thousand FSO's working
their way through the promotion structure, as well as a somewhat
uncertain sense of purpose within the department as a whole.

The State Department has three quasi-autonomous organisations
attached to it: the US Information Agency (the major informational
and propaganda agency), the International Development Cooperation Agency (embracing AID, the Agency for International
Development) and the Arms Control and Disarmament Agency. The
latter agency in particular has involved the State Department in yet
more bureaucratic battles, this time against the Defence Department.
Though the State Department has a legitimate interest in arms control, the Pentagon has long resented State's involvement in this
area.[33]

(c) *Sources of weakness*   The State Department has not adapted well
to the intensification of interdependence in international relations,
nor to the growing intermingling of foreign and domestic concerns.
Richard Allen, Reagan's first NSA, noted in 1983 that Secretary of
State Alexander Haig's working definition of 'diplomacy' as virtually
synonymous with 'national security' (itself defined in terms of 'foreign
policy and defense matters') was inappropriate:

> In reality, it must include virtually every facet of international activity, includ-
> ing (but not limited to) foreign affairs, defense, intelligence, research and
> development policy, outer space, international economic and trade policy,
> monetary policy and reaching deeply even into the domains of the Depart-
> ments of Commerce and Agriculture.[34]

The rise of interdependency has allowed rival bureaucratic players into State's traditional 'turf', an area which the department has not been able successfully to redefine. In 1985, only about one in three of 15,000 Americans working in missions abroad actually worked for the State Department; substantial numbers of departmental employees also service and support other agencies.[35] Interdependence has also intensified the tendency for interdepartmental networks of influence and loyalty to develop and cut across traditional institutional identifications. Economic and trade policy specialists within the State Department may, for example, look for bureaucratic allies not to their own department, but to the Treasury, the Office of Management and Budget (in the President's Executive Office) and to relevant staffers in Congress.[36]

Modern communications and the rise of the international economic agenda has also tended to damage the prestige of the institution at the heart of State's operational prerogative: the ambassador and his embassy staff. Reporting from foreign embassies has acquired a reputation for serving vested interests and is often (and often unwisely) ignored. FSO clientism – the close identification with host regimes and local interests – is, of course, a real phenomenon. It is often said that the State Department suffers from having no constituency except foreign governments. President Johnson is reported to have told an Indian ambassador in 1968 that the Indian leader ('Madame Gandhi') did not know how lucky she was: 'She's got two ambassadors working' for her ... you here and (American Ambassador Chester) Bowles out there.'[37] Embassies do, however, have local knowledge and should not, any more than the State Department itself, be ignored. Washington's reaction to the growing crisis in Iran in 1978–79 is, in part, a story of deaf ears being turned to ambassadorial warnings.[38] It should also be remembered, however, that ambassadorial prestige has also declined alongside the continued practice (clearly visible in the early months of the Bush Presidency) of 'selling' ambassadorships in return for campaign contributions.

The State Department's internal compartmentalisation, and also its actually very small budget, fits it ill for bureaucratic battling. Robert Pringle, an FSO writing in the late 1970s, noted that the Secretary of State is 'charged (in theory) with responsibility for the coordination of all foreign policy activities'; he presides, however, 'over a bureaucratic midget'.[39] Its annual budget is typically something in the region of one per cent of that of the Pentagon. Foreign policy and diplomacy is also, unlike defence, an area without substantially inhibiting technical jargon. Its apparent openness to all, combined with State's reputation for slowness and caution, seems positively to invite bureaucratic invaders.[40]

According to Leslie Gelb, there are two iron laws of US bureaucracy: first, 'that operations drive out policy'; second, 'that administering, regulating, and coordinating drives out operations'.[41] This leads to the most paradoxical of all charges made against the State Department: that far from being an agency capable of developing long-term policy it has simply become an agency of implementation and day-to-day administration.[42] Even the Policy Planning staff, so the argument goes, has – since its heyday under Kennan – become irrelevant precisely to the extent that it has become removed from operations. State's very immersion in incremental management has rendered it ineffective as a maker of policy.

The golden age of the Policy Planning staff occurred during the period when the policy of containment, the philosophical keystone of the post-1945 'Pax Americana', was being developed and promulgated. It may be that any major reorientation in US foreign policy, consequent upon relative American decline and upon rapid liberalisation in Eastern Europe and the Soviet Union, will similarly involve something of a regeneration of State Department planning. During the first year of the Bush Presidency, Secretary of State James Baker gave considerable publicity to the twenty-five member staff, apparently using it as a personal advisory staff. More publicity accrued from the publication of staff member Francis Fukuyama's article, 'The end of history', proclaiming a new 'end of ideology': the triumph of American liberalism over its competitors. Dennis Ross, staff director, was understandably anxious to play down Fukuyama's triumphalism, and to emphasise the range of opinion within the Policy Planning Council. According to Ross, there were major parallels with the late 1940s: 'The world is changing in very big ways, hour by hour. That keeps you humble when someone says, "Please draw me up three scenarios for the future of Europe." '

Ross, in November 1989, described the three areas being worked upon: plans to transform established institutions such as NATO for the 'new era'; plans for reunification between Western and Eastern Europe (especially Germany); and plans to enhance US leadership in Europe in new conditions.[43]

3 The Pentagon

Sections below (in Chapters 5 and 8) will consider the interaction between the Pentagon and Congress over defence budgeting, and the Pentagon's relationship with defence contractors and the 'military industrial complex'. The intention here is to concentrate on the impact of the military in general, and of the Defence Department in particular, upon foreign policy.

The use of threat of force has been a continuous theme within American foreign policy since 1945.[44] Post-war Presidents have presided over a 'warfare' or 'national security' state. The developing Cold War saw a blurring of the distinction between 'defence' and 'foreign policy'.[45] Nonetheless, the United States has not developed a praetorian military on the Latin American model. President Truman's dismissal of General MacArthur in 1951 underlined the principle of civilian control. The US remains a clear prototype of the liberal model of civilian control of the military.[46]

At the level of bureaucratic politics, however, civilian-military conflicts have been a persistent theme. They form one inescapable dimension of intra-Defence Department pulling and hauling. James Forrestal, the first chief of the Defense Department upon its creation in 1947, declared that the 'peacetime mission of the Armed Services' was to 'destroy the Secretary of Defense'.[47] With no direct authority to dismiss or promote serving officers, the civilian Secretary frequently finds himself pitted against formidable military-Congressional alliances. James Schlesinger (Defence Secretary 1973–75) observed in 1983: 'The Office provides the (Defence) Secretary simply with a license to persuade outside parties. Even within the (Pentagon) building, quite frequently, it's only a license to persuade.'[48]

Failure to win over military opinion, as embodied in the Joint Chiefs of Staff (JCS), will severely damage the political and bureaucratic position of the Secretary. The Joint Chiefs maintain channels of influence to the Congressional Arms Services Committees. In the past, this has given them, in effect, the power of veto over arms control proposals. At the very least, Presidents may be forced to make significant concessions – such as Carter's promised deployment of MX and Pershing II – to gain Pentagon support.[49] Even Caspar Weinberger, the Defence Secretary who presided over the massive defence increases of the early Reagan years, found himself compromised over his MX (especially the so-called 'dense pack') proposals by his failure to gain JCS backing.[50]

The Secretary is not confronted by a unified military, but one riven by inter-service and intra-service rivalries. In a 1989 manual written for Pentagon employees, Major General Perry Smith describes such rivalries as almost the defining characteristic of life at the Defence Department: 'each of the four services has its own separate history, culture, clan, uniforms, training establishment, staff colleges, bases and, with the exception of the Marine Corps, service academy and war college'.

In some bureaucratic battles, the joint staff (accountable to the chairman of the JCS) constitutes another power base, making five-way contests common.[51] Intra-service rivalries can also surface at the level of defence procurement politics: for example, rivalry between the strategic and tactical air commands. Perry Smith comments:

when a service can buy only one new weapons system within a mission area and must choose between a new attack submarine or a new missile launching submarine ... these rivalries surface strongly. If you find someone pushing a new weapons system hard, you might ask yourself what subcommunity that individual comes from.[52]

Equally destructive of rationality in the procurement process is inter-service logrolling (mutual project support on a *quid-pro quo* basis). Inter-service rivalry has also been at the heart of the many widely publicised examples of military incompetence in the field. Perhaps the best known example was during the 1983 Grenada invasion when – due to the imcompatibility of army and air force radio nets – an advancing army unit made a credit card telephone call back home to request air cover![53]

The paralysing effect of inter-service rivalry and logrolling stimulated a major defence reorganisation in 1986. A Congressional staff report prepared for Senators Nunn and Goldwater in the previous year highlighted these problems, and argued for an enhanced role for the JCS chairman. The report also criticised the 'limited mission integration' at Defence Department 'policymaking level' and the 'imbalance between modernisation and readiness': 'current warfighting capabilities are robbed to pay for hardware in the distant future'.[54] The military's fetish for technology is a familiar theme within military reform circles. New weapons systems frequently originate in interstices of bureaucratic compromise, inter-service rivalry and the coincidental development of particular technologies, rather than in any objective military need. The 1986 reforms attempted to encourage more coherent planning by providing career incentives to those engaged in trans-service (joint staff) duties. Most importantly, they awarded the JCS chairman important functions previously ascribed to the Joint Chiefs severally.[55]

No Secretary of Defence since the 1960s has attained the position of foreign policy influence occupied by Robert McNamara in the years of the escalation of the Vietnam conflict. McNamara's activist management style and determination to assert civilian control at the Pentagon both upset service sensibilities and reinforced his position as policy adviser.[56] Caspar Weinberger certainly held an important position within Reagan's decision-making structure, although the structure itself was so confused as almost to defy accurate description. Weinberger's advice was not consistently hawkish; indeed, the Reagan experience illustrates the folly of automatically identifying the Pentagon with hard-line adventurism and the State Department with a more cautious, softer approach. The Pentagon did develop its own covert operations facility in the early 1980s.[57] Yet in the developing tension between Weinberger and Secretary Shultz (after Haig's 1982 resignation), it was the former who tended to counsel caution: in the Lebanon in 1982, Grenada in 1983 and Libya in 1986. In November 1984, Weinberger set out six criteria which should be met before American troops were sent into combat: the vital nature of relevant US interests; the presence of a 'clear intention of winning'; clearly defined objectives; continued monitoring and reassessment of the commitment; the reasonable certainty of popular and Congressional support; and the presumption that force was a weapon of last resort.[58]

Weinberger's apparent caution reflected the military's determination to avoid repeating the mistakes of the Vietnam conflict. Even before Vietnam, however, it is worth recalling that it was the State Department which led the way, against the doubts of Defence Secretary Louis Johnson, towards accelerated levels of defence spending in the years 1949–50.[59] During the Vietnam war itself, figures like retired General Gavin frequently counselled in favour of cautious realism.[60] Ultimately the problem is not one of an over-influential, hawkish and praetorian military. Rather, it revolves around the extent to which the Cold War stimulated and embraced the institutionalisation of high, and accelerating, levels of defence spending in the name of 'national security'. The failure in Vietnam provoked a temporary setback for the 'warfare state'. In constant dollars, military budget projections were cut by 22 per cent between 1968 and 1975. By the early 1980s, however, the party had resumed. A Pentagon official involved in the formulation of defence procurement requests in 1981 recalled: 'I was in the Office of the Secretary, working for the readiness accounts. Carter had given us a lot. The Weinberger team came in and said, Add more. Find room to add. Find places to put more money.'[61]

The military were willing recipients of the Cold War largesse. The whole process, however, was driven by civilians (notably Presidents Truman, Kennedy and Reagan) and by civilian willingness to defer to military values and military expertise.[62]

In such an environment, it is not surprising that the Pentagon has become a bureaucratic machine for generating defence spending. Explaining the Pentagon's apparent antipathy to the testing of military technology, an Air Force colonel told the journalist Hedrick Smith: 'The reason the Pentagon doesn't like testing is that testing may interrupt the money flow to its programs. That's the strategy in the Pentagon: Don't interrupt the money flow.'[63]

The political and economic conditions of the 1990s – transformed conditions in the Soviet Union and Eastern Europe, high federal deficits in the United States – require a transformation also in the culture and expectations of the military and its bureaucratic allies. In November 1989, Defense Secretary Richard Cheney ordered the armed services to draw up plans to cut one hundred and eighty billion dollars in 1992–94 projected spending. Sean O'Keefe, Pentagon Comptroller, spoke of the need to alter the assumption that spending would always steadily increase. Representative Les Aspin spoke of the 1990 defence budget as the first 'Gorbachev-driven budget'.[64] Along with its assumptions regarding unlimited resources for defence, the military also needs to modify its characteristic 'oppositional culture'.[65] Even during the slowdown of the 1968–75 period, the military tended to meet spending reduction requests in a spirit of cynicism. The military has been notoriously reluctant, for example, to scrap whole programmes rather than to shave off (easily restored) excess. Reformers have been condemned as anti-military. The position of the United States in international politics in the 1990s requires a reorientation of military culture: a change more profound than simply adopting the view that a brief retrenchment may be needed before the spending tap is turned on once again.

Notes

1 *The White House Years*, Boston, 1979, p. 30. See also L. H. Gelb, 'Why not the State Department?', in C. W. Kegley and E. R. Wittkopf, eds., *Perspectives on American Foreign Policy*, New York, 1983, pp. 282–95; I. M. Destler, *Presidents, Bureaucrats and Foreign Policy*, Princeton, 1974.

2 Cited in I. M. Destler, 'The rise of the national security assistant, 1961–1981', in Kegley and Wittkopf, eds., *Perspectives*, pp.260–81, p. 268.

3 Z. Brzezinski, *Power and Principle*, New York, 1983, p. 63.

4 J. A. Nathan and J. K. Oliver, *Foreign Policy Making and the American Political System*, Boston, 2nd ed., 1987, p. 48.

5 See I. M. Destler, 'National Security Management', *Political Science Quarterly*, 95, 1980–81, pp. 573–89;P. Williams, 'The President and foreign relations', in M. Shaw, ed., *Roosevelt to Reagan: The Development of the Modern Presidency*, London, 1987, pp. 206–43, p. 219; J.G. Bock, *The White House Staff and the National Security Assistant*, New York, 1987, pp. 173–4.

6 See B. H. Patterson, *The Ring of Power*, New York, 1988, p. 109.

7 See E. C. Hargrove, *Jimmy Carter as President*, Baton Rouge, 1988, p. 149.

8 A. Haig, *Caveat*, New York, 1984, pp. 306, 352–8. See also R. J. Barilleaux, *The Post-Modern Presidency*, New York, 1988, p. 115.

9 L. Speakes, *Speaking Out*, New York, 1988, p. 265. See also S. Hess, *Organizing the Presidency*, Washington D.C., rev. ed., 1988, pp. 165–6; J. Mayer and D. McManus, *Landslide: The Unmaking of the President, 1984–1988*, Boston, 1988; Nathan and Oliver, *Foreign Policy Making*, p. 82.

10 J. Spanier and E. M. Uslaner, *American Foreign Policy and the Democratic Dilemmas*, Pacific Grove (California), 5th ed., 1989, pp. 55–6.

11 C. G. Menges, *Inside the National Security Council*, New York, 1988.

12 R. E. Hunter, *Presidential Conduct of Foreign Policy: Management or Mishap?*, Washington D.C., 1982, p. 29.

13 Destler, 'The rise', p. 262;B. H. Patterson, *The Ring of Power*, New York, 1988, ch. 7; E. C. Hargrove, *Jimmy Carter as President*, Baton Rouge, 1988, p. 115.

14 Patterson, *The Ring of Power*, p. 104.

15 *Ibid.*, p. 125.On Eisenhower's NSC system and its demise, see P. G. Henderson, *Managing the Presidency: The Eisenhower Legacy from Kennedy to Reagan*, Boulder (Colorado), 1988.

16 *The Tower Commission Report*, New York, 1987, p. 94. See also W. R. Farrell, 'The National Security Council and the Iran-Contra crisis', in N. C. Livingstone and T. E. Arnold, eds., *Beyond the Iran-Contra Crisis*, Lexington (Massachusetts), 1988.

17 See B. Rubin, *Secrets of State*, New York, 1987, p. ix; also, Barilleaux, *The Post-Modern Presidency*, p. 115.

18 B. A. Rockman, 'America's departments of state', in D. C. Kozak and J. M. Keagle, eds., *Bureaucratic Politics and National Security*, Boulder, 1988, pp. 174–201, p. 189. On plans for Senate confirmation of the NSA, see J. Hart, *The Presidential Branch*, New York, 1987, p. 143; *The Tower Commission Report*, pp. 94–5. See also, generally, C. V. Crabb and K. V. Mulcahy, *Presidents and*

Foreign Policy Making, Baton Rouge, 1986.

19 Bock, *The White House Staff*, pp. 118, 157–66.

20 'Why not the State Department?', p. 284. See also I. M. Destler *et al.*, *Our Own Worst Enemy*, New York, 1984.

21 P. Bushnell, 'Leadership at State', *Foreign Service Journal*, September 1989, pp. 30–1.

22 V. Huddleston, 'State's image on the Hill', *Foreign Service Journal*, September 1989, p.35.

23 D. T. Regan, *For the Record*, London, 1988, p. 294.

24 *Inside the National Security Council*, p. 17.

25 See D. D. Newsom, 'The executive branch in foreign policy', in E. S. Muskie *et al.*, *The President, the Congress and Foreign Policy*, New York, 1986, pp. 93–119;G. C. Mackenzie,ed., *The In-and-Outers*, Baltimore, 1987.

26 Destler *et al.*, *Our Own Worst Enemy*, p. 100.

27 C. Vance, *Hard Choices*, New York, 1983, p. 43.

28 Rubin, *Secrets of State*, pp. 233, 240; on the 'dissent channel', see Vance, *Hard Choices*, pp. 42, 126.

29 See Z. Steiner, 'Decision-making in American and British foreign policy', *Review of International Studies*, 13, 1987, pp. 1–18, p. 11. On departmental organisation, see C.V. Crabb, *American Foreign Policy in the Nuclear Age*, New York, 5th ed., 1988, pp. 73–7; also, Vance, *Hard Choices*, pp. 39–44.See also J. C. Whitehead, 'The Department of State', *Presidential Studies Quarterly*, 19, 1989, pp.11–23.

30 Nathan and Oliver, *Foreign Policy Making*, p. 38.

31 *Ibid.*, p. 40.

32 D. Luppi, 'Studies aim at personnel reform', *Foreign Service Journal*, July-August 1989, pp.29–34.

33 See M. J. Sheehan, *Arms Control: Theory and Practice*, Oxford, 1988, pp. 86–7; R. Burt, 'Defence policy and arms control', in R. Burt, ed., *Arms Control and Defence Postures in the1980's*, London, 1982, pp. 1–12.

34 Cited in Spanier and Uslaner, *American Foreign Policy Making*, p. 52.

35 See C. W. Kegley and E. R. Wittkopf, *American Foreign Policy: Pattern and Process*, New York, 3rd ed., 1987, p. 375.

36 See Newsom, 'The executive branch', p. 96.

37 Cited in R. Morris, 'Working for the other team: clientism in the Foreign Service', in C. Peters and J. Fallows, eds., *Inside the System*, New York, 3rd ed., 1976, pp. 171–81,p. 171.

38 See Steiner, 'Decision-making', p. 2;M. Ledeen and W. Lewis, *Debacle: The American Failure in Iran*, New York, 1981.

39 R. Pringle, 'Creeping irrelevance at Foggy Bottom', *Foreign Policy*, 29, 1977–78, pp. 128–39, p. 133.

40 See Gelb, 'Why not the State Department?', p. 286; Rockman, 'America's departments', p.182.

41 'Why not', p. 293.

42 This is the conclusion advanced in J. H. Esterline and R. B. Black, *Inside Foreign Policy: The Department of State Political System and its Subsystems*, Palo Alto (California), 1975.

43 T. L. Friedman, 'In quest of a post-Cold War plan', *New York Times*,

17 November 1989, p. 12; F. Fukuyama, 'The end of history', *The National Interest*, 1989.

44 See B. M. Blechman *et al.*, *Force without War*, Washington D.C., 1978.
45 See A. R. Millett and P. Marlowski, *For the Common Defense*, New York, 1984.
46 See E. Nordlinger, *Soldiers and Politics*, Englewood Cliffs, 1977.
47 R. A. Stubbing, *The Defense Game*, New York, 1986, p. 261.
48 *Ibid.*, p. 262.
49 See R.E. Powaski, *March to Armageddon*, New York, 1987, p. 230.
50 Stubbing, *The Defense Game*, p. 384.
51 P. M. Smith, *Assignment :Pentagon*, Washington D.C., 1989, p. 157.
52 *Ibid.*, p. 159.See also C. Jeffries, 'Bureaucratic politics in the Department of Defence', in Kozak and Keagle, eds.,*Bureaucratic Politics*, pp. 109–21.
53 On the record of incompetence, see J. Record, 'Why our high-priced military can't win battles', in Kozak and Keagle, eds., *Bureaucratic Politics*, pp. 462–8. See also J. Record, *Beyond Military Reform*, Washington D.C., 1988.
54 'The Goldwater-Nunn defense organization staff study', in Kozak and Keagle, eds., *Bureaucratic Politics*, pp. 490–5, p. 492.See also D. C. Hendrick, *Reforming Defense*, Baltimore, 1988.
55 J. G. Kester, 'The 1986 defense reorganization: a promising start', in Kozak and Keagle, eds., *Bureaucratic Politics*, pp. 378–89; The Joint Staff, *United States Military Posture for FY1989*, Washington D.C., 1988, p. 55; also F. Hampson, *Unguided Missiles: How America Buys its Weapons*, New York, 1989.
56 See G. Piller, 'DOD's Office of International Security Affairs', *Political Science Quarterly*, 98, 1983, pp. 59–78.For a summary of the records of Secretaries since McNamara, see Stubbing. *The Defense Game*, chs. 16–19.
57 See S. Emerson, *Secret Warriors: Inside the Covert Military Operations of the Reagan Era*, New York, 1988.
58 W. LaFeber, *The American Age*, New York, 1989, pp. 672–3; Nathan and Oliver, *Foreign Policy Making*, p. 95.
59 LaFeber, *The American Age*, p. 481.
60 See B. Buzzanco, 'The American military's rationale against the Vietnam War', *Political Science Quarterly*, 101, 1986, pp. 559–76.
61 Stubbing, *The Defense Game*, p. 391.
62 President Nixon remarked in 1969: 'I do not presume to be a specialist in this field and I am going to rely, when it comes to purely military matters, on what military advisers tell me should be done' (cited in J. Clotfelter, *The Military in American Politics*, New York, 1973, p. 191).See also A. Yarmolinsky, *The Military Establishment*, New York, 1971; E. Regehr, 'What is militarism?', in A. Eide and M. Thee, eds., *Problems of Contemporary Militarism*, London, 1980, pp. 127–39; D. E. Rosenblum, 'Pentagon savings',*New York Times*, 22 November 1989.
63 H. Smith, *The Power Game*, London, 1988, pp. 166–7. See also J. Gansler, *Affording Defense*, Cambridge (Massachusetts), 1989; A. E. Fitzgerald, *The Pentagonists*, New York, 1989; T. L. McNaugher, *New Weapons, Old Politics*, Washington D.C., 1989.
64 *New York Times*, 18 November 1989, pp. 1, 8.

65   See N. Lemman, 'Whistling in the Pentagon', *New York Review of Books*, 26 October 1989, pp. 3–5; J. K. Galbraith, 'Friendly advice to a shrinking military', *New York Times*, 22 November 1989.

5

Congress

Key Administration witnesses in the Iran-Contra hearings appeared to believe that foreign policy was, and should be, solely the concern of the executive. For Admiral Poindexter, for example, the failure of Congress to appropriate funds for desired projects was unfortunate, but was not the final word. Poindexter and Oliver North seemed to regard it as self-evident that Congress was not to be taken seriously as an actor in the foreign policy process.[1]

In some respects, this attitude, although constitutionally alarming and absurd, is unsurprising. Denigration of Congress has a long history in American culture. References to Congress in American literature tend to be to a Senate of unrelieved windbaggery and cynical power-brokerage, and to a House of Representatives of mindless parochialism and corruption.[2] Mark Twain considered Congressmen to represent the only 'distinctly native American criminal class'.[3] Feature films like *The Seduction of Joe Tynan* (1979) portray Congress as a place where principle is sacrificed to ambition. Public perceptions of Congress as an institution – although not necessarily of individual Members – are consistently negative.[4]

It is, therefore, especially important to remind ourselves of the impressive constitutional grant of power to Congress. Congress alone has the power to declare war. It has important powers relating to the regulation of foreign commerce. Ultimately, it has the 'power of the purse', potentially a fundamental influence on foreign as on domestic policy. This grant of power is not simply a constitutional obstacle, to be pushed aside by an executive which sees Congress simply as an irritant. It is also the case that Congress has representational and democratic virtues with which the executive cannot compete.

This is not to suggest that much criticism of Congress is

undeserved, nor that it is likely to cease. In no other policy area is there a stronger tradition of scepticism as to the desirability of a strong Congressional role as in the area of foreign affairs. These doubts rest not so much on grounds of constitutional propriety as on the presumed practical superiority of Presidential discretion. From Alexander Hamilton and John Jay, in their contributions to *The Federalist*, to advocates of a strong Presidency in the 1980s, opponents of Congressional influence have grounded their case in considerations of expediency.[5] Loud voices have held that successful foreign policy peculiarly requires secrecy, firm leadership and expeditious crisis-management, along with a transcendence of local and regional interests. Such qualities do not readily attach themselves to Congress. Rather, to cite John Lehman's 1976 catalogue of Congressional deficiency, legislative foreign policy has traditionally been hindered by 'multipolarity, diffuse authority, paucity of machinery, thinness of expertise and personnel, lack of intelligence sources, plodding and workaday character, freedom from secrecy, lack of continuity, and above all localism and parochialism.'[6]

Many observers would see these deficiencies as particularly acute in the decentralised, 'new Congress' of the 1970s and 1980s. Though fundamentally supporting a strong Congressional role, this chapter will discuss the recent history of legislative foreign policy in the light of these criticisms.

1   Determinants of Congressional influence

It is received wisdom that the making and conduct of foreign policy tends to be dominated by the executive. President Eisenhower once reportedly advised a freshman Representative to seek assignment to the Ways and Means Committee rather than Foreign Affairs. Ike declared that, whereas Ways and Means was 'King' in tax policy, in foreign affairs that title belonged to the President.[7]

Despite the general perception of executive dominance, the extent of Congressional influence varies considerably both over time and across policy areas. The period from Pearl Harbor (1941) to the emergence of widespread legislative dissent over Presidential conduct of the Vietnam war (*c.* 1968–71) clearly represented a high point of Congressional deference. Legislative pliancy was rooted in consensus over foreign policy aims (anti-communist containment) and in the relative and apparent success of Presidential initiatives.[8] The consensus, with its implicit invocation of executive superiority in crisis-management and in formulating consistent policy, was shattered by the early 1970s. In Alton Frye's words, the Vietnam war provoked the realisation that 'the constitutional system itself must be insulated from the perils of an overweening Presidency'.[9] Even in the years of Congressional passivity, however, it is worth noting that Presidents were not entirely immune from criticism in certain areas, and that the ability of Congress to initiate foreign policy was not entirely lost. Thus, while President Truman was able to exploit Cold War certainties and his putative crisis powers to embark upon an undeclared war in Korea in 1950, he was soon exposed to violent Congressional criticism regarding his conduct of the war. Even during the Eisenhower Presidency, Congress managed to retain the ability to initiate policy (one may cite the dominant legislative role in the creation of the International Development Association in 1958).

In fact, in periods both of Congressional quiescence and activism, the degree of legislative influence will tend to vary considerably across the range of US foreign and defence policy. To adopt the terminology used by R.B. Ripley and G. A. Franklin,[10] Congressional impact in the actual decision-making process is likely to be greatest in the areas of 'structural' and 'strategic' policies. The former refers to the incremental administration of long-term commitments – most notably the defence budget – which Congress tends to deal with in a highly decentralised fashion, in co-operation with executive and private sector personnel. 'Strategic' policy decisions, involving important departures in defence and foreign policy, tend to involve Congress in a less decentralised fashion, with the legislature inclining to a considerable degree of deference to the executive. In the case of Ripley and Franklin's third category, 'crisis policy', the normal decision-making structure consists of the President and major executive advisers, with perhaps (as in the Grenada invasion of 1983) some peremptory and belated consultation with a few specially selected legislators. While the President is not immune from criticism after the event, and may alter policy accordingly, Congress has not managed historically to secure a major role in the management of real, imagined (or, indeed, Presidentially-manufactured) crisis.

Presidents, along with State Department and other defence and foreign policy bureaucrats, are not unmindful of Congress's role as a reflector of public opinion,[11] and as an agency capable of publicising flaws and inconsistencies in the executive's conduct of policy. Democratic Senator Frank Church observed of President Johnson's reaction to Senate foreign affairs hearings that LBJ feared the 'Klieg lights' rather than any 'misgivings ... expressed behind closed doors'.[12] The executive is aware, however, that public opinion is often contradictory and (except on a highly salient issue like Vietnam) often of very low intensity. The fact that few constituents – often those with particular ethnic, religious or economic interests[13] – maintain a consistent concern with foreign policy, tends to diminish the extent to which Congress is regarded by the executive as representative of public opinion across the whole range of issues. In such circumstances, something of a 'culture of hostility'[14] has grown up between executive officials and Congress. Legislative pretensions in foreign policy tend to be seen by the executive as tedious and as constituting yet another obstacle to successful policy. Especially resented are attempts by Congress to involve itself in policy implementation, to 'micro-manage' foreign policy. J.B. Martin has noted that neither the State Department nor Congress 'thinks highly of the other': 'State thinks that the members of Congress engage in sordid politics and drink too much. Congress considers the department elitist and unable to comprehend political realities.'[15] Against this background, the executive is tempted, with varying degrees of subtlety, to propagate the notion that legislators are little more than country bumpkins, with no interest in, or knowledge of, foreign affairs.

It is, of course, inevitable that Congressional foreign policy will be significantly shaped by local, domestic considerations. It is a common criticism that legislators tend to see foreign policy as a slightly specialised branch of domestic policy.[16] Where they exist, constituency concerns – for example, employment prospects at a local defence plant – are bound to predominate. Where they do not, Members' concern with foreign policy may be either absent or simply concerned with empty publicity-seeking.[17] Constituency casework, an increasing Congressional concern in the 1970s and 1980s, does not typically yield problems of international moment.[18] (Nonetheless, immigration problems do rank highly. Staff at a Minnesota Senator's district office in 1988 regarded immigration problems as possibly the most time-consuming and important of all their duties.)[19] As an issue at Congressional elections, foreign affairs are often reduced to bland constituency-oriented sloganising by incumbents, with challengers attempting to establish an often spurious distance on particular issues from their opponents.[20]

In this context, policies which may involve a relocation of resources away from the domestic arena, or which have a major domestic economic impact, will tend to provoke an especially assertive legislative reaction.[21] Historically, Congress has taken particular interest in tariff and trading policies. While the increasing complexity and success of US trade inclined Congress to take a more passive role in the post-1945 period, reawakened protectionist pressures in the later 1970s and 1980s revived legislative interest. (The ninety-ninth Congress, 1985–86, saw the introduction of 782 trade bills, 248 with clear protectionist intent.)[22] The burgeoning 'intermestic' agenda, with the increasing difficulty in distinguishing 'foreign' from 'domestic' issues, had a major impact on Congress. The oil price rises and world energy crisis of the early 1970s alerted Congress to the onset of the new agenda. More generally, the perception of potential American vulnerability in a world of shrinking resources concentrated the legislative mind upon the domestic implications of international policies.

In those areas – foreign policy with clear domestic impact, trade and tariff matters – where Congress shows particular concern, it is often alleged that Capitol Hill is improperly responsive to 'special interests'. The post-Vietnam years witnessed a huge increase in the intensity and extent of lobbying of Congress on foreign-related issues. This was due partly to the perceivedly greater importance attached to Congressional foreign policy-making, and also increasing decentralisation, during the 1970s. It was also connected with the energy crisis and new perceptions of the domestic effects of foreign decisions, together with the tendency for higher interest group profiles to emerge in a period of party decline. Coalitions of business interest, single industry lobbies, foreign governmental pressure, labour and 'citizens' interest and domestic ethnic lobbies have all had important influence on Congressional foreign policy since Vietnam.[23]

2   The foreign policy Congress

The burgeoning influence of wealthy interest groups, and their associated Political Action Committees, forms part of the contemporary case against Congressional 'interference' in foreign policy. The decentralised Congress of the 1970s and 1980s is regularly depicted as the creature of moneyed organisation: 'the best Congress money can buy'.[24] Opponents of a strong legislative role in foreign policy-making would argue that Congress has traditional, inherent defects in this area: slowness, lack of secrecy, irrational parochialism, and so on. They would consider, however, that, during the 1970s, Congress reached a condition of virtual anarchy. Reforms, ostensibly designed to enhance international democracy and break the power of unaccountable committee chairmen, simply – according to this view – promoted chaos. The 1970s thus saw the rise of 'subcommittee domination' at the expense of 'committee government';[25] there emerged a new generation of individualistic party disloyalists operating in an electoral environment of constant campaigning and increasing localism. Incumbent Congressmen shored up their local base by prioritising narrowly-defined constituency service. The much vaunted 'staffing revolution' on Capitol Hill led to further irresponsible unaccountability and atomisation. The House of Representatives obviously, but also, in more subtle ways, the Senate, had become unfit and unwilling to perform a responsible foreign policy role.[26]

It is not here the intention to ridicule or parody the view that Congress became excessively decentralised during the 1970s. This argument, as will be made clear in the concluding section of this chapter, does need modification; nonetheless, to a considerable extent, it is correct. This can be seen if we examine the record of the major Congressional foreign policy committees during recent years.

A clear sign of changing times was the relative decline in importance of the Senate Foreign Relation Committee. As C. V. Crabb puts it, in the early post-war period, under the chairmanship of figures like Arthur Vandenberg and Tom Connally, 'the voice of this committee' was 'usually *the voice of Congress* in foreign affairs'.[27] By the 1980s, membership of the Committee was widely regarded as an electoral liability. At one level, integration on the Committee was undermined by increasing subcommittee autonomy – a product both of 1970s decentralisation and of the chairmanship of John Sparkman. Staffing increases – from twenty-five in 1960 to fifty-nine in 1981 – buttressed intra-Committee atomisation, rather than enhancing the authority of the full Committee.[28] The policy agenda of the 1970s and 1980s had a similar effect. Multiple referrals for bills among several panels became increasingly common with the rise of the 'intermestic' agenda.[29] The centrality of budgetary politics in the 1980s also had a deleterious effect on the Committee's prestige. Most damaging of all, however, was the perception that the acquisition of a reputation for foreign policy specialisation could be a harbinger of electoral defeat. In 1980 four prominent Foreign Relations Committee liberals were unseated, including chairman Frank Church and ranking Republican Jacob Javits. These members were vulnerable to the Reaganite sweep, but were also deemed to have suffered as a result of having identified themselves with international rather than constituency concerns.[30] Charles Percy, the Illinois Republican who became chairman in 1981, was himself defeated in the 1984 elections. Unsurprisingly, by the later 1980s, membership of the Committee was seen as anything but a desirable power base. Indeed, during the hundredth Congress (1987–88), the Committee actually operated with one (Democratic) vacancy. Church and Percy were high-profile liberal chairmen in the post-Vietnam mould. Richard Lugar, the Indiana Republican who took over in 1985, was much closer to Reagan than Percy had been (although he was easily outflanked on the right by Republican Jesse Helms, who made conservative position-taking on foreign issues a major priority). Lugar attempted to reinvigorate the Committee by embarking upon a wide-ranging review of US foreign policy. His 1987 Democratic successor, Claiborne Pell of Rhode Island, seemed to lack any such ambition. No longer did the chairman of the Foreign Relations Committee purport to speak as the leader of Congressional foreign policy. If anyone sought such a role in the later 1980s, it was Senator Sam Nunn, chairman of the traditionally more conservative Armed Services Committee.[31]

Many of the forces affecting the Senate Foreign Relations Committee in the 1970s and 1980s also reverberated upon the House Foreign Affairs Committee. The increasing incidence of multiple referring – even more pronounced in the House than the Senate – tended to erode the Committee's authority.[32] The early 1980s saw the rise in influence of the Committee's eight subcommittees.[33] Alternative centres of power (for example, Clarence Long's House Appropriations subcommittee on Foreign Operations) began to emerge.[34] The advantages of House incumbency meant that there were no spectacular defeats for 'foreign policy Representatives' to match those in the Senate. However, the Committee was perceived as offering few re-election benefits.[35] Members tended to come from safe, urban constituencies, with junior Congressmen joining the Committee in order to attain seniority. During the 1970s and 1980s, the House Foreign Affairs Committee continued to be designated a 'minor' committee assignment by the party organisations. Dante Fascell, the

Florida Democrat who became chairman in 1983, attempted, like Lugar in the Senate, to reinvigorate the Committee's prestige; however, its influence remained low. In particular, the biennial foreign aid authorisation bill – the main formal work of the Committee – tended to decline in importance along with the authority of the Senate Foreign Relations Committee.[36] Nonetheless, a conspicuous example of how to thrive in the new environment was provided by Stephen Solarz, the New York Democrat who assumed chairmanship of the Asian and Pacific Affairs subcommittee in 1981. Solarz identified himself with highly visible foreign policy debates, on which he took clear positions: for example, opposing the Marcos regime in the Philippines, or calling for a tough US response to the Beijing student massacre of June 1989. That foreign policy activism need not be an electoral liability was revealed by the fact that, by 1989, Solarz had accumulated the second largest campaign fund in the House: over 1.2 million dollars, raised principally from first generation Asian-Americans.[37]

The degree of anarchic decentralisation in the 'new Congress' has been exaggerated. Nonetheless, it manifestly is a major factor in assessing the ability of Congress to make effective foreign policy. In particular, Congressional decentralisation impinges upon (though does not necessarily negate) the efficacy of the two central pillars which support legislative power in foreign affairs: information-gathering and the 'power of the purse'.

The problem of Congressional access to sensitive foreign policy information is almost as old as the Republic itself. The investigative and oversight functions of Congress depend upon a prior right to secure information from the executive, as does the need of the House of Representatives to collect information relevant to impeachment investigations. On the other hand, there are practical arguments which may be used to buttress the putative need for a qualified 'executive privilege' over information. These would include the argument that the knowledge that ostensibly private conversations might be transmitted to Congress would hardly encourage frankness of advice, and would simply encourage the executive to erect new barriers of secrecy. While rejecting President Nixon's claim of an absolute, blanket, discretionary power to withhold information, the Supreme Court in *U.S.* v. *Nixon* (1974) did countenance the existence of a qualified 'executive privilege', with 'military, diplomatic or sensitive national security secrets' enjoying special status.[38] While legislative-executive tension in this area subsided during the Carter Presidency, they emerged once more under President Reagan. Major disputes developed over access to information relating to Central Intelligence Agency operations. Claims made by Reagan Administration officials recalled the autocratic attitudes of the Nixon years. In the Bruce Blair case, for example, a report (on US communications systems vulnerability), commissioned by Congress itself, was eventually withheld after reclassification.[39]

Without access to potentially sensitive information, an effective legislative role in foreign policy becomes impossible. Absolute executive discretion in this area is a concept disallowed both by constitutional tradition and by modern experience of unaccountable Presidential power. During the 1980s, Congress encountered a Supreme Court which was generally unsympathetic to arguments rooted in the democratic desirability of enhanced legislative access. Nonetheless, Congress has a strong constitutional case in this area, and should assert it.[40] Inevitably, however, legislative decentralisation militates against the efficacy of any such assertion. Congress does not have an integrated, unified information-gathering and processing system on the lines of the State Department. Individual members and committees fight their own battles with the executive over information access. Yet, as Stanley Heginbotham has argued, Congress is not a bureaucracy and should not be judged as such.[41] The very multifacetedness of the Congressional information process can be an asset. The pluralist, multi-dimensional Congress may be able to probe, and keep issues alive, in a way impossible for a centralised bureaucracy. The 1970s staffing revolution on Capitol Hill, its centrifugalist consequences notwithstanding, did strengthen the capacity of Congress to garner information. Also, it should be emphasised that Congress is not entirely dependent on the executive for information. It has been estimated that the House Foreign Affairs Committee gathers 60 per cent of its information from open sources, 25 per cent from the State Department, 5 per cent from the intelligence community, and 10 per cent from other, foreign sources.[42]

Perhaps even more than access to information, the 'power of the purse' lies at the heart of the legislative prerogative. Recognition of the need to defend this prerogative in the face of attacks upon it by the Nixon Administration was central to the emergence and passage of the 1974 Congressional Budget and Impoundment Control Act.[43] The Act gave Congress an integrated budget process, set up the

Congressional Budget Office and attempted to control executive discretion over the disbursement of funds. For here lies the nub of the problem: the practical advantages enjoyed by the executive, the operating branch, over the legislature, the enabling branch. In practice, the executive can make decisions over the timing of spending, or on transfers between accounts, which undermine the Congressional money power. There is a grey area where legitimate executive discretion shades into irresponsibility and illegality. The history of the CIA is replete with examples of this. Reprogramming, covert funding, the accumulation of 'pipeline' funds, the use of 'discretionary' money (as in the early stages of the Peace Corps under President Kennedy): these are some of the quasi-legal devices used by the executive to evade legislative control of spending.[44]

As with information access, the ability of Congress successfully to assert its spending power tends to be undermined by legislative decentralisation. Again, however, it should be emphasised that decentralisation (within certain bounds at least) is not automatically harmful and 'inefficient'. The two-step authorisation-appropriation process may be lengthy and labyrinthine. It also provides opportunities for oversight, detailed scrutiny and criticism. It should also be set in the context of the broadly integrative, concentrating effects of the 1974 budgetary reforms and of budgetary politics generally in the 1980s.[45] There is also no escaping the fact that the constitutional case underpinning strong Congressional control of spending is overwhelming. When Congress acts unambiguously on money matters, the executive has either to comply or to break the law.[46]

3   Congress and US foreign policy since 1964

(a)   *Congress and the Vietnam war*   Although a few unrepentant hawks have tried to blame failure in Vietnam on excessive Congressional interference,[47] it had become received wisdom by the mid-1970s that Vietnam represented the nadir of irresponsible legislative acquiescence in executive domination. Congress appeared to have failed in its constitutional duty to act as a check upon the President, and in its representative function of reflecting changing public attitudes towards the war.

The putative need for a united, bi-partisan Cold War foreign policy bedevilled the ability of Congress to control the executive's conduct of the war. While the legislature's abject, and constitutionally improper, failure over Vietnam is not doubted, a few less obvious points about Congressional action on Vietnam may nonetheless be noted. In the first place, Congressional action was decisive in ending American military involvement. Secondly, despite frequent assertions to the contrary, it is far from clear that Congress was seriously out of kilter with public opinion on the war. Poll evidence indicates that public support for the war only began seriously to evaporate after 1968, and, indeed, remained at high levels even in the early 1970s. Only after the Cambodian invasion of 1970 can it be argued at all convincingly that Congress – or, more particularly, the House – lagged significantly behind public opinion as reflected in poll evidence.

It would also be erroneous to assume that Congress had no impact on the actual course of the war. Given the state of legislative and public opinion in the 1960s, this impact was, however, as likely to be hawkish as doveish. In 1967, for example, Johnson was arguably converted to a policy of bombing previously restricted targets by bi-partisan Congressional criticism.[48] The Joint Chiefs of Staff regularly utilised contacts with right-wing legislative sub-committees as a means of pressuring the administration.[49] On the side of the Vietnam doves, the Senate Foreign Relations Committee hearings of 1966 and 1968 provided the most public of all fora for elite critics of the Administration. Throughout the war, Congressional investigations also helped illuminate some dark areas: for example, war crimes, the plight of refugees and the condition of prisoners in South Vietnam.

While not wishing in any sense to 'excuse' the failure of Congress to exercise responsible and effective oversight, it must be appreciated that many legislators did combine real doubts about the war with the refusal to indulge in behaviour which could in any sense be interpreted as an abandonment of troops already committed. Johnson consistently and effectively evoked the 'boys-in-the-field' and the need to support them with continuing appropriations, just as Nixon later claimed that precipitate withdrawal would amount to an abandonment of American prisoners-of-war. Nixon's espousal of 'Vietnamisation' – the gradual handing over of the war to South Vietnamese forces – also effectively defused Congressional opposition.[50]

(b) *Reassertion: 1973–80* In retrospect, the Nixon years now seem a period of transition towards greater Congressional impact on foreign policy, rather than years of executive dominance. However, it was during the Ford and Carter Administrations that Congress seemed, in certain policy areas at least, either to seize the initiative or to be subjecting the executive to new controls. By 1976, Secretary of State Kissinger was accusing Congress of having dangerously hamstrung the President, depriving him of 'indispensable flexibility'.[51]

During the period 1973–80, legislative reassertion was most obvious in a series of Congressional conflicts with the White House, and in new techniques intended to enhance control over executive discretion. The Ford Administration found its policies successfully opposed not only in Southeast Asia, but also in Cyprus (where Congress imposed an arms embargo after the Turkish invasion of 1974) and Angola.[52] Everywhere loomed the memory of Vietnam and the remembered nightmare of uncontrolled Presidential discretion. Although, as T.M. Franck and E.W. Weisband have written, often 'maddeningly inconsistent' in ideology,[53] Congress tended to oppose the interventionist conservatism of the Ford Administration and to lead the 'human rights' orientation of the early Carter Presidency. However, increasing Congressional conservatism in the late 1970s engendered fierce inter-branch conflicts over the Panama Canal treaty and the normalisation of relations with China. Above all, the Senate appeared poised to reject the second Strategic Arms Limitation Treaty (SALT II), before Carter abandoned it in the wake of the 1979 Soviet invasion of Afghanistan.[54]

The most celebrated of the new techniques introduced in an attempt to inhibit executive discretion was the 1974 War Powers Act. Here Congress made use of the legislative veto, an increasingly popular and constitutionally controversial mode of control. The legislative veto – applied for example, to arms sales in the mid-1970s – allows Congress a second bite at the executive cherry. The executive is authorised to take certain action subject to veto by the whole Congress, by one chamber, or even by one committee. The legislative veto formed part of the so-called 'new oversight'. This was designed to give Congress the right of prior and ongoing veto and consultation in foreign policy decisions, rather than simply the ability to scrutinise past policies. It also involved a new involvement in foreign policy by the House of Representatives and its Foreign Affairs Committee (known between 1975 and 1979 as the Committee on International Relations).[55]

The impact of these changes should not be exaggerated. The effect of the War Powers Act was, at best, ambivalent. The legislative veto was soon to be subjected to major constitutional challenge, and, at least in connection with major arms sales (under the 1974 Bingham amendment), was not taken up by the entire Congress until 1981. Similarly, initiatives such as the requiring of executive reports on arms control (1975) were met by Presidential evasion. Carter succeeded in exporting nuclear fuels to India in 1978 despite prior restrictions placed upon his power in this area. It now appears that the 1970s witnessed, not a new Congressional dominance, but – as S. J. Baker has written – a newly 'complex pattern of interaction' between the branches.[56] The 'new oversight' also intersected with the new decentralisation. Reviewing the period, ex-Congressman C. W. Whalen complained that the newly assertive House was operating as 'a flotilla of 147 sub-committee vessels . . . without a compass'.[57]

Whatever its limits, the years of reassertion did see positive gains: in expertise, confidence, intra-Congressional democracy and, above all, in serving notice on the White House that unilateral and unaccountable foreign policy is bound eventually to stimulate legislative reaction.

(c) *Congressional foreign policy: 1981–88*   In October 1980, Presidential candidate Reagan promised to 'restore leadership to US foreign policy'.[58] Though primarily an attack upon the Carter Administration's supposed failure to speak with one voice, the promise also implied the need for a newly firm direction of Congress. In the first two years of the Presidency, Congress was largely content to allow Reagan the new flexibility. At one level, Congressional leaders appeared to accept that executive discretion had become unduly fettered. Senator Percy, the new Foreign Relations Committee chairman, spoke of the need to restore bi-partisanship – a clear invocation of the need for a strong Presidential role.[59] In addition, Reagan's high poll ratings combined with the institutionalised weakness of oppositional leadership in Congress to promote a new docility. Highly questionable measures, such as the 'reprogramming' of funds to aid the government of El Salvador, were accepted with little protest. With a Republican majority in the Senate, White House foreign policy-makers seemed in a stronger position than any White House team since the mid-1960s.

Problems did, however, begin to surface in the Democratic House. Even in 1981, the House rejected Reagan's plan to sell AWAC radar

planes to Saudi Arabia. In December 1982, the House adopted the
first Boland amendment, disallowing covert US military aid to the
anti-government *contra* forces in Nicaragua; and, in May 1983, the
House adopted a resolution requiring a nuclear freeze. All these
measures were reversed or killed in the Senate, and, indeed, the
AWAC sale was trumpeted as a great Administration victory. Nonetheless, the stage was set for the major foreign policy battles of
Reagan's Presidency: especially over *contra* aid and funding for the
MX missile. Respectable Democratic performances in the 1982, 1984
and 1986 Congressional elections also tended to alter legislative
perceptions of the nature of Reagan's mandate. The Administration
began to adopt the tactic of moving to meet anticipated Congressional
action: for example, in removing marines from the Lebanon in
February 1984 (after Congressional invocation of the War Powers
Act five months earlier), and in reducing support for President Marcos in the Philippines in February 1986.[60]

It would, therefore, be a gross exaggeration to depict the period
between Reagan's inauguration and the onset of the Iran-Contra
crisis (November–December 1986) as one of overwhelming executive
domination. In 1985, for example, Congress forced the abandonment
of proposed arms sales to Jordan and some modest changes in the
Administration's stance towards South Africa. The overriding (in
October 1986) of Reagan's veto of the South African sanctions bill was
a major White House defeat. The final two years of Reagan's Presidency, after Irangate and with a Senate Democratic majority, were
inevitably difficult for the Administration. In September 1987, the
Senate hindered the advance of the Strategic Defence Initiative (SDI)
by effectively disallowing Administration interpretations of the 1972
Anti-ballistic missile treaty. In February 1988, the House rejected the
President's request for 36.25 billion dollars in new military aid to the
contras. Nonetheless, attempts to invoke the War Powers Act over US
action in the Persian Gulf failed, and the Senate voted in May 1988 to
accept (with certain provisos) the INF (Intermediate Nuclear Force)
treaty.

Overall, and certainly for the first six years of the Reagan Presidency, foreign policy emanated from the White House rather than
Capitol Hill. The South African sanctions bill of 1986 was the first
major exception to this. Despite a major fight over the MX missile,
and unease about SDI and swollen federal deficits, Congress voted
huge increases in Pentagon spending. The 1983 Grenada invasion

and 1986 Libyan bombings ultimately received strong majority Congressional support. Widespread anxieties notwithstanding, Congress did vote substantial sums to guerrilla movements in Afghanistan, Angola, Cambodia and Nicaragua. Above all, the conduct of East-West relations remained firmly in the White House.[61]

4 War powers, advice and consent

(a) *War powers* The 1974 War Powers Act emerged against the background of perceived Presidential usurpation of the Congressional war power. Although Congress has sole constitutional authority to declare war, only five wars in American history have actually been formally declared as such. Under the Act, Presidents must report to Congress the involvement of US troops in 'hostilities' within forty-eight hours. Unless Congress specifically authorises the troops to stay, the President must withdraw them in sixty days (or, in especially difficult circumstances, in ninety days). The President is also instructed to consult Congress 'in every possible instance'.

The fate of the 1973 War Powers Resolution and Act of 1974 has mirrored the fate of the entire effort of the 1970s to reassert legislative control in foreign policy. Presidents have been able to exploit the existence of putative crises, requiring swift and secretive action, as well as the rather patchy nature of Members' interest in and knowledge of foreign affairs. The War Powers Act itself, however, has many inherent weaknesses. It is unclear exactly with whom the President is supposed to consult 'in every possible instance'. The whole Congress? Party leaders? The relevant committee chairmen? The word 'hostilities' is far too vague and positively invites executive dissimulation.[62] Senator Eagleton also noticed at the time of passage that the war powers provisions effectively allow the President 'an open-ended blank cheque for ninety days of war-making'. The Act also allows Presidents to implicate Congress in policy failures.[63] The Act raises doubts as to the constitutionality of the legislative veto, and effectively invites Presidents to invoke their 'Commander-in-Chief' powers. (Congress has elsewhere recognised the constitutional authority of Presidents to take action to rescue endangered US citizens abroad.)[64] During periods of perceived national crisis, Congress may be only too willing to acquiesce in whatever the President thinks fit. As Senator Javits described his own position during the *Mayaguez* incident of 1975: 'The overwhelming temptation is to wait and see, to let the dust settle.'[65]

During President Reagan's first term, the Act seemed in danger of becoming a dead letter. For one thing, the Supreme Court's *Chadha* decision (1983) cast doubt on the propriety of the Act's use of the legislative veto. At the very least, it seemed to require that Congress use joint resolutions (subject to veto) rather than concurrent resolutions to operate under the Act.[66] Administration action in the Lebanon and Grenada violated both the spirit and letter of the Act. Reagan did offer reports which he held to be 'consistent' with the Act, but which made clear that the White House did not accept its constitutionality. The circumstances of the 1983 Grenada invasion ensured that Congress was, as M. Rubner has put it, offered the choice of 'putting up or shutting up'.[67] Major Congressional protest did, emerge, however, in connection with the presence of US troops in the Lebanon in 1983, and concerning action in the Persian Gulf in 1987. As noted above, the War Powers Act was actually invoked in 1983, but with the proviso that the President be allowed to keep troops in the Lebanon for eighteen months. In 1987, 110 members of the House unsuccessfully brought a lawsuit seeking to trigger the war power procedures.

On the one hand, there is the argument made succinctly in President Nixon's original veto message on the War Powers Resolution. This held it to be unconstitutional (a breach in separation of powers) and unworkable: an attempt 'to take away, by a mere legislative act, authority which the President has properly exercised for almost 200 years'.[68] Congressman McCain, a Republican from Arizona, during the 1987 debate on the Persian Gulf, identified the central mistake of the War Powers Act as 'the idea that Congress should have control over tactical military decisions'.[69] Senator Larry Pressler, ranking Republican on a special Senate subcommittee on war powers, argued in July 1988 that the Framers knew well the difference between 'war' and 'hostilities'. The latter condition was to be province of executive direction.[70]

The opposing argument stresses the need for accountability and democratic control. Louis Fisher, for example, has argued that the War Powers Act intended 'not to encroach upon the president but to reintroduce some semblance of balance between the branches'.[71] During the Reagan Presidency, there also emerged the question of executive good faith. Senator Lowell Weicker, the maverick Republican, put the point with characteristic bluntness: 'Why should there be blind trust in a policy devised by those who were not hesitant to sell arms to Iran?'[72] In April 1983, Defence Secretary Weinberger assured Senator Kennedy that US forces in Central America were not involved in 'combat activities within the meaning of the War Powers Resolution'.[73] Such statements presume a degree of legislative acceptance of executive good faith.

(b) *Treaties* The powers of Congress regarding treaties provide another example of a potentially impressive grant of constitutional authority, which has to considerable extent been abdicated to Presidential discretion. According to Article II, Section 2 of the Constitution, the President 'shall have Power, by and with the Advice and Consent of the Senate, to make Treaties, provided two thirds of the Senators present concur'. A report commissioned by the Senate Foreign Relations Committee in 1977 held that the 'original concept' of the Senate's role was that 'it would share fully in the process', rather 'as a council sitting to make decisions on treaty problems presented by the President'.[74] It is also at least eminently arguable that the 'original concept' included a significant role for the House of Representatives.[75]

In modern times, the 'original concept' has become moribund. Certainly, some Presidents have sought the aid of important Senators. For example, Congressional 'advisers' participated in the 1978 SALT II talks. During the Panama Canal treaty negotiations of 1977–78, a group of Republican Senators, led by Howard Baker, virtually indulged in their own, private treaty-making process with General Torrijos of Panama.[76] Speaker Jim Wright's role in the Central American peace plan (1987) may also be cited. Nonetheless, as Franck and Weisband point out, Presidential dominance in treaty negotiation has actually been enhanced by the 'façade of selective senatorial participation'.[77] Congressional participation has often simply been a function of the prestige and political requirements of the White House.[78] In particular, the use of executive agreements – not requiring advice and consent – has decisively altered the treaty process as envisioned in the Constitution.

By the mid-1980s, the United States was party to almost one thousand treaties, but to over four thousand executive agreements. White House preference for executive agreements has increased enormously since 1945.[79] The constitutional case for executive agreements rests on Supreme Court interpretation (notably

Curtiss-Wright (1936) and *Belmont* (1937)), and on invocation of 'inherent' and 'Commander-in-Chief' Presidential authority. Many executive agreements are, in a formal sense, authorised by statute. Nonetheless, the scale of contemporary usage of executive agreements – 343 were concluded in 1982 – really does seem at variance with constitutional intent. However, and certainly since the narrow failure of the Bricker amendment in 1954, Congress has not been sufficiently united to address this problem satisfactorily. The 1972 Case Act dealt only with the question of executive agreement secrecy. It required that agreements be reported within sixty days, the most sensitive being referred only to the specialist Congressional foreign policy committees. More forceful action was sidetracked by the failure of House and Senate to agree upon acceptable procedures. As it was, the Case Act could do nothing to prevent the Vietnam peace document of 1973, nor the Sinai accords of 1975, being promulgated without advice and consent. By 1976, it had become obvious – for example, in the case of agreements between the US and South Korean intelligence services – that even the reporting requirements of the Case Act were not being followed. The experience of the Reagan Presidency was one of further evasions.[80]

In the case of treaties actually submitted for advice and consent, Presidents sometimes argue that they must either be accepted or rejected *in toto*. Tinkering or amending would, as Carter argued over SALT II for example, destroy the delicately negotiated balance of the treaty. In fact, the Senate does have the power to take limiting action: 'amendment, reservation, understanding, interpretations, declaration, and statement'.[81] These can form the substance of further negotiation with the treaty partner. Presidents may also argue that anything short of wholesale acceptance will destroy the international standing of the White House. While considering SALT II, the Senate Foreign Relations Committee explicitly considered the impact on international opinion of the Senate's failure to support Carter. The Democratic majority on the Committee was also aware that rejection would undermine the President's 'effectiveness as a leader and consensus-builder ... not only internationally but domestically as well'.[82] During the INF treaty ratification debate of 1988, the Foreign Relations Committee, prodded by Senator Helms, also explicitly addressed the question of possible reinterpretation of the treaty after the application of advice and consent.[83]

(c) *Appointments*   Senate advice and consent regarding Presidential appointments similarly involve the examination of nominees rather than prior consultation. The importance of the confirming power is tied to expectations that the President will consider anticipated Senate reaction before making the nomination.

Most appointments are subject to a simple majority vote on the Senate floor, and are confirmed without difficulty. In addition, most White House (as distinct from Cabinet) officials are not subject to confirmation at all. For most Senators, the appointment confirmation process is valued less for the opportunity to exercise a veto, than for providing opportunities (especially during the confirmation hearings) to initiate relationships with appointees, to acquire information and to publicise grievances.[84] Attempts were made during the 1970s to revamp committee procedures for examining nominees, as well as to increase the number of posts requiring confirmation. Despite this, the confirmation process is widely regarded as unsatisfactory. The 'sale' of ambassadorships in return for campaign assistance has long been recognised as a patent abuse of Presidential authority. Yet the Senate has not been prepared to use the confirmation power to remedy it.

Confirmation hearings can provide a forum for the articulation of Senate criticism of Administration foreign policy. Under President Carter, for example, the nomination of Leonard Woodcock as the first US ambassador to the People's Republic of China stimulated an extended debate on the normalisation of US-Chinese relations. In 1982, the William Clark confirmation (as Undersecretary of State) hearings revealed the nominee's ignorance of foreign affairs, and proved embarrassing to the Reagan Administration. However, both Woodcock and Clark were eventually confirmed. Ernest Lefever's rejection as human rights assistant at the State Department did discomfort the Reagan Administration. It signalled Congressional displeasure and drew attention to the Administration's low prioritisation of human rights issues. The rejection of John Tower as Defence Secretary in 1989 was a major humiliation for the incoming Bush Administration. It was the first time in American history that a President's Cabinet-level nominee had been rejected at the start of his first term. It was only the second time that the Senate had turned down an ex-Senator nominated to the Cabinet. The debate on Tower, of course, hinged not only on his hawkish record on defence, but also on Tower's personality, drinking and private life. The personality and personal prestige of his chief adversary, Senator Nunn, was also a factor. It has also been argued that the very fact that Tower's rejection was 'driven neither by ideology nor by outside pressure' meant that a precedent especially damaging to the executive had been set.[85] The case's unique features – Tower's personality and also the bitterness resulting from Bush's controversial 1988 campaign – make it difficult to generalise. Nonetheless, it did illustrate the potency of the constitutional grant of power to Congress, and also the tendency for this power to be used in an apparently negative, reactive fashion.

5   Foreign aid and defence budgeting

In many areas of foreign policy, Congress tends to lose the initiative because it has no 'handle': no annual, ongoing process specifically designed to develop new approaches. Rather, it reacts to crises, which themselves are managed and defined by the executive. In the case of foreign aid, which may cover everything from Peace Corps funds to support for right-wing guerrillas in Central America, there is such a process: the annual foreign aid authorisation and foreign assistance appropriations measures.

The lack, except in exceptional cases like Israel, of any obvious constituency for the bulk of foreign aid has tended to orient Congress towards a confrontational budget-cutting role *vis-à-vis* executive requests. A Congressman, interviewed by C.W. Whalen, said that he had opposed every foreign aid for twenty years: 'It is unpopular in my district, which is very poor. Had I voted for it, it would have become a campaign issue.'[86]

Nonetheless, Congress is influenced by shifting actions about the purpose and efficacy of aid: ideas articulated around the concepts of national security and moral responsibility. During the Reagan Presidency, especially pre-Irangate, the Administration view that foreign aid should be used consciously as an instrument of US foreign policy gained ground on Capitol Hill. Congress has been affected by 'donor fatigue' regarding the Third World, and also by the view that aid should be applied selectively to prevent left-wing takeovers.[87] Congress has used the aid process to make policy changes, and during the 1970s fought major battles to ensure that aid spending by the executive was closely controlled.[88] Congress has used the lever of aid to force specific courses of action on foreign countries. For example, a 1984 Senate rider to an aid appropriation prevented Turkey receiving 215 million dollars unless part of the city of Famagusta was returned to Cypriot government control.[89] Nonetheless, there is no question that the aid process suffers from centrifugalism and excessive deference to special pleading from the White House. Between 1981 and 1985, Congress did not even manage to finalise an annual foreign aid authorisation bill, dispensing aid by means of *ad hoc* appropriations and continuing resolutions.[90]

As with foreign aid, annual consideration of defence spending provides Congress with an opportunity to develop policy on a coherent basis. Congressional impact upon executive defence requests is far from negligible, with the legislature moving to a more activist position in the post-Vietnam period. Between 1960 and 1968, there were only three examples of Congress making changes of over 5 per cent in the procurement, research, developing, testing and evaluation titles of the President's defence budget. The years 1969–1977 saw seventeen such changes.[91] Even changes of less than 5 per cent may, given the huge sums involved, be of significance. In the mid-1970s, conspicuous anti-Pentagon Democrats even began to gain assignment to the traditionally docile House and Senate Armed Services Committees.

Despite what an opponent of Congressional reassertion in this area has called these attempts 'to intrude too deeply in the national security policy-making process',[92] the legislative defence budget yet again exhibits the strengths and weaknesses of centrifugalism. Opportunities for detailed scrutiny and multiple access are balanced by the politics of the 'pork barrel'. The defence budget in Congress typically has at least twenty-two stages at which votes are taken. Individuals and sub-groups compete to gain lucrative contracts for states and districts. The final House-passed authorisation bill for fiscal year 1981, for example, provided a job-creating defence project for every single member of the Armed Services Committee.[93]

The politics of the 'pork barrel' are not conducive to coherent policy-setting. With huge sums at stake – between 1970 and 1980, the top seven US defence contractors received over one hundred billion dollars in Pentagon contracts – contractors devote enormous resources to legislative lobbying. Congress is also lobbied openly by the military itself. Members who consistently support high defence spending very often receive substantial defence contracting Political Action Committee (PAC) contributions. Philip Stern quotes the case of Senator Dan Quayle, before his elevation to the Vice-Presidency. Quayle, chairman of a military procurement subcommittee which enacted a defence cost reporting measure in 1985, reversed his position after receiving contractors' PAC money.[94] In this environment, causes such as arms control, which may have little obvious centrifugal benefit, often take second place. Too often Congress is content to direct its attention to aspects of the defence budget with high constituency saliency, while deferring to the Pentagon on wider issues. The long lead-time of weapons systems research and development also militates against effective Congressional action.[95]

Nonetheless, the situation is not hopeless. As Cox and Kirby's case study on procurement of the AV-8B aircraft (1976–81) illustrates, Congress can act responsibly and effectively if political conditions favour such an outcome.[96] Maverick 'Pentagon gadflies' like Senator Proxmire of Wisconsin and (Republican) Congressman Denny Smith of Oregon do manage to build careers on their criticisms of bloated defence budgets.[97] It is also manifestly the case that strong ideological coalitions develop on defence; it is not simply the province of the 'pork barrel'. Above all, the obvious deficiencies of legislative defence budgeting should not be used as an argument to exclude Congress from those areas – especially detailed line-item and cost effectiveness scrutiny – where it has shown itself able to operate effectively.[98] Nothing could be more dangerous than the wholesale abandonment of defence budgeting to unaccountable executive discretion.

6 Concluding remarks

Normative arguments for a strong legislative role in foreign policy relate essentially to the multifarious representative virtues of Congress, as compared to the executive. Presidents may tell the public, as J.F. Kennedy told the National Press Club in 1960, that only the President represents the national interest. However, if the President can exploit the virtues of the highly concentrated and unitary kind of representation held to be embodied in the Chief Executive, then Congress can point to the strengths of a decentralised representational base. Congress may, in fact, be said to 'represent' the United States in ways in which the executive would find impossible. Members can, for example, attempt to balance the 'delegate' and 'trustee' aspects of representation; in other words, to combine the virtues of reflecting the views of the constituency with the freedom to weigh those views against other (national and party) considerations. Congress can also present itself as a nation-in-miniature, proclaiming the virtues of 'microcosmic' representation: the degree to which the membership of the legislature mirrors the characteristics – regional, racial, religious, and so on – of the entire population.

In point of fact, of course, Members, eager for re-election, may allow the 'delegate' role to predominate over the 'trustee'. Hispanics, women and African Americans are notoriously under-represented in Congress, and especially in the Senate. Yet these considerations do not entirely negate the potential benefits of a strong Congressional foreign policy role, rooted in multifarious representative capacity. At the very least, Congress is far more likely than the relatively unitary executive publicly to air policy alternatives. Policy which is the product of a strong legislative input could also be the basis of a firmer and more democratically oriented consensus than one dictated by executive policy preferences. Legislative consistency in policy is not necessarily a contradiction in terms.[99] Intra-bureaucratic and inter-departmental rivalries, Presidential inconsistency and executive failures of intelligence may, on a day-to-day basis, seem less deep-seated than defects in Congress; they do exist, however, and, in the long run, may be more dangerous, especially if not checked by Capitol Hill.

This is not to suggest that major problems, deriving from legislative centrifugalism, do not exist. At one level, institutional tinkering can address these problems and help reverse any counter-productive tendencies of the 1970s reform movement. Rationalisation of overlapping committee jurisdictions, greater institutionalised House-Senate co-operation, annual reviews of foreign policy, the use of bi-partisan legislative groups as crisis-management teams, effective controls on PACs, the creation of a new Committee on National Security: all these changes could be beneficial. There have for a long time been strong arguments for having four-year terms for Congressmen, and for Congressional participation on the National Security Council.[100] Even more importantly, a regeneration of party responsibility – provided it did not degenerate into insipid pro-Presidential bi-partisanship – would help effect a diminution of harmful centrifugalism.

In fact, the outlook is not so black as many commentators on the 'new Congress' have painted. In the face of the mass of literature on party decline and Congressional individualism, there has been a tendency over-eagerly to report the demise of party coherence and ideological consistency on Capitol Hill.[101] The moves of the 1970s and 1980s towards anarchism, in fact, were balanced, as R.H. Davidson indicates, by:

> contraction of the legislative workload; limitations in the numbers of participants at crucial junctures; resort to omnibus 'mega-bills' to enact controversial policies; high levels of partisanship in voting; resurgence of leadership, especially in the House; and subtle shifts in power within the two chambers, primarily away from authorising committees and toward fiscal committees.[102]

Prior to Jim Wright's resignation in 1989, the House Speaker had attained a position of strength probably not seen in the post-1945 period. The use of 'substitute amendments' was one of several successful tactics employed by the House leadership in foreign policy.[103]

When Congressman Dick Cheney was nominated by President Bush as Secretary for Defence in 1989, Cheney declared that while 'Congress has a role in shaping foreign policy ... the president has to be the architect' and also 'has to manage it on a day-to-day basis'.[104] Here was a classic example of the executive attempting to have its cake and eat it. On the one hand, Congress is too parochial to be allowed a say in overarching foreign policy questions; on the other, it does not have the expertise to involve itself in detail. Congress has a role provided it does not impinge upon executive discretion. Such a view must be resisted in the name of democratic accountability and constitutional propriety. The 'new Congress', especially in its moves towards resource strengthening and internal democracy, created the opportunity for a new, and newly responsible, legislative foreign policy activism.

Notes

1   See L. Fisher, 'Foreign policy powers of the President and Congress', *Annals of the American Academy*, 500, 1988, pp. 148–62.

2   See, e.g., H. Adams, *Democracy: An American Novel*, London, 1882, p. 14; G. Vidal, *Washington DC*, London, 1967, p. 25; R.H. Davidson *et al.*, *Congress in Crisis*, Belmont, 1966, p. 38.

3   J. Kaplan, *Mr. Clemens and Mark Twain*, London, 1967, p. 69.

4   See, e.g., G. Orfield, *Congressional Power*, New York, 1975, p. 3; G.R. Parker and R.H. Davidson, 'Why do Americans Love their Congressmen so much more than their Congress?', *Legislative Studies Quarterly*, 4, 1979, pp. 125–48.

5   See, e.g., B. F. Wright, ed., *The Federalist*, Cambridge (Massachusetts), 1961, pp. 442, 477; J. Spanier and J. Nogee, eds., *Congress, the Presidency and*

American Foreign Policy, New York, 1981; J. G. Tower, 'Congress versus the President', *Foreign Affairs*, 60, 1981–82, pp. 229–46; L. G. Crovitz and J. A. Rabkin, eds., *The Fettered Presidency*, Washington D.C., 1989.

6   J. Lehman, *The Executive, Congress and Foreign Policy*, New York, 1976, p. 30.

7   See R. F. Fenno, *Congressmen in Committees*, Boston, 1979, p. 30.

8   See F. R. Bax, 'The legislative-executive relationship in foreign policy', *Orbis*, 20, 1977, pp. 881–904.

9   A. Frye, *A Responsible Congress: The Politics of National Security*, New York, 1975, p. 225.

10   R.B. Ripley and G. A. Franklin, *Congress, the Bureaucracy and Public Policy*, Homewood (Illinois), 3rd ed., 1984, ch. 7.

11   See B.C. Cohen, *The Public's Impact on Foreign Policy*, Boston, 1973, p. 115.

12   Cited in J. Rourke, *Congress and the Presidency in U.S. Foreign Policy*, Boulder, 1983, p. 119.

13   See A. Clausen, *How Congressmen Decide*, New York, 1973, p. 225.

14   See R. G. Sutter, *The China Quandary*, Epping, 1983, pp. 103–7.

15   J. B. Martin, *U.S. Policy in the Caribbean*, Boulder, 1978, p. 123.

16   See, e.g., S. Hoffman, *Dead Ends: American Foreign Policy in the New Cold War*, Cambridge (Massachusetts), 1983, p. 105.

17   See C. W. Kegley and E.R. Wittkopf, *American Foreign Policy: Pattern and Process*, London, 1987, p. 429; also A. Platt, *The U.S. Senate and Strategic Arms Policy, 1969–1977*, Boulder, 1978, p. 101.

18   See J. R. Johannes, *To Serve the People*, Lincoln (Nebraska).

19   Visit by author to district office of Senator R. Boschwitz, Minneapolis, 7 July 1988.

20   See C. W. Whalen, *The House and Foreign Policy*, Chapel Hill (North Carolina), ch. 6.

21   Rourke, *Congress and the Presidency*, p. 239.

22   D. B. Yoffie, 'American trade policy: an obsolete bargain?', in J. E. Chubb and P. E. Petersen, eds., *Can the Government Govern?*, Washington D.C., 1989, pp. 100–38, p. 113.

23   See N. J. Ornstein, 'Interest groups, Congress and American foreign policy', in D. P. Forsythe, ed., *American Foreign Policy in an Uncertain World*, Lincoln (Nebraska), 1984, pp. 49–64.

24   P. M. Stern, *The Best Congress Money Can Buy*, New York, 1988.

25   See J. Spanier and E.M. Uslaner, *American Foreign Policy Making and the Democratic Dilemmas*, New York, 4th ed., 1985, p. 112.

26   A. King, 'The American polity in the late 1970's', in A. King, ed., *The New American Political System*, Washington D.C., 1978, pp. 371–96. See also T. E. Mann and N. J. Ornstein, ed., *The New Congress*, Washington D.C., 1981; G. C. Jacobson, *The Politics of Congressional Elections*, Boston, 1983; L.C. Dodd and B.I. Oppenheimer, eds., *Congress Reconsidered*, Washington D.C., 3rd ed., 1985; H. Smith, *The Power Game*, London, 1988, ch. 7; G. R. Parker, *Characteristics of Congress*, Englewood Cliffs, 1989; and C.J. Bailey, *The U.S. Congress*, Oxford, 1989.

27   C. V. Crabb, *American Foreign Policy in the Nuclear Age*, New York, 5th

ed., 1988, p. 181.

28 See S. W. Hammond, 'Congress in foreign policy', in E. S. Muskie *et al.*, *The President, the Congress and Foreign Policy*, New York, 1986, pp. 67–93, at p. 78.

29 *Ibid.*, p. 77.

30 See E. M. Uslaner, 'The case of the vanishing liberal Senators', *British Journal of Political Science*, 11, 1981, pp. 105–13.

31 See *Congressional Quarterly Weekly Report, (CQWR)*, 46, 1988, p. 3257.

32 See Spanier and Uslaner, *American Foreign Policy Making*, p. 103; also R. H. Davidson *et al*, 'One bill, many committees', *Legislative Studies Quarterly*, 13, 1988, pp. 3–28.

33 See Whalen, *The House and Foreign Policy*, p. 55.

34 Spanier and Uslaner, *American Foreign Policy Making*, p. 105.

35 Meeting with M. Van Dusen (Staff Director, subcommittee on Europe and the Middle East, House Committee on Foreign Affairs), Washington D.C., 24 June 1988.

36 *CQWR*, 46, 1988, p. 3276.

37 *CQWR*, 47, 1989, p. 501. See also B. Sinclair, 'Committee positions in the U.S. Senate', *American Journal of Political Science*, 32, 1988, pp. 276–301, p. 299.

38 418 U.S. 683: 41 L Ed 2d 1039, at 1063.

39 See J. A. Nathan and J. K. Oliver, *Foreign Policy Making and the American Political System*, Boston, 2nd ed., 1987, pp. 246–7.

40 See R. Berger, *Executive Privilege*, Cambridge (Massachusetts), 1974, and L. Fisher, *The Constitution between Friends*, New York, 1978, pp. 139–65.

41 S.J. Heginbotham, 'Foreign policy information for Congress', *The Washington Quarterly*, 10, 1987, pp. 149–61.

42 Meeting with M. Van Dusen (note 35).

43 See J. Dumbrell, 'Strengthening the legislative "power of the purse" ', *Public Administration*, 58, 1980, pp. 479–502.

44 See L. Fisher, *Presidential Spending Power*, Princeton, 1975.

45 See R. H. Davidson, 'The new centralisation on Capitol Hill', *Review of Politics*, 50, 1989, pp. 345–64, at p. 355; also J. W. Ellwood, 'The greater exception: the Congressional budget process in an age of decentralisation', in Dodd and Oppenheimer, *Congress Reconsidered*, pp. 315–42.

46 See T. M. Franck and E. Weisband, *Foreign Policy by Congress*, New York, 1979, ch.1 (on termination of Vietnam war).

47 See, e.g., H. Kissinger, *White House Years*, London, 1981, p. 513.

48 See *Congressional Quarterly Almanac*, 1967, p. 918.

49 See J. C. Thompson, *Rolling Thunder: Understanding Policy and Program Failure*, Chapel Hill (North Carolina), 1980, p. 56.

50 See J. Dumbrell, 'Congress and the antiwar movement', in J. Dumbrell, ed., *Vietnam and the Antiwar Movement*, Aldershot, 1989, pp. 101–12.

51 S. Brown, *The Faces of Power*, New York, 1983, p. 436.

52 See K.R. Legg, 'Congress as Trojan horse? The Turkish embargo problem, 19674–1978', in Spanier and Nogee, eds., *Congress, the Presidency and American Foreign Policy*, pp. 107–31; and Franck and Weisband, *Foreign*

Policy by Congress, pp. 46–57.

53 P. 35.

54 See F. Halliday, *The Making of the Second Cold War*, London, 1986, pp. 214–33.

55 See Franck and Weisband *Foreign Policy by Congress*; also J. D. Lees, 'Techniques of Congressional oversight of foreign policy in the 1970's', in G. Rystad, ed., *Congress and American Foreign Policy*, Sweden, 1981, pp. 201–26. But see also R. S. Baker, *House and Senate*, New York, 1989, p. 164.

56 S. J. Baker, 'Evaluating Congress' foreign policy performance', in H. Purvis and S. J. Baker, *Legislating Foreign Policy*, Boulder (Colorado), 1984, pp. 1–24, p. 15. See also C. V. Crabb and P.M. Holt, *Invitation to Struggle: Congress, the President and Foreign Policy*, Washington D.C., 1980; F. O. Wilcox, 'Cooperation versus confrontation', in L.W. Koenig *et al.*, eds., *Congress, The Presidency and the Taiwan Relations Act*, New York, 1985, pp. 37–62.

57 *The House and Foreign Policy*, p. 80.

58 Cited in I. M. Destler, 'The evolution of Reagan's foreign policy', in F. I. Greenstein, ed., *The Reagan Presidency: An Early Assessment*, Baltimore, 1983, pp. 117–58, p. 118.

59 C. H. Percy, 'The partisan gap', *Foreign Policy*, 45, 1981–82, pp. 82–103. See also C.D. Tompkins, 'Bi-partisanship', in A. De Conde, ed., *Encyclopaedia of American Foreign Policy*, 1, New York, 1978, pp. 78–89.

60 See J. Dumbrell, 'President Reagan and Congress', *Teaching Politics*, 16, 1987, pp. 243–52.

61 See I.M. Destler, 'Congress', in J.S. Nye, ed., *The Making of America's Soviet Policy*, New Haven, 1984, pp. 107–31.

62 See M. Rubner, 'The Reagan Administration, the 1973 War Powers Resolution and the invasion of Grenada', *Political Science Quarterly*, 100, 1985–86, pp. 627–47, p. 645.

63 J.L. Sundquist, *The Decline and Resurgence of Congress*, Washington D.C., 1981, p. 258. Also, Nathan and Oliver, *Foreign Policy Making*, pp. 168–9, 189.

64 See R. D. Clark *et al.*, *The War Powers Resolution*, Washington D.C., 1985, pp. 36–7. See also C. V. Crabb and K. V. Mulcahy, *Presidents and Foreign Policy Making*, Baton Rouge, 1986, p. 34.

65 J. K. Javits, 'War powers reconsidered', *Foreign Affairs*, 64, 1985, pp. 130–40, p. 138.

66 G. Rystad, 'Who makes war?', in D. K. Adams, ed., *Studies in U.S. Politics*, Manchester, 1989, pp. 49–77, p. 72. See also J. L. Sundquist, *Constitutional Reform and Effective Government*, Washington D.C., 1986, pp. 220–4 and B. H. Craig, *Chadha*, New York, 1988.

67 P. 644. See also D.P. Franklin, 'War powers in the modern context', *Congress and the Presidency*, 14, 1987, pp. 77–101.

68 Clark *et al.*, *The War Powers Resolution*, p. 1.

69 *Congressional Digest*, 66, 1987: 'The War Powers Act and the Persian Gulf', p. 229.

70 Statement of Senator Pressler, Seminar on the War Powers Act, Washington D.C., 14 July 1988 (session attended by the author).

71   L. Fisher, extract from *National Law Journal*, 1983, printed in Hearing before the Subcommittee on Administrative Practice and Procedure, Senate Judiciary Committee, *Legislative Veto and the 'Chadha' Decision*, 20 July 1983, p. 154.

72   *Congressional Digest*, 1987, p. 298.

73   *Congressional Quarterly Almanac*, 1983, p. 1239.

74   Staff Memorandum to the Senate Foreign Relations Committee, *The Role of the Senate in Treaty Ratification*, 1977, p. 28.

75   See Fisher, *The Constitution between Friends*, pp. 197–204.

76   See W. L. Furlong, 'Negotiations and ratification of the Panama Canal treaties', in Spanier and Nogee, eds., *Congress, the Presidency and American Foreign Policy*, pp. 77–106, p. 89.

77   *Foreign Policy by Congress*, p. 138.

78   See N. A. Graebner, 'Negotiating international agreements', in G. Edwards and W. E. Walker, *National Security and the Constitution*, Baltimore, 1988, pp. 202–33, p. 228.

79   See D. S. Clemens, 'Executive agreements', in A. De Conde, ed., *Encyclopaedia*, 1, pp. 339–58; L. Margolis, *Executive Agreements and Presidential Power in Foreign Policy*, Westport (Connecticut), 1986.

80   See Nathan and Oliver, *Foreign Policy Making*, p. 131; Franck and Weisband, *Foreign Policy by Congress*, pp. 149–50; C. J. Stevens, 'The use and control of executive agreements', *Orbis*, 20, 1977, pp. 905–31; and L. K. Johnson, *The Making of International Agreements*, New York, 1984.

81   1977 Staff Memorandum, *The Role of the Senate*, p. 3.

82   Committee print, Subcommittee on European Affairs of the Senate Foreign Relations Committee, *SALT II: Some Foreign Policy Considerations*, June 1979, pp. 14, 20.

83   Report of the Senate Foreign Relations Committee, 100–15, *INF Treaty*, April 1988, pp. 240–55, 437–41.

84   See G. C. MacKenzie, *The Politics of Presidential Appointments*, New York, 1981; M.L. Mezey, *Congress, the President and Public Policy*, Boulder (Colorado), 1987, p. 64.

85   S. Garment, 'The Tower Precedent', *Commentary*, 87, 1989, pp. 42–8.

86   *The House and Foreign Policy*, pp. 146. See also J. W. Kingdon, *Congressmen's Voting Decisions*, New York, 1973, p. 59.

87   See G. M. Guess, *The Politics of United States Foreign Aid*, London, 1987, pp. 115–16.

88   See I. M. Destler, 'Congress as boss?', *Foreign Policy*, 42, 1981, pp. 167–80.

89   *CQWR*, 42, 1984, p. 959.

90   *Congressional Quarterly Almanac*, 1983, p. 112.

91   See J. A. Nathan and J. K. Oliver, *The Future of the United States Naval Power*, Bloomington, 1979, p. 136.

92   L. J. Korb, *The Fall and Rise of the Pentagon*, Westport (Connecticut), 1979, p. 175.

93   S. Kirby and A. Cox, 'Defence budgeting and accountability in Britain and America', in M. Shaw, ed., *War, State and Society*, London, 1984, pp.

231–60, p. 248. See also P. Williams, 'United States of America', in G. M. Dillon, ed., *Defence Policy Making*, Leicester, 1988, pp. 53–82.

94 *The Best Congress Money Can Buy*, pp. 149–50. See also P. Navarro, *The Policy Game*, New York, 1984, pp. 264–65.

95 See A. Cox and S. Kirby, *Congress, Parliament and Defence*, London, 1986, p. 124; also S. McLean, ed., *How Nuclear Weapons Decisions are Made*, London, 1986, p. 71; D. L. Clarke, *Politics of Arms Control*, New York, 1979, p.59; R. J. Art, 'Congress and the defense budget', *Political Science Quarterly*, 100, 1985, pp. 227–48; and J.M. Lindsay, 'Congress and the defense budget', *Washington Quarterly*, 11, 1988, pp. 57–74.

96 *Congress, Parliament and Defence*, ch. 5.

97 See Smith, *The Power Game*, pp. 164–68.

98 See S. J. Heginbotham, 'Congress and defense policy making', in R. L. Pfaltzgraff and U. R. Ra'anan, eds., *National Security Policy: the Decision-Making Process*, Hamden (Connecticut), 1984, pp. 250–61.

99 Baker, 'Evaluating Congress' foreign policy performance', p. 15. See also L. Fisher, 'The efficiency side of separated powers', *Journal of American Studies*, 5, 1971, pp. 113–31; and L. Hamilton and M. Van Dusen, 'Making the separation of powers work', *Foreign Affairs*, 57, 1978, pp. 17–39.

100 See Destler, 'Congress'; L. Cutler, 'To form a government', *Foreign Affairs*, 59, 1980, pp. 126–43; and D.L. Robinson, 'Adjustments are needed in the system of checks and balances', *Polity*, 19, 1987, pp. 660–6.

101 For studies which emphasise party and ideological consistency, see W. R. Shaffer, *Party and Ideology in the United States Congress*, Washington D.C., 1980; and J. E. Schneider, *Ideological Coalitions in Congress*, Westport (Connecticut), 1979. See also K. A. Shepsle, 'The changing textbook Congress', in Chubb and Peterson, eds., *Can the Government Govern?*, pp. 238–66, p. 264.

102 'The new centralisation', p. 345.

103 Whalen, *The House and Foreign Policy*, pp. 155–56. On the positive changes and opportunities provided by the various reforms, see N. J. Ornstein, 'The open Congress meets the President', in A. King, ed., *Both Ends of the Avenue*, Washington D.C., 1983, pp. 185–211, p. 209; and R. J. Barilleaux, *The Post-Modern Presidency: The Office after Reagan*, New York, 1988, p. 76.

104 *CQWR*, 47, 1989, p. 531.

6

The intelligence community

Although this chapter will focus almost exclusively on the Central Intelligence Agency, it is worth emphasising that the sprawling American intelligence community extends well beyond the CIA. Exact figures are difficult to ascertain; nonetheless, the CIA was reckoned, as of 1988, to have between 16,500 and 20,000 employees in the D.C. area, with an annual budget of up to one and a half billion dollars.[1] Yet some estimates suggest that the CIA makes up less than 15 per cent of the intelligence community.[2] What directs particular attention to the CIA is its extraordinary reputation at home and abroad, its involvement in innumerable covert political operations, its visibility, centrality and relative bureaucratic independence.

Beyond the CIA, intelligence work is principally concentrated within the Defence Department. Army, navy, marine corps and air force all have their intelligence arms, while the Defence Intelligence Agency (set up by Secretary of Defence McNamara in 1961) attempts a co-ordination role. The largest portion of the Pentagon's intelligence budget appears, however, to be accounted for by the National Security Agency. Headquartered at Fort George Meade, Maryland, the NSA's home budget has been estimated at three billion dollars.[3] The agency is principally concerned with signals intelligence (SIGINT). Throughout its history it has been blanketed in secrecy, spending the first five years of its life (1952–57) in a kind of ontological limbo, its existence unacknowledged by the US government. Its enormous communications interception capabilities have stimulated anxieties about domestic surveillance, an issue which the Foreign Intelligence Surveillance Act of 1978 attempted to address. As it is, the NSA is, in J. Bamford's words, 'free to pull into its massive vacuum cleaner every telephone call and message entering, leaving or transiting the country, as long as it is done by microwave interception'.[4] Other intelligence capabilities are located in, for example, the Departments of State, the Treasury and Energy, and the Intelligence Division of the Federal Bureau of Investigation (FBI).[5]

With intelligence costs running at somewhere around six billion dollars annually, and with more than 150,000 intelligence employees,[6] co-ordination is clearly vital. The President, operating through the National Security Council, is, of course, formally responsible for co-ordination and control. Within the intelligence community itself, however, it is the CIA and its head (the Director of Central Intelligence or DCI) which attempts to perform this role. The DCI chairs the National Foreign Intelligence Board, whose membership and elaborate committee structure encompass all elements of the intelligence community. He occupies a position within the intelligence community bolstered by deference rather than direct control. Some DCIs, like James Schlesinger in 1973, have consciously tried to take the reins.[7] Others, tacitly acknowledging the quasi-feudal structure of the community, and the fact that the CIA's budget is dwarfed by that of the intelligence wing of the Defence Department, have virtually admitted defeat.

1 The CIA from Truman to Reagan

(a) *1947–77* The CIA was established, under its first director, R. H. Hillenkoettler, by the 1947 National Security Act. The CIA embodied those Cold War concerns which elevated 'national security' over 'foreign policy'. Like the National Security Council itself, the CIA was an institutional embodiment of the 'trend towards non-accountable, subterranean policy-making and security operations'.[8]

The CIA was preceded by Truman's Central Intelligence Group of 1946 and the wartime Office of Strategic Services (OSS), led by 'Wild' Bill Donovan. McGeorge Bundy later described the OSS as 'half cops-and-robbers and half faculty meeting',[9] and much of this ethos was to survive into the CIA. Nonetheless, although Donovan no doubt deserved his cowboy-adventurer reputation, he was also concerned that the new intelligence should have fixed bureaucratic standing. (Donovan, in fact, did apparently see the CIA's role much more in terms of intelligence-gathering rather than covert military adventures.)[10] Bureaucratic standing was to some extent achieved in the 1947 Act and the 1949 Central Intelligence Act, which virtually exempted the Agency from normal oversight. Nonetheless, the very permissiveness of these acts, especially the 1947 Act's mention of 'other functions' (besides intelligence-gathering), was to prove a double-edged sword. William Colby (DCI, 1973–76) later complained that the absence of a 'clear charter' had led to uncertainty and confusion.[11] What was clear, both in the 1947, and certainly in the 1949, Act was that the CIA should not indulge in domestic intelligence. There should be no American Gestapo.[12] Yet even this clear prohibition can hardly be said to have operated satisfactorily. On the one hand, it became evident by the late 1960s and early 1970s that the CIA had long been involved in domestic surveillance, and in sponsoring domestic organisations. CIA funding of the National Student Association became a *cause célèbre* when revealed in *Ramparts* magazine in 1967.[13] On the other hand, the domestic prohibition has worked to the disadvantage of the CIA's strategic intelligence work. CIA intelligence estimates of Soviet military strength have always lacked an authoritative comparative element. The agency has not enjoyed access to raw Pentagon data on US military force, despite the view expressed in Sherman Kent's influential 1949 study[14] that it should have such access.

Kent, OSS veteran and head of the CIA's Office of National Estimates between 1952 and 1967, foresaw a CIA role that would be greater than simply *primus inter pares* within the intelligence community: more a monitor, co-ordinator, controller and disseminator of information than a competitive producer of intelligence.[15] In the early Cold War period, however, the agency was a new bureaucratic actor searching for roles and for Presidential favour. Production of its own intelligence, effectively in competition with the State and Defence departments, was one avenue of advancement. Another was covert political operations. By 1953, major covert military and/or propaganda operations were under way in forty-eight countries.[16] Cold War and the contemporary vogue for 'psychological warfare' provided the context for increasingly unaccountable CIA adventures.

In particular, the agency enjoyed success in two apparently successful attempts to install pro-American administrations in Iran in 1953 and in Guatemala in 1954. It is often noted that these two adventures greatly encouraged both the CIA's buccaneering spirit and its bureaucratic credibility. What should also be stressed, however, is that both the Mossadegh regime in Iran and the Arbenz government in Guatemala had formidable domestic opposition, quite apart from any CIA involvement.[17] American sponsorship of the Shah, of course, was eventually to rebound upon the United States in the Iranian revolution of 1979, a year which also saw the citing by the Sandinista revolutionaries in Nicaragua of 'Guatemala 1954' as part of a long record of CIA interference in Central America. It may also be observed that, while Iran and Guatemala were undoubtedly short-term CIA 'successes', many early Cold War covert operations were bungled. For example, attempts in the late 1940s to establish guerrilla operations in Albania and in the Ukraine failed miserably.[18]

The early Cold War ethos encouraged irresponsibility. For example, by the time Allen Dulles became DCI in 1953, several ex-Nazis, including Reinhard Gerhard (a senior intelligence officer in Nazi Germany), were on the CIA's payroll.[19] Former Secretary of State Dean Rusk was later to testify that the CIA had vied with the Soviets 'in the back alleys of the world'.[20] The second commission on executive organisation, chaired by ex-President Hoover, reported in 1954 that, if the U.S. were to survive, 'American concepts of "fair play" must be reconsidered.'[21] It was an atmosphere which promoted the bizarre. In 1953, a civilian scientist, Frank Olson, jumped to his death from a hotel window following his participation in hallucogenic drug experiments.[22] The incident was not made public until 1975. Assassination plots, often with the CIA role geared to the exigencies of 'plausible denial', proliferated. Fidel Castro, Rafael Trujillo (in the Dominican Republic), General Schneider (in Chile), Patrice Lumumba (in the Congo), Colonel Abdul Kassem (Iraq) and Diem in Vietnam were all the subject of such plots, some of them almost unbelievably bizarre.[23] During the 1950s, the CIA's internal bureaucracy even boasted a 'Health Alteration Committee'![24]

By the time of John Kennedy's inauguration in 1961, the agency had acquired the reputation as a home for what former deputy DCI director for intelligence Ray Cline called 'romantic ... "cowboy" types of covert action officers'.[25] Its Cold War activism had enabled the agency to fight off attacks levelled by McCarthyites; indeed, the fear of such attacks partly explains the CIA's 'gung ho' ethos. However, it had also acquired a reputation on the right as a haven for Ivy League liberals, inclined to underestimate Soviet strength. Recurring crises of 'intelligence failure' – what the CIA saw as the inability to predict the unpredictable – had also been experienced. When riots interrupted the creation of the Organisation of American States in Bogotá in 1948, the CIA took the blame for not anticipating them. The Korean invasion of June 1950 and the Bay of Pigs fiasco in 1961 were two more famous examples. The CIA became especially vulnerable to unexpected, precipitate developments in apparently obscure or 'safe' countries. The impact upon the CIA of perceived 'intelligence failure' could itself be unpredictable. Kennedy treated the agency to a public, verbal laceration after the Bay of Pigs failure; the non-prediction of the Iranian revolution of 1979 was to prove the backdrop to a huge transfer of resources to the CIA.

The Kennedy Presidency saw a significant deterioration in White House-CIA relations.[26] At first, however, JFK was enthusiastic about the agency, telling McGeorge Bundy in 1961: 'if I need some material fast or an idea fast, CIA is the place I have to go. The State Department takes four or five days to answer a simple yes or no.'[27] Kennedy also never lost his enthusiasm for covert operations. However, 'intelligence failures' – not only over the Bay of Pigs, but over failure to predict the construction of the Berlin Wall – soured the relationship. JFK even apparently resented the fact that DCI John McCone was 'right' in anticipating the Soviet build-up in Cuba.[28] Things did not improve under President Johnson, who ignored the CIA's continuous pessimism over Vietnam. LBJ appeared unenthusiastic about assassinations, but covert operations continued, notably in Chile and in Indochina. The CIA's domestic surveillance role increased with the unfolding tragedy in Vietnam. Johnson instructed DCI Richard Helms in 1967 to mount a programme of disruptive monitoring against the antiwar movement. (The nature of White House-CIA relations was neatly encapsulated when LBJ falsely disseminated the view that the CIA considered the movement to be a communist front.)[29]

According to Henry Kissinger, President Nixon distrusted the CIA, associating it and Helms with 'the liberal Georgetown set to which Nixon ascribed many of his difficulties'.[30] Using the National Security Council staff to double-check and interpret CIA raw data, Kissinger managed to establish a new control on intelligence.[31] As Marchetti and Marks point out,[32] Kissinger had been managing the CIA's affairs for four years when he remarked in 1973 that the agency was not sufficiently competent to manage the coup which ousted Allende in Chile.

The destabilisation in Chile shocked liberal world opinion. By the mid- to late 1970s, the agency stood accused of a range of acts of illegal intervention, murder and subversion: acts undertaken in the name of democracy, but actually contemptuous of the democratic process and of human rights.[33] The CIA's putative role in the Kennedy assassination and actual role in Watergate became major news stories across the globe. Ex-CIA agents like Marchetti and Philip Agee[34] wrote books exposing the agency's record and, in the latter case, actually listing active agents. Europeans became alarmed to learn of clandestine CIA backing for the journal *Encounter* and for the Congress on Cultural Freedom. In Britain, the revelations damaged the reputation of right-wing Labour party figures who had, often inadvertently, been associated with CIA-backed organisations. Anxieties also began to be expressed regarding CIA influence over British foreign and intelligence policies.[35]

In the teeth of the anti-CIA gale, President Ford set up a commission under Vice-President Rockefeller. Like the Katzenbach inquiry of 1967, the commission's findings were largely cosmetic. Recommendations centred on a commitment to greater frankness and oversight, and support for an enhanced DCI role.[36] Ford issued a public moratorium on assassinations and began moves to clarify the agency's legal status. The 'Forty Committee', which had formally considered covert action proposals, was replaced by a smaller Operations Advisory Group: a move widely interpreted as a public signal that Henry Kissinger's authority over covert operations would be diminished. Following revelations about the secret war waged in Laos by the CIA during the 1960s, Congress passed the Hughes-Ryan amendment (1974), requiring the reporting of covert operations to designated legislative committees.[37] (In so doing, Congress did, of course, paradoxically, extend legitimating recognition to covert operations.) Special committees in the Senate (under Frank Church) and the House (under Otis Pike) examined the CIA record. Intelligence oversight committees were established in both houses in 1975 and 1976. DCI Colby complained:

by mid-1975, appearances on the Hill had become a pervasive aspect of my job as DCI, and I was going up there to report on every new step taken in the Angola, Kurdish and other covert operations currently underway as well as testifying on practically everything the CIA had ever done during the last three decades.

As Colby indicated, even in the hostile climate of the mid-1970s, covert operations were not abandoned. They simply ceased to be formally 'covert' as, according to Colby, 'secrets, if they are to remain secret cannot be given to more than a few Congressmen'.[38]

(b)   *From Stansfield Turner to William Casey*   President Carter came to the White House in 1977 having made promises that the CIA excesses would be curbed, and that the agency would, above all, be constrained by the law. Yet in 1980, amidst the shocks of Iran, Nicaragua and Afghanistan, he declared: 'We need to remove unwarranted restraints on America's ability to collect intelligence.'[39]

Carter's handling of the DCI appointment – the firing of George Bush (who had succeeded Colby in 1976) and the hastily withdrawn nomination of Theodore Sorensen – was scarcely sure-footed, and raised inevitable accusations that the office was becoming excessively politicised. Stansfield Turner, the eventual choice, determined to put the 'CIA's much criticised past behind us'. Countering the agency's institutional culture, he urged rapid adaptation to the new Congressional oversight and even proclaimed the value of oversight in promoting CIA responsibility. Turner made significant personal changes: early on, for example, firing two middle-level CIA 'rogue elephants'.[40] Yet the contrast with the past should not be exaggerated. Jimmy Carter himself was ambivalent about the CIA: aware of the past horrors, but also anxious about impeding effective intelligence. He was not prepared to condemn covert operations *per se*.[41] On Capitol Hill also, as the Carter Presidency progressed, the concern became one of combining oversight with enhancement of CIA effectiveness. The 1978 Foreign Intelligence Surveillance Act did attempt to control domestic spying; yet it also explicitly recognised the utility of electronic surveillance in domestic counter-espionage. The 1980 Intelligence Oversight Act weakened the reporting requirements of the Hughes-Ryan amendment, implicitly accepting Colby's point about Members' inability to keep secrets.[42]

The frenetic atmosphere of the later Carter years, along with the 'intelligence failure' over Iran in 1979, provided the backdrop to President Reagan's appointment of William Casey as DCI in 1981. The new President spoke in cavalier terms of 'unleashing' the CIA. Under Casey, all the familiar CIA abuses were redoubled. The budget forged ahead, apparently uncontrollably, increasing at a probable compound rate of over 20 per cent annually. David McMichael estimated that covert operations – the majority of which remained unreported to Congress – increased five times over during the first Reagan Administration. McMichael, who quit the CIA in 1983, calculated that over twenty such operations were under way in Africa alone.[43] According to Stansfield Turner, Reagan and Casey regarded oversight as an 'impediment rather than a necessity for good intelligence'.[44]

By the early 1980s, Casey, who had acted as Reagan's campaign manager in the 1980 election, was widely regarded as probably the most overtly politicised director in CIA history.[45] Casey's appointment was at Cabinet level. He was part of the innermost White House foreign policy-making circle.[46] John Ranelagh has written:

In the early days, DCIs were important because of the CIA. During the 1970's, the CIA became important because of the DCI. William Casey epitomised the change. He was much more than just a director, he was an ambassador for the agency (thirty years earlier the agency did not need one), and he personally gave the CIA access to the president.[47]

Casey was a close Presidential confidant, prioritising the CIA's role against international terrorism and in support of anti-Soviet forces in Afghanistan.[48] Above all, there was Central America. Casey had chaired a foreign policy advisory board for Reagan in 1980, and had expressed shock at the lack of CIA interest in El Salvador.[49] Between 1980 and 1985, over two billion dollars of US aid went to the El Salvador government. Much of this money came under the control of the CIA, whose total expenditures in the 'secret' wars against leftist guerrillas and the government of Nicaragua are virtually incalculable.[50]

The intelligence environment of the early 1980s was revealed in the successful legislative requests emanating from Casey and Reagan: the 1982 Intelligence Identities Protection Act, designed to protect CIA security, and the 1984 Freedom of Information Act amendments, which further protected the CIA from public scrutiny. An Executive Order, issued in 1981, actually set down conditions for CIA infiltration of private and academic institutions within the United States.[51] It represented an open flouting of the 1947 and 1949 prohibitions on domestic activity.

The great irony of the close Reagan-Casey relationship lay in the degree to which the Administration actually chose to ignore CIA analysis. Despite the widespread fear that intelligence under Casey would become hopelessly politicised, CIA analyses – especially after Robert Gates became deputy intelligence director in 1982 – failed automatically to confirm White House perceptions of the Soviet threat. Information, for example about the extent to which SALT II had slowed down Soviet arms development, tended to be discounted by the Administration.[52] Casey may, however, have suppressed evidence concerning the shooting down of the aircraft KAL 007 in 1983. The idea that the Soviets had genuinely (mis?)taken it for a spy plane did not serve the Administration's polemical ends.[53]

2   Covert operations

Some commentators approach the question of covert operations as essentially an organisational problem. The central issue is seen not as the admissibility of covert operations as such, or even the justification for particular operations, but centres on the appropriateness of the CIA's clandestine role. Ray Cline, for example, has recommended that a revamped Central Institute of Foreign Affairs Research should take over the CIA's Langley (Virginia) headquarters. The new agency would take over analytic intelligence work from the CIA and State and Defence departments. Clandestine operations might be controlled in a general sense by the new body, but would be managed elsewhere.[54]

Although the agency gained considerable kudos as a result of the Iran and Guatemala operations in the early 1950s, there is no question that clandestine adventures have damaged the CIA's credibility and its intelligence function. The CIA is regularly (and plausibly) accused of being involved in activities such as drug dealing and illegal arms traffic. During a 1982 Irish republican gun-smuggling trial in the United States, Ralph McGehee, a former CIA case officer, testified that the CIA itself might run such an arms network.[55] Little wonder that some defenders of the CIA, like Cline, have looked to the formal distancing of covert operations from intelligence as a way of escaping embarrassment. Separating the two functions would also seem to satisfy a fundamental tenet of public administration. As Marchetti and Marks put it:

Intelligence should not be presented to the nation's policy-makers by the same men who are trying to justify clandestine operations. The temptation to use field information selectively and to evaluate information to serve operational interests can be irresistible to the most honest men – let alone to the clandestine operatives.[56]

Covert operations and intelligence evaluation may be separated within the agency's internal directorate system,[57] but inevitably come together at DCI, Deputy and Executive Director levels. Stansfield Turner pointed to 'a fundamental conflict between any covert action and the accepted practice that intelligence must stay clear of policy and its executive'. (Turner did not, in fact, favour removing covert operations from the CIA. He argued that the 'CIA's intelligence agents overseas are often the same people needed for covert action. It would be confusing, and at times dangerous, to have two agencies giving them orders'.)[58]

At another level, the debate on covert operations hinges upon the concept of control: both by Congress and by the President. The idea that the CIA provided a home to 'rogue elephants' figured prominently in the early deliberations of the Church Committee, although was to some extent dropped in the final report. The Pike Committee, which undertook a survey of covert operations between 1965 and 1975, concluded that 'the CIA, far from being out of control, has been utterly responsive to the instructions of the President and the Assistant to the President for National Security Affairs'. The report did add that it was the DCI himself who determined 'which CIA-initiated covert action projects are sufficiently "politically sensitive" to require Presidential attention'. The 'Forty Committee' was described as a rubber stamp for the President and National Security Adviser. Having studied election support projects, propaganda, organisational support and paramilitary actions, the Committee concluded: 'they are irregularly approved, sloppily implemented, and at times have been forced on a reluctant CIA by the President and his National Security Adviser'. The CIA initiated far fewer projects than was generally supposed and often had far from complete control over implementation. In one of three projects considered in detail, the Committee noted that funding of pro-American forces in the 1972 Italian elections was administered, against CIA wishes, by Ambassador Graham Martin.[59]

As a general theory, the 'rogue elephant' interpretation of the CIA is not very satisfactory. Undoubtedly, cowboy-adventurers have played their part and the CIA has been anything but scrupulous in its recruitment policies. The world of a James Angleton or an Ed Wilson is not far removed from spy fiction.[60] Accounts of the CIA 'offloading' or 'contracting out' operations to avoid oversight and control are profoundly alarming. During the Reagan years, a network of ex-CIA employees and Cuban exiles operated in this manner, in an environment untouched by the law or democratic accountability.[61] It is also true that many minor covert projects, defined by the CIA as of secondary importance, are never properly reported.[62] Nonetheless, the balance of the evidence suggests that, for most of its history, the

CIA has been an integral part of the National Security Council system and a consciously integrated arm of White House foreign policy. In some respects, the CIA appears a remarkably disciplined organisation. Defection and Soviet penetration, for example, have been rare,[63] especially when contrasted with the almost comically aberrant record of the British intelligence services. The 'rogue elephant' theory of the CIA tends simply to strengthen the ability of Presidents plausibly to disclaim responsibility for failed, embarrassing or illegal projects.

Where the 'Forty Committee' consisted of senior White House, State Department, CIA and Pentagon personnel – and was dominated by the President and National Security Adviser – Ford's Operations Advisory Group was designed to facilitate more circumspect consideration of projects. Under Carter, the responsible body was an NSC Special Co-ordination Committee, headed by Brzezinski. President Reagan relied initially on a National Security Planning Group, whose membership included senior foreign policy and intelligence officers, but with a minimum of expert and staff attendance. As covert operations increased, management tended to be taken on by an elite, intelligence-oriented '208 Committee'.[64]

The need for high-level executive (not to mention Congressional) control of the CIA is obvious, despite the degree to which the 'rogue elephant' thesis has been over-stated. Yet discussion about hiving off or controlling covert operations does not address the central issue. Is there any justification for covert action and, if there is, what criteria may be employed?

A number of points are relevant here. Firstly, there is Dean Rusk's remark about the politics of the world's back alleys. In his memoirs, Richard Nixon wrote that CIA intervention against Allende in Chile had been justified by the fact that the Soviets operate covertly; the United States cannot be expected to operate with too many self-imposed restraints.[65] This argument affects an air of sad, worldly wisdom, but actually sails very close to a crassly relativistic view of the difference between democratic and totalitarian societies. How can 'freedom' be defended by illegal, blatant interference in the democratic procedures of foreign countries? East-West detente and the declining world status of the United States may militate against future interventions. The construction of loyal, ideologically committed militias – especially in fundamentalist Iran – considerably constrained the CIA in the 1980s, and contrasted sharply with the situation in the 1950s. It should also be emphasised that the United States is party to a number of treaties and agreements (not least the United Nations charter) which are inimical to, for example, CIA activity in Central America during the Reagan Presidency.[66]

Does the US need covert actions capabilities at all, either within or outside the CIA? Covert operations are scarcely an acceptable substitute for coherent foreign policy; they are inimical to the democratic process and antagonise world opinion; their outcomes are difficult to predict or control. There is also the question of from whom covert actions are meant to be concealed. Congress? The Soviet Union? World opinion? The people most directly affected? The American public? There may have been some operations which have remained genuinely 'secret', but exceedingly few.[67] The Reagan Administration's CIA interventions in Central America were scarcely even intended to be secret. As Gregory Treverton has argued, given that covert action is virtually a contradiction in terms, 'why not act openly?'[68]

Few within the American political process would wish to debar covert operations altogether. Senator Abourezk's 1974 proposal so to do floundered, even in the anti-CIA context of the time. The Hughes-Ryan amendment countenanced covert action if 'important to national security'. Cyrus Vance has said that there are occasions 'when no other means will do'.[69] It does not take too much imagination to envisage such circumstances, although again one has to raise the question of from whom exactly the action is designed to be secret. (There is also the related question of avoiding embarrassment to allies who may not wish to acknowledge their involvement.) However, in a democratic system, decisions about covert actions must be resolved by the democratic process. In the American governmental context, this necessitates an important role for Congress.[70]

3 Congressional control of the CIA

The traditional attitude of Congress towards the CIA was summarised by Senator Stennis, chairman of the Armed Services Committee, in 1971: 'You have to make up your mind that you are going to have an intelligence agency and protect it as such, and shut your eyes and take what is coming.'[71] throughout the 1960s and early 1970s, CIA appropriations were disguised in monies made available to the Pentagon, while the House and Senate Armed Services subcommittees responsible for intelligence oversight rarely bothered even to convene.

There were abortive attempts to set up intelligence committees in 1956 and 1966, but most Members simply did not wish seriously to tackle the issue.[72]

The new intelligence oversight of the mid-1970s did attempt to confront the problem of CIA irresponsibility, and to demystify the agency. Congress even began to appreciate the need to scrutinise intelligence budgets. However, the moves to construct a new legislative charter for the agency failed in the political atmosphere of the late 1970s. As noted above, the 1980 Intelligence Oversight Act reduced the reporting requirements of the Hughes-Ryan amendment. In special circumstances, the number of Members who were to be informed of covert operations could be as low as eight. This provision was, in fact, no more than a realistic attempt to respond to anxieties about excessive information dissemination. (Senator Barry Goldwater once famously declared that the Hughes-Ryan amendment required the President and CIA to brief fifty Senators and 120 Congressmen on national security issues.)[73] The weakness of the 1980 Act lay not so much in the lesser numbers of Congressional reportees, but rather in the ambiguity of language and in the various escape routes offered to the President. The definition of conditions – 'extraordinary circumstances affecting vital interests' – for allowing less than full disclosure to the intelligence committees is (perhaps necessarily) vague. More importantly, Presidents may actually neglect to inform Congress in advance of covert action, provided they report later 'in timely fashion'. There is also an ambiguous reference to the need to protect 'sources and methods' when reporting. The Act did not really address the issue of CIA budgetary scrutiny. In a study published in 1989, Berkowitz and Goodman acknowledged that the CIA budget was 'almost entirely invisible'.[74]

DCI Casey's attitude towards Congress was one of minimum co-operation, rooted in the tactic of volunteering no information and exploiting the fact that many Members simply do not know the right questions to ask. (William Webster, Casey's successor as DCI, deliberately cultivated a less confrontational style, while still stressing the need for 'flexibility' – especially in covert operations.) 'Limit access. Don't go brief', were Casey's instructions.[75] Congressman Mineta, a member of the House intelligence panel, declared in 1983 that the CIA 'keep us in the dark and feed us a lot of manure'.[76] Congressional exasperation came to the surface in 1983 with the Boland amendment on Central America, and in 1984 with the discovery of

CIA mining of Nicaraguan harbours. On the latter occasion, Senator Goldwater, traditionally a staunch CIA ally, lost patience: 'The President has asked us to back his foreign policy. Bill [Casey], how can we ... when we don't know what the hell he is doing?'[77]

The 1984 minings provoked the CIA and Goldwater's Senate intelligence panel into adopting more stringent reporting requirements, especially regarding detailed developments within wider covert programmes.[78] However, the intelligence committees have no effective power of prior veto, especially since covert operations are generally funded in their early stages from the CIA contingency fund, over which the Congress does not choose to exercise more than token control. The constant invocation of national security, and the genuine desire of Members not to compromise sensitive areas of activity have seriously blunted the cutting edge of responsible oversight.

The problems of Congress in this area go back to familiar arguments about legislative parochialism and myopia. There are also the related issues of clientism and the desire to duck responsibility. As he resigned as leading Democrat on the Senate Intelligence Committee in 1986, Senator Moynihan remarked: 'Like other legislative committees, ours came to be an advocate for the agency it was overseeing.'[79] Members – and also staff[80] – may be too easily sucked into client relationships. Nonetheless, renewed Congressional activism appeared to be signalled in November 1989 with the incorporation into the intelligence community spending bill of a provision for a statutory CIA inspector general. He would be the agency's third-ranking officer, with the duty to report to Congress. The provision was predictably criticised by former DCI's Helms and Schlesinger as 'micromanagement at its worst'.[81]

Congressional activism on intelligence oversight does tend to be a function of the current state of public opinion regarding the Administration's foreign policy and the international situation generally.[82] Both public and Congress need to be convinced of the need for an active legislative role. The alternative is bureaucratic abuse, evasion and justified international suspicion about the ends and methods of US foreign policy.

4 Strategic intelligence and analysis

The central dilemma of intelligence analysis revolves around the problem of objectivity. On the one hand, 'pure' objectivity is an illusion. Lawrence Freedman has described the position of the intelligence officer, attempting to estimate the military strength of a potential adversary, thus:

As an estimator is usually faced by a mass of confusing and contradictory data, in order to avoid a paralysing eclecticism he needs a 'point of view', a conceptual framework to enable him to select and organise the data and so create order out of chaos. This is why ... the conventional distinction between 'estimates of capabilities' and 'estimates of intentions' breaks down in practice.[83]

On the other hand, politicisation of intelligence – the skewing of data to serve perceived (or unconscious) institutional, political or ideological ends – is probably the most common cause of intelligence failure.[84] Bureaucratic agencies have institutional and teleological biases which may distort information processing over generations. This is why some authorities proclaim the virtues of the US system of having different agencies – notably the Pentagon and the CIA – produce different, competing intelligence estimates.[85] Henry Kissinger, unusually for a consumer of intelligence, actually encouraged such competition during his period as chief foreign policy adviser to Presidents Nixon and Ford.[86]

Among many academics, the CIA has a high reputation for avoiding excessive politicisation. According to Freedman, for example, the CIA's weaknesses include 'rigid adherence to professional norms and procedures, even when they inconvenience and irritate the clientele' and 'contempt for rivals who are considered less professional in their approach'. Nonetheless, for Freedman, it 'is hard ... to find examples where the CIA analyses have been distorted to satisfy the preconceived notions of its clientele'.[87] The CIA probably has avoided the cruder over-simplifications of the Pentagon's intelligence analysis. This is not to suggest that CIA estimates have not been frequently mistrusted. Putative CIA underestimation of Soviet strength became a familiar theme in the rhetoric of neo-conservative critics of the Carter Administration in the late 1970s. Under Ford, DCI George Bush initiated an experiment whereby a team led by Professor Richard Pipes provided a parallel estimate to that produced by the official CIA team. This 1976 experiment did cause the CIA to increase its estimates of Soviet strength, though, as Freedman writes, this was a function of 'the politics in the estimating process rather than any new information concerning Soviet forces'.[88]

The intelligence process typically consists of four stages, all of which are prone to distortions and abuses: 'tasking' (the identification and determination of the intelligence needs of the foreign policy process – the 'consumers' of intelligence); intelligence collecting; data processing and analysis; and dissemination of completed analysis to the consumers. At the 'tasking' stage, consumers (notably the National Security Council) may become complacent in certain areas, or become obsessed with others. Thus, in the early 1970s, US policy-makers, unaware of the importance of problems being encountered in Soviet grain production and unused to giving attention to such matters, did not request CIA data in this area. The information collection stage is prey to a host of technical and human difficulties. The processing and analysis stage is typically liable to distortion through the operation of institutional 'groupthink' or 'mirror imaging' (the attribution to potential opponents of characteristics derived from US political and intelligence processes). Failure may even occur at the dissemination stage, with information failing to be delivered to the appropriate people at the appropriate time.[89]

Global interdependence raises new problems for US intelligence.[90] Failure may be alleviated by awareness of common sources of distortion, and also possibly by continuing and extending competition within the intelligence community. (Concomitant problems of controlling this sprawling structure need also to be addressed, however.) Ultimately, nonetheless, the CIA is the servant of political masters and cannot be held responsible for misconceived policies. During 1989, with the Felix Bloch case focusing attention on spying and the Senate Intelligence Committee under Senator Boren raising criticisms, William Webster (Casey's successor) set up a new CIA counter-intelligence capability. The future, however, should lie with intelligence analysis and collection, especially if the CIA is at long last becoming more regularised and cautious in its procedures.[91] The danger is that, as with Iran-Contra, illegal adventures are simply transferred elsewhere.

Notes

1   See J. T. Richelson, *The U.S. Intelligence Community*, 2nd ed., Cambridge (Massachusetts), 1989, p. 13. For a more conservative estimate, see J. Ranelagh, *The Agency*, London, 1986, p. 17.

2   C. W. Kegley and E. R. Wittkopf, *American Foreign Policy*, 3rd ed., London, 1987, p. 399.

3　Richelson, *The US Intelligence Community*, p. 26.

4　J. Bamford, *The Puzzle Palace*, London, 1982, p. 372. See also A. Theoharis, *Spying on Americans*, Philadelphia, 1978.

5　For a full catalogue of US intelligence capabilities, see Richelson, *The U.S. Intelligence Community*, chs. 2–6.

6　This is the estimate given in L. Freedman, *U.S. Intelligence and the Soviet Strategic Threat*, 2nd ed., London, 1986, p. 8.

7　See R. Jeffreys-Jones, *The CIA and American Democracy*, New Haven, 1989, p. 191; and V. Price, *The DCI's Role in Producing Strategic Intelligence Estimates*, Newport (Rhode Island), 1980.

8　G. W. Reichard, 'The domestic politics of national security', in N. A. Graebner, ed., *The National Security*, New York, 1986, pp. 243–74, p. 261. See also S. Landau, *The Dangerous Doctrine: National Security and U.S. Foreign Policy*, Boulder, 1988. For a wide-ranging account of the CIA's relations to the democratic process see L. K. Johnson, *America's Secret Power: The CIA in a Democratic Society*, New York, 1989.

9　R. Winks, *Cloak and Gown*, London, 1987, p. 115. See also F. B. Smith, *The Shadow Warriors*, London, 1983.

10　See Jeffreys-Jones, *The CIA*, pp. 26, 250. See also A. C. Brown, *The Last Hero: Wild Bill Donovan*, London, 1982.

11　W. Colby, *Honourable Men: My Life in the CIA*, London, 1978, p. 201.

12　Jeffreys-Jones, *The CIA*, p. 30.

13　See Final Report of the Senate Select Committee to Study Governmental Operations with Respect to Intelligence Activities, 1976 (Church Committee Report), Book 1, *Foreign and Military Intelligence*, pp. 184–85.

14　S. Kent, *Strategic Intelligence for American World Policy*, Princeton, 1949.

15　See B.D. Berkowitz and A.E. Goodman, *Strategic Intelligence for American National Security*, Princeton, 1989, pp. 118–19.

16　See S. Turner, *Secrecy and Democracy*, London, 1985, p. 76; also, Church Committee Report, Book 1, ch. 8.

17　See G. F. Treverton, 'Covert action and open society', *Foreign Affairs*, 65, 1987, pp. 995–1014, p. 995. See also B. Rubin, *Paved with Good Intentions: The American Experience and Iran*, New York, 1980; G. Sick, *All Fall Down: America's Tragic Encounter with Iran*, New York, 1985; R. H. Immerman, *The CIA in Guatamala*, Austin, 1982; J. A. Bill, *The Eagle and the Lion*, New Haven, 1988, ch. 2.

18　See V. Marchetti and J. D. Marks, *The CIA and the Cult of Intelligence*, London, 1974, p. 23; also T. Powers, *The Man who kept the Secrets: Richard Helms and the CIA*, New York, 1979, pp. 39–40.

19　See C. Simpson, *Blowback: America's Recruitment of Nazis and its Effect on the Cold War*, London, 1988, pp. 246, 248.

20　Church Committee Report, Book 1, p. 9.

21　*Ibid.*, Book 4, *History of the Central Intelligence Agency*, pp. 52–3.

22　Ranelagh, *The Agency*, p. 209.

23　See Church Committee Interim Report, 1975, *Alleged Assassination Plots Involving Foreign Leaders*.

24 L. Mosley, *Dulles*, London, 1978, p. 459. The Committee appears to have been concerned with toxic weapons for use in espionage.

25 R. S. Cline, *The CIA under Reagan, Bush and Casey*, Washington D.C., 1981, p. 211.

26 Jeffreys-Jones, *The CIA*, ch. 7.

27 H. Wofford, *Of Kennedys and Kings*, New York, 1980, p. 358.

28 Jeffreys-Jones, *The CIA*, pp. 136–37.

29 C. DeBenedetti, 'Johnson and the antiwar movement', in R. A. Divine, ed., *The Johnson Years*, Volume Two, Lawrence (Kansas), 1987, pp. 23–53, p. 41; also, C. DeBenedetti, 'A CIA analysis of the anti-war movement', *Peace and Change*, 9, 1983, pp. 30–9.

30 H. Kissinger, *The White House Years*, Boston, 1979, p. 169.

31 Ranelagh, *The Agency*, p. 501; Marchetti and Marks, *The CIA*, pp. 102–03.

32 *The CIA*, p. 20.

33 See, e.g., H. Frazier, ed., *Uncloaking the CIA*, New York, 1978.

34 P. Agee, *Inside the Company*, Harmondsworth, 1975. On the CIA in the 1970s, see also E. J. Epstein, 'Secrets from the CIA archive in Tehran', *Orbis*, 51, 1987, pp. 33–42.

35 See R. Fletcher, 'How CIA money took the teeth out of British socialism', in P. Agee and L. Wolf, ed., *Dirty Work: The CIA in Western Europe*, London, 1978, pp. 188–200. See also J.T. Richelson, *The Ties that Bind: Intelligence Cooperation between the UKUSA Countries*, London, 1985.

36 Jeffreys-Jones, *The CIA*, pp. 203–4.

37 See T. M. Franck and E. Weisband, *Foreign Policy by Congress*, New York, 1979, pp. 117–25.

38 Colby, *Honourable Men*, p. 423. See also J. Prados, *President's Secret Wars*, New York, 1986, pp. 310–20.

39 G. Smith, *Morality, Reason and Power*, New York, 1986, p. 230.

40 S. Turner, *Secrecy and Democracy*, London, 1985, pp. 39, 150, 56–7; also, H. H. Ransom, 'Secret intelligence in the United States, 1947–1982: the CIA's search for legitimacy', in C. M. Andrew and D. Dilks, eds., *The Missing Dimension*, London, 1984, pp. 199–226, at pp. 218–19.

41 J. Carter, *Keeping Faith: Memoirs of a President*, New York, 1982, p. 143; Ransom, 'Secret Intelligence', p. 220.

42 See J. M. Oseth, *Regulating U,S. Intelligence Operations*, Lexington, p. 170; Turner, *Secrecy and Democracy*, pp. 155–62; L.K. Johnson, 'Legislative reform of intelligence policy', *Polity*, 17, 1985, pp. 549–73, p. 569.

43 *Guardian*, 12 June 1984 (cited in R. W. Johnson, *Shootdown: The Verdict on KAL 007*, London, 1986, pp. 94–5).

44 Turner, *Secrecy and Democracy*, p. 172.

45 See Johnson, *Shootdown*, pp. 94–5; also, B. Woodward, *Veil: The Secret Wars of the CIA 1981–1987*, London, 1987, *passim* and p. 385; L. K. Johnson, 'Seven sins of strategic intelligence', *World Affairs*, 146, 1983, pp. 176–204; and A. E. Goodman, 'Dateline Langley: Fixing the Intelligence Mess', *Foreign Policy*, 37, 1984–85, pp. 160–79.

46 J. A. Nathan and J. K. Oliver, *Foreign Policy Making and the American Political System*, Boston, 1987, p. 86.

47   *The Agency*, p. 712.

48   Berkowitz and Goodman, *Strategic Intelligence*, pp. 12, 44.

49   Woodward, *Veil*, pp. 38–9.

50   See Woodward, *Veil*, and Nathan and Oliver, *Foreign Policy Making*, p. 185. See also T.W. Walker, ed., *Reagan versus the Sandinistas*, London, 1987.

51   See S. D. Breckinridge, *The CIA and the U.S. Intelligence System*, Boulder (Colorado), 1986, p. 308.

52   Jeffreys-Jones, *The CIA*, p. 242.

53   Johnson, *Shootdown*. See also S. Hersh, *The Target is Destroyed*, London, 1986 for the view that Casey was instrumental in suppressing NSA intelligence that the Soviets genuinely considered KAL 007 to be a spy plane.

54   R. S. Cline, *Secrets, Spies and Scholars*, Washington D.C., 1976, pp. 265–8. See also Goodman, 'Dateline Langley'.

55   See J. Holland, *The American Connection*, Dublin, 1989, p. 105. On drugs, see L. Cockburn, *Out of Control: The Story of the Reagan Administration's Secret War in Nicaragua, The Illegal Pipeline and the Contra Drug Connection*, London, 1988. For an excursion to the wilder shores of CIA conspiracy theory, see F. Bresler, *The Murder of John Lennon*, London, 1989. See also J. Pilger, *A Secret Country*, London, 1989 (on CIA involvement in the 1975 dismissal from office of Australian Prime Minister Gough Whitlam).

56   *The CIA and the Cult of Intelligence*, p. 375.

57   The four major components of the CIA (as of 1988) were the directorates of administration, operations, science and technology, and intelligence (see Richelson, *The U.S. Intelligence Community*, p. 113).

58   Turner, *Secrecy and Democracy*, pp. 174–5.

59   *CIA: The Pike Report*, Nottingham, 1977, pp. 189, 188, 186, 193–4. The other projects studied were support for the Kurdish rebellion in Iraq and assistance to pro-American forces in Angola.

60   Angleton was CIA counterintelligence head, 1947–74; Wilson was a 'free-lance CIA operative and arms dealer' during the 1970s and early 1980s (Ranelagh, *The Agency*, p. 630).

61   J. Marshall *et al.*, *The Iran Contra Connection*, Boston, 1987.

62   See Johnson, 'Legislative reform', p. 561.

63   On CIA defections, see D. Wise, *The Spy who got away: The inside story of Edward Lee Howard*, New York, 1988; I. Corson *et al.*, *Widows*, London, 1989.

64   *Pike Report*, p. 188; Richelson, *The U.S. Intelligence Community*, pp. 407–9; Kegley and Wittkopf, *American Foreign Policy*, p. 404. The '208 Committee' met in room 208 of the Old Executive Office building.

65   R. Nixon, *The Memoirs of Richard Nixon*, London, 1978, pp. 489–90.

66   See, e.g., W. Q. Morales and H. E. Vanden, 'Relations with the nonaligned movement', in T. W. Walker, ed., *Nicaragua: The first five years*, New York, 1985, pp. 467–84, p. 476.

67   Treverton, 'Covert action', p. 999.

68   *Ibid.*, p. 1007. See also G. F. Treverton, *Covert Action: The Limits of Intervention in the Postwar World*, 2nd ed., New York, 1989.

69   Turner, *Secrecy and Democracy*, p. 173; Treverton, 'Covert action', p. 1013.

70 See L. K. Johnson, 'Covert Action and Accountability', *International Studies Quarterly*, 33, 1989, pp. 81–110, p. 105.

71 Colby, *Honourable Men*, p. 18.

72 See N. D. Sandler, *Twenty-eight Years of looking the other way: Congressional oversight of the Central Intelligence Agency*, Cambridge (Massachusetts), 1975.

73 Jeffreys-Jones, *The CIA*, p. 198.

74 *Strategic Intelligence*, p. 138. See also (on the 1980 Act) Johnson, 'Legislative reform', p. 561, and T. G. Paterson, *Meeting the Communist Threat*, New York, 1988, p. 249.

75 Woodward, *Veil*, p. 200. See also *Financial Times*, 18 October 1989 (article on Webster by L. Barber).

76 Johnson, 'Legislative reform', p. 566.

77 *Congressional Quarterly Weekly Report*, 1984, p. 833.

78 *Ibid.*, 1985, p. 120.

79 Paterson, *Meeting the Communist Threat*, p. 254.

80 Woodward, *Veil*, pp. 196–200.

81 R. Helms and J. Schlesinger, 'CIA watchdog – or mole?', *New York Times*, 22 November 1989.

82 See H. H. Ransom, 'Strategic intelligence and intermestic politics', in C. W. Kegley and E. R. Wittkopf, eds., *Perspectives on American Foreign Policy*, New York, 1983, pp. 299–319.

83 *U.S. Intelligence and the Soviet Strategic Threat*, p. 184.

84 See H.H. Ransom, 'Producing foreign intelligence', in G. Edwards and W. E. Walker, eds., *National Security and the Constitution*, Baltimore, 1988, pp. 50–70, p. 69; also J. Prados, *The Soviet Estimate*, Princeton, 1986.

85 See, e.g., Breckinridge, *The CIA*, p. 319.

86 Freedman, *U.S. Intelligence*, p. 189.

87 *Ibid.*, p. 187. See also B. D. Berkowitz, *American Security: Dilemmas for a Modern Democracy*, New Haven, 1986, p. 247.

88 *Ibid.*, p. 197. See also A. Wohlsetter, 'Is there a strategic arms race?', *Foreign Policy*, 29, 1974, pp. 62–91.

89 Berkowitz and Goodman, *Strategic Intelligence*, pp. 185–92, 91. See also R. N. Lebow, 'Misconceptions in American strategic assessment', *Political Science Quarterly*, 97, 1982, pp. 187–206.

90 See Berkowitz and Goodman, ch. 1, on contemporary intelligence problems.

91 See Treverton, *Covert Action*, ch. 7.

7

Public opinion

Arguments against public involvement in foreign policy-making are similar to those advanced against Congressional foreign policy. Speed, crisis management and informed judgement are widely held to be the province of the executive. Walter Lippmann held that 'governments' generally knew what was wise and expedient. The 'people' had forced governments to be 'too late with too little ... too pacifist in peace and too bellicose in war, too neutralist or appeasing in negotiation or too intransigent'.[1] In *The Public Philosophy*, Lippmann argued that the executives of Western democracies had become enfeebled by the irrationality of mass opinion, and its natural allies in legislatures.[2]

To some extent such sentiments may be countered by the same arguments which support a strong legislative role in foreign policy. The historical record shows that unaccountable executive discretion leads to irrationality and the abuse of power. Of course, democracy should not be equated with simple majoritarianism or 'tyranny of the majority'. Popular participation is partly exercised through representative organs of government – notably the Congress – but also through organised groups and vehicles for minority dissent. It is facilitated through the widest possible dissemination of information and high levels of public education.

1 Public opinion on foreign policy issues

Opponents of extensive public involvement in the foreign policy process point to evidence demonstrating public ignorance of foreign affairs. In 1983, apparently only 8 per cent of the American public knew that the US supported the government of El Salvador against guerrilla forces, but supported anti-government guerrillas in Nicaragua. Even those with some information may have no opinion, even after long periods of public debate.[3]

As the hearings which confirmed William Clark as Under-Secretary of State in 1981–82 indicated, ignorance is not the prerogative of the masses. Nonetheless, there is no question that the 'average' American citizen, like the 'average' British citizen, is ill-informed on foreign issues. For long periods, foreign affairs do not impinge on people's everyday lives. T. G. Paterson quotes a blue-collar worker interviewed in the late 1940s: 'Foreign affairs, that's for people who don't have to work for a living.'[4] People confronted with the problems of having to make a living, especially those facing economic hardships, may (understandably if not rationally) lack interest in 'remote' issues like elections and foreign politics.[5] This, however, is an argument for increasing public education levels and alleviating hardship, not for maximising executive discretion.

William Schneider has argued that a majority of Americans want the United States to be the toughest kid on the block, but in a defensive sense, rather than as a world policeman. They want both peace and strength, with the stress on either one varying over time.[6] Recent US public opinion on foreign policy has typically been a product of countervailing forces: notably, suspicion of Soviet expansionism, anxiety about nuclear weapons, concern for foreign policy issues with domestic economic impact, and (especially after Vietnam) caution about committing troops abroad.[7] The early Cold War invocation of Soviet aggression, arguably used by President Truman in order to gain domestic support for expensive internationalist policies,[8] has had a long-term impact on public opinion. Although dented by detente in the 1970s and by US public perceptions of President Gorbachev in the 1980s, distrust of the Soviet Union appears deep-seated.[9] Americans typically perceive nuclear war as more likely than do other nationalities, and have exhibited increasingly pessimistic notions, since the early 1960s, about the survivability of such a war.[10] Arms control and peace initiatives tend to gain automatic support. Yet, notably in the late 1970s, nuclear anxiety may also contribute to demands for higher military spending to gain advantages over the USSR.[11] Public concern for the impact on jobs and prices of events abroad can be easily documented, for example, in the reaction to the 1974 Arab oil embargo.[12] On troop commitment, public opinion has arguably acted as an inhibitory force upon Presidents, even before

Vietnam. It was a factor in the US decision not to send troops to Indochina after the 1954 French defeat at Dienbienphu. In May 1961, 65 per cent of Americans opposed using troops to support anti-Castro forces in Cuba.[13] After Vietnam, it was noticeable that the hardening of public attitudes towards the Soviet Union in the 1970s did not extend to enthusiasm for military intervention. Typically, no more than 34 per cent of Americans favour intervening in foreign wars.[14]

The view that public opinion is quixotic, capricious and unstable does not bear much examination. Wars – above all, war casualties – do alter opinion dramatically, as was demonstrated in the Korean and Vietnam conflicts.[15] There certainly were major fluctuations over public support for high levels of military spending in the 1970s and 1980s.[16] Nonetheless, the problem for students of public opinion is really one of explaining change-within-stability, rather than mercurial, unpredictable shifts. To this end, various cyclical and generational theories have been developed.[17] The most obvious explanation of relatively stable opinion, prone to periodic shifts, however, relates to Presidential manipulation. The relatively uninformed nature of public knowledge of foreign affairs allows Presidents to indulge in symbolic political leadership. They may, in a sense, actually feed off public ignorance. As Graebner puts it: 'The better informed the public, the more threatening it becomes.'[18] Crises become occasions to achieve a 'rally-round-the flag' effect. Presidents take initiatives in the knowledge that they generate short-term enthusiasm, and that this may deflect public attention from failed or embarrassing policies. Such tactics are powerful, especially given the President's ability to control the flow of information. However, they do not always work, and may be subject to a law of diminishing returns.[19]

An alternative approach to this problem is that encapsulated in Shapiro and Page's notion of the 'rational public'.[20] The debate here is akin to that between the tradition set by the 1960 study of the American electorate, *The American Voter*, and the perspective embodied in V. O. Key's *The Responsible Electorate*.[21] According to the 1960 study, voters form an ill-informed body, politically unsophisticated and basing choices largely upon leadership cues. Key argued that voters are not fools. They act 'on the basis of widely varying quantities of information' and fulfil 'roles both of bewilderment and wisdom'.[22] Voters do exhibit some ideological consistency and do concern themselves with candidates and issues, on the basis of such information as they acquire. Similarly, Shapiro and Page, who associate their view with that of Key and use comprehensive data,[23] hold that foreign policy preferences are generally consistent. Changes may be described as 'reasonable, given the unfolding of events … as reported and interpreted by the media and political leaders'. Thus, public attitudes towards the Middle East in the 1980s showed strong traces of traditional support for the state of Israel, but also 'sympathy for the Palestinians and a more critical view of Israeli foreign policy, later accentuated somewhat by revelations of the Israeli role in the Iran-contra affair'.[24]

Adult members of the American public, no less than the policy-makers, are conceptual consistency-seekers, capable of suppressing information which challenges established notions. Nonetheless, early political socialisation neither fixes adult opinions irrevocably, nor destroys the capacity for rational choice.[25] Above all, while recognising public ignorance of foreign events as a major problem, foreign policy leaders should not regard the public as an inert mass, capable of infinite manipulation. To do so would be both foolhardy and impolitic.

The relationship between mass and elite opinion is central to the question of leader manipulation. Mueller depicts the President as moulding mass opinion through the agency of attentive elites.[26] The relatively uninformed 'mass' may be estimated at about 30 per cent of the population. 'Attentive publics', with some knowledge of and interest in foreign affairs, would comprise 45 per cent, and community 'opinion leaders' 25 per cent.[27] Elite opinion may lead tendencies toward change in opinion. J. S. Nye thus sees the relative stability of mass opinion as a constraining force on elite excesses – a neat reversal of notions of a volatile public.[28] Regarding actual opinion content, Susan Welch has summarised research findings from the early 1980s as follows: 'Leaders were more likely to favor selling military equipment, giving military aid and defending our allies, while the public more often agreed that an important foreign policy goal was containing communism and was less supportive of a nuclear weapons freeze.'[29]

2 Policy and public influence

Studies of both public and elite opinion in the 1970s tended to identify three strands within the post-Vietnam dissensus. Firstly, Cold War internationalism, hostile to the Soviet Union and stressing

US military strength; secondly, liberal or post-Cold War internationalism, emphasising peace, arms control and aid to the Third
World; and, lastly, noninternationalism or quasi-isolationism.[30] The
anxieties and events of the later 1970s and early 1980s either accompanied or stimulated a hardening of attitudes, in the direction being
advocated by the Committee on the Present Danger, and underpin-
ned the election of Ronald Reagan.[31]

The new President seemed to exemplify and feed off the public
mood. Yet, by the late 1980s, sweeping claims could be made about
the way that public opinion had reversed the policies of the Reagan
White House. According to Barry Sussman, for example, the 1984
withdrawal of US marines from the Lebanon, the erosion of support
for President Marcos in the Philippines and moves against South
Africa were all the product of public opinion pressures. Most important of all, the 1987 arms control agreements echoed public sentiments, as well as being an attempt to recapture public support after
Irangate.[32]

This simple attribution of developments within the Reagan
Administration's foreign policy to the force of public opinion is not
entirely convincing. For one thing, it tends to ignore the mediating
role played by Congress, and also the extent to which the views of the
Administration changed alongside, rather than in direct response to,
public opinion. It is very difficult to disentangle direct causes and
effects with clarity. Yet shifting public opinion and activism –
especially over South Africa – were major factors in these policy shifts.
The relationship between Administration policy and public opinion
on Central America is especially interesting. The inhibitory impact of
public attitudes may be hypothesised with some confidence. Despite
the public ignorance on this issue already noted, and in face of
consistent worries about communism in the region, the polls showed
public opposition to direct military intervention. Gallup polls
between 1981 and 1983 showed, typically, that 68 per cent of those
aware of the situation in El Salvador felt that it 'could turn into a
situation like Vietnam'. CBS and *New York Times* polls between 1983
and 1985 showed majority opposition to intervention against the
Nicaraguan government. The figure dropped somewhat during the
1986 White House campaign for *contra* aid, but rose again to over 70
per cent opposition after the Irangate revelations.[33] Of course, it
could be argued that here was an example of an Administration
persisting with an unpopular policy in the face of public opposition.

Certainly the relatively low saliency of the Central American issue for most respondents[34] would have encouraged the White House. However, the state of public opinion at least appeared to rule out the possibility of invading Nicaragua. It also demonstrated that conscious White House attempts to mould public opinion – in this case to mobilise it against the menace of communism in the Western hemisphere – do not always succeed.

The shift in the Reagan Administration foreign policies towards greater pragmatism[35] may be explained in a variety of ways. It reflected an adjustment to the uncertainty of the international political environment.[36] Robert Tucker has expressed doubt whether Reagan ever seriously believed in the possibility of restoring a new Cold War consensus.[37] The pragmatism of the second phase of the Reagan Presidency was also undoubtedly associated with the outcome of the intra-Administration conflicts and bureaucratic 'pulling and hauling' of the period. Public opinion polls, however, consistently sent messages to the White House and, on the face of it, there seems to have been a response. When faced by a lengthy and unpopular commitment in the Lebanon, forces were withdrawn. With Congress and the polls turning against Marcos, policy changes followed.

The Reagan years did not see a restoration of the pre-Vietnam consensus. Nonetheless, while the direction of post-Cold War public opinion is uncertain, the Gorbachev era has given President Bush the chance to forge a new consensus rooted in detente. In this sense, Reagan bequeathed a relatively settled climate of opinion. Fluctuations in attitudes over military spending seemed by the late-1980s to have developed into steady support for reducing or keeping spending constant. As T. L. Deibel writes, it was a paradox of the Reagan period, that a President 'as far from the mainstream as any in recent history ended up ameliorating many of the public divisions that brought him to power'.[38]

Conventional wisdom has it that public opinion may have a role in shaping long-term foreign policy, but that it scarcely affects day-to-day management. State Department officials do not typically see it as part of their job to keep abreast of public opinion.[39] Yet the State Department does undertake scrupulous poll analysis, and itself samples public opinion. It has since 1954 conducted a systematic survey of European public opinion on US policy.[40] Poll analysis is regularly undertaken at White House level, as, for example, scrutiny of the White House Central Files during the period of Vietnam war escalation will bear out.[41] Most observers see public opinion responding to governmental leadership, rather than *vice versa*. However, there are specific instances where public opinion may be seen to be leading executive action. One such case was public support for the normalisation of relations with the People's Republic of China in the 1970s. Support for recognition of mainland China increased by thirty-one percentage points between 1968 and 1977. President Carter extended recognition in 1978, using public opinion as a lever against Congressional and bureaucratic opposition.[42]

As in the Red China case, public opinion shifts can be crucial in developing a climate of opinion conducive to policy change, and can be powerful weapons in the hands of those within the foreign policy process who choose to follow 'popular' policies. Above and beyond all this, of course, the public has the ultimate sanction implicit in the Presidential election. Again, the conventional view is that Presidential elections (much less Congressional ones) are not really foreign policy events at all. There is also the related point that in many Presidential elections, voters are not offered clear alternatives. To some extent the role of foreign policy in Presidential elections turns on the degree to which voters are seen as making choices on the basis of issues, candidate appeal, party or, for example, attachment to a 'reference group'.[43] Generally, however, it is clear that foreign policy issues are rarely prominent in Presidential campaigns. Robert Tucker noted 'the virtual absence of any serious discussion of foreign policy in the 1988 presidential elections'.[44] The 1988 campaign contrasted strongly with the virtually simultaneous elections in Israel and Canada, where foreign policy issues (the Middle East peace process and the US free trade agreement) predominated.[45]

Foreign and defence issues regularly cause problems for Presidential candidates. One thinks of the 'missile gap' in 1960, President Ford's 1976 gaffe over Soviet influence in Poland, and the 'window of vulnerability' (to Soviet nuclear strike) issue in the 1980 campaign. Candidates, however, are generally content to attempt to project images of managerial competence, while (like President Johnson in 1964) attributing dangerous consequences to the election of an opponent. There was little detailed discussion of the foreign policy differences between Bush and Dukakis, notably over SDI and Nicaragua, in 1988. This was not due to a conspiracy between the candidates. Dukakis at one point attempted to shift the debate towards foreign policy in a speech to the Council on Foreign

Relations in Chicago. He attacked Reagan's interventionism and outlined five areas within which to test Soviet good intentions. The Bush camp produced Zbigniew Brzezinski to claim that Dukakis's views were 'closer to Jesse Jackson and Jane Fonda', than to those of Democratic centrists like Senator Nunn.[46]

Throughout most of the Cold War era, the Republican party tended to gain support as the party of military strength, the Democrats (despite Vietnam) as the party of peace. Schneider has pointed out that when the GOP won the Presidential races of 1952, 1956, 1968 and 1972, they, in effect, used positive foreign policy images to compensate for disadvantage on economic issues. The 1980s have seen changes in this pattern. In 1980, the Democrats had an unusually strong lead on the peace issue, though suffered greatly in the area of economic policy.[47] By 1988, the GOP seemed to be ahead on both the 'peace' and 'strength' fronts.[48] Future Presidential elections seem likely to involve foreign policy considerations that extend beyond the traditional, Soviet-oriented peace *versus* strength debate. Reactions to terrorism and attitudes towards the Third World may figure more prominently. Issues appropriate to declining economic hegemony – notably the protectionist cause which formed the basis of Richard Gephardt's 1988 campaign for the Democratic nomination – will also be firmly on the agenda.

3 American women and foreign policy

Women have tended disproportionately to support Democratic candidates in recent Presidential elections.[49] There is evidence that this tendency is related to defence and foreign issue preferences. In 1980, 53 per cent of men declared themselves to be 'closer to Reagan' on defence spending, compared with 40 per cent of women. Polls on Reagan's Central America policies tended to find women in support of them some 10 per cent scarcer than men. The invasion of Grenada in 1983 increased President Reagan's approval rating among men by eight points, but only by two points among women.[50]

The 1980s saw the emergence of a new generation of female peace activists, building on the tradition set by older groups such as Women Strike for Peace. Many of the newer activists linked their peace activities to feminist theory, and to the campaigns of European women (notably the Greenham Common peace camp in England). Women's Pentagon Action, founded in 1980 at Hartford

(Connecticut), organised a demonstration at the Defence Department in November 1982. Forty-three arrested women issued a statement from prison: 'We acted because we fear for our lives, and because we oppose the military mentality: that of rule by the biggest weapons, of penetration and domination, and of appropriation of our lives to keep this power structure intact.'[51]

Other groups, such as Women's Party for Survival, distanced themselves from radical feminism. The peace cause was frequently linked to ecological and social justice imperatives, as, for example in statements issued from the Puget Sound peace camp. Female activists have also been prominent in both religiously-oriented and more secular Central American solidarity organisations like the Committee in Solidarity with the People of El Salvador.

Moving towards the political centre, the Women's Foreign Policy Council was established in 1986 as part of Women USA Fund.[52] Attempts to increase the influence of women *within* the foreign policy process have to confront both apathy and inherited traditions of male domination of the process. Despite changing roles and within the limits of polling errors and misperceptions, women appeared to demonstrate less interest than men in political affairs over the period 1960-84; this phenomenon may be attributed to childhood and adolescent socialisation.[53] Regarding male domination of the policy process, Jeane Kirkpatrick (appointed as Ambassador to the United Nations in 1981) declared on her departure from the Reagan Administration: 'I was the only woman in our history, I think, who ever sat in regularly at top-level foreign policy meetings.' In 1985, she described seeing a mouse in the Situation Room: 'That mouse is no more surprising a creature to be in the Situation Room than I am.'[54]

The State Department has a well-documented history of discriminating against women in employment practices.[55] Eleanor Lansing Dulles (sister of Allen and John Foster) was in charge of State's Berlin desk from 1952 to 1959. Pat Derian's role in the Carter State Department is discussed in Chapter 9. More recently, Rozanne Ridgway served as First Assistant Secretary of State for European Affairs under Reagan. The Bush Administration also saw women at senior levels at State (notably Assistant Secretaries Tutwiler and Mullins) and on Brent Scowcroft's NSC staff (notably Condoleeza Rice). The State Department has operated equal opportunity and affirmative action programmes for women and minorities. By 1987, women made up 27.5 per cent of the career Foreign Service, but only 4.8 per cent of top-level Foreign Service employees.[56] In 1981 the proportion of tenured minority women in the Foreign Service Officer Corps was 0.8 per cent.[57]

The debate over enhancing the role of women in the foreign policy process centres not only on strategies to increase female involvement, but also on speculation as to the effect of a stronger feminine input. (It should be stressed that many of these points about female involvement apply equally to minorities.) The position of Madeleine Albright, of Georgetown University, as a leading foreign policy adviser to candidate Dukakis in 1988 stimulated debate on the role of women in future Democratic Administrations. The familiar stereotype of women as more pacifistic than men is not entirely convincing if one considers the careers of those few females who have gained entry into foreign policy inner circles. Dulles or Kirkpatrick would hardly fit the stereotype, for example; neither would Frances Willis (1899–1964, the first woman to gain Class One rank as career diplomat and senior Foreign Service Officer). On the other hand, one may cite the career of Jeannette Rankin (1880–1973), the first woman elected to the House of Representatives and the only legislator to oppose US entry into both World Wars.[58]

During a 1987 informal Congressional hearing organised by the Women's Foreign Policy Council, Vivian Derryck, of the Democratic Institute for International Affairs, addressed the assumption that 'women in decisionmaking roles will necessarily be more interested in equality, economic advancement, and social justice'. According to Derryck, this is not always the case:

Because by the time that a woman gathers the expertise to be effective in these kinds of jobs ... she has come through a male system. She has learned concepts and learned language that are gender-neutral or that connote maleness.[59]

Former Representative Bella Abzug countered:

My experience ... is that large numbers of [women], even those with conservative views, tend to be more willing to question policies that they have not been associated with ... They didn't create the atom bomb, they are not responsible for developing the various theories of the Cold War ... I think women can make a difference.[60]

4 Citizen lobbying: the case of the nuclear freeze movement

Efforts to measure the impact on policy, and on wider public opinion, of direct citizen action tend to detect only minimal, if not actually counter-productive effects.[61] The hypothesis that anti-Vietnam war protest stimulated the mobilisation of the Silent Majority is well known. However, far more positive interpretations of direct action and lobbying may be advanced. Marches, petitions, occupations and teach-ins may shake complacency and slowly alter the decisional climate. Melvin Small suggests that the anti-Vietnam war movement had an important role to play in presenting credible information on the war, slowly undermining the official version of events. (He also speculates that demonstrations and disruptions may have made voters and leaders 'want to end the war so that they could return to' a society where 'hippies and other ne'er-do-wells did not threaten domestic tranquillity'.)[62]

Far more representative of 'middle' or 'respectable' America, but widely acclaimed as the most important citizens' movement on foreign policy since Vietnam days, was the nuclear freeze campaign of the early 1980s. The movement sprung from the Massachusetts referendum proposals for a bilateral, verifiable moratorium on nuclear weapons acquisition and development, fostered by Randall Forsberg and Randy Kehler.[63] It gathered strength from growing public disquiet about Reagan's stance on nuclear weapons. By November 1983, polls were showing 86 per cent in favour of a freeze on nuclear weapons, with the popularity of the notion that the US should 'get tough' with the Soviet Union dropping from 74 per cent in January 1980 to 40 per cent in May 1982.[64] To use Robert Osgood's terminology, Americans tend to be 'mitigators' rather than 'rejectionists' or 'abolitionists' over nuclear arms:[65] that is, they tend to favour strategies designed to ameliorate the danger of war, rather than either accepting the idea of a winnable nuclear war or seeking to abolish nuclear weapons altogether. By 1983, Reagan's hawkish reputation appeared significantly out of line with public sentiment.

The nuclear freeze movement exploited modes of political activism, such as direct mailing, often associated with the New Right. A freeze petition acquired nearly two million signatures in a fifteen-month period. The June 1982 rally in New York's Central Park attracted over half a million people. Eventually, in May 1983, the House of Representatives passed a joint resolution requiring the President to negotiate a mutual halt to the arms race with the Soviet Union. The significance of the resolution should not be exaggerated (as it is, to some extent, in the account offered by D. C. Waller, legislative director to E. J. Markey, the resolution's House sponsor).

The proposal was for a mutual freeze; when the press scented a whiff of unilateralism at the 1983 freeze conference in St Louis, it threatened to harm the movement. Moreover, the resolution had no chance of passing the Republican-controlled Senate. It was also subjected, prior to House passage, to significant amendment. In particular, the amendment proposed by Elliot Levitas made the freeze dependent on achieving arms reductions.[66]

After 1983, the movement lost impetus and voted in 1986 to merge with the pre-existing Committee for a Sane Nuclear Policy (SANE). Part of the reason for decline was undoubtedly the changed Administration's attitude towards arms control. As Waller puts it: 'Mr. Reagan finally regained the momentum after four years of clumsy attacks on the freeze movement, and did so by at least appearing to be concerned about arms control. In a way, the freeze movement became a victim of its own success.'[67]

Did the freeze movement, along with associated developments in Congressional and public opinion, force the shift in Administration policy? The changing climate was exemplified by the pastoral letter on war and peace issued by the National Council of Catholic Bishops in May 1983.[68] The freeze issue appeared to offer hope to the Democrats, who endorsed a version of the resolution at a midterm convention in June 1982. Administration policy changes were one way of responding to the changed elite and public opinion. Policy shifts ran in tandem with public opinion. The 'zero option' for European arms reductions (widely thought, in fact, to be virtually unnegotiable) was proposed as early as November 1981. Substantial strategic arms reductions were proposed by Reagan in May, 1982. These were dismissed by freeze supporters as a transparent and cynical attempt to undermine support for the resolution. Michael Hayes has noted that Presidential proposals 'brought the President valuable time, permitting most – if not quite all – of his proposed defense build-up to go forward'.[69] In March 1983, Reagan announced the Strategic Defence Initiative in a speech clearly designed to appeal to deep-seated public desire to establish an absolute security. Further developments were linked to continuing public support for arms control and to growing perceptions of the nature and intentions of the new leadership in Moscow.[70]

Some freeze activists felt that the movement had been co-opted by political leaders: to some extent in Reagan's arms control policies, but more so by Democrats who took up the freeze cause in the 1984 elections. It was felt that only Jesse Jackson and Alan Cranston seriously believed in it. According to Forsberg, 'Mondale didn't really support the freeze, and neither did Hart, and neither did the Democratic party as a whole ... It was a sort of lip-service campaign.'[71] The experience of the freeze movement did illustrate the ability of the White House to respond to shifts in public opinion by re-setting the agenda, and also indicated the degree to which grass-roots activism can come to serve more compromised electoral interests. Nonetheless, the freeze movement did at least come near to making a reality of the pretence to public participation in a democratic foreign policy process.

5 Sensitised public opinion: the ethnic lobbies

Although the contribution of ethnic lobbying to the shaping of US foreign policy has probably been exaggerated in the voluminous literature on the subject,[72] there is no doubt as to the potency of such pressure in certain policy areas. The role of the Greek-American lobby in orchestrating support for the post-1974 Turkish arms embargo was highlighted by the Ford Administration for propaganda purposes, but was nonetheless important. Greek-American activists were able to marshal and target information supportive to their cause.[73]

As in the case of the Greek-American lobby, ethnic group lobbies tend to succeed in situations where there is, through poor organisation, funding or the nature of immigration patterns, an absence of a countervailing organised interest. Above all, the pro-Israeli lobby (especially AIPAC, the American Israeli Public Affairs Committee) has long had the ability to mobilise support well beyond the ranks of the Jewish community, or of Members of Congress with significant numbers of Jewish constituents. There simply was no comparable pro-Arab organisation. The situation became more complex in the 1980s with, on the one hand, widespread US public hostility to Muslim fundamentalism and, on the other, growing sympathy for the Palestinians. Even American Jewish opinion has shown signs of dissatisfaction with Israeli policy in this area.[74] According to Republican ex-Congressman Paul Findley, in a polemical study published in 1985, AIPAC was 'the pre-eminent power in Washington lobbying'.[75] (Findley, widely identified in Congress as friendly to the Palestinian cause, was defeated in 1982 in an Illinois campaign which saw the mobilisation of pro-Israeli forces against him.) Legislators without special Jewish constituency interests may be influenced by the efficiency of the information services offered by AIPAC, by sensitivity to charges of anti-Semitism, and by the fact that (traditionally at least) public opinion has tended to be either pro-Israeli or uniformedly neutral. M. C. Feuerwerger quotes a member of the House Appropriations subcommittee on Foreign Operations to the effect that Israel succeeds in Congress because 'two or three per cent of voters care intensely about it, and the rest are uninformed and don't care'.[76] It should not, however, be supposed that the pro-Israeli lobby is omnipotent. For example, Congress displayed caution about a strong pro-Israeli commitment during the 1967 Arab-Israeli war.[77] The 1974 passage of the Jackson-Vanik amendment, which attempted (largely in vain) to use trade as a lever to liberalise Soviet policy on Jewish emigration, was a victory for AIPAC; however, in pressing for the amendment, the Jewish lobby formed only part of a wider coalition of largely independent labour, academic and scientific interests.[78]

As will be evident from the above remarks, it is easier to trace the influence of ethnic lobbying on Congress than on the executive. Members of Congress often indulge in 'no lose' policy stances designed to impress small, influential sections of opinion, without alienating any significant countervailing interest. George Kennan in 1967 drew attention to the impact on Congress of 'ethnic groups ... representing compact voting groups in large cities'.[79] Turning to the executive branch, it is almost as easy to point to examples of the executive exploiting ethnic loyalties as to examples of ethnic influence. Thus, for example, Washington organised a campaign by Italian-Americans to use their influence on behalf of non-Communist candidates in the 1948 Italian elections.[80] The Assembly of Captive European Nations was, since its foundation in 1954, the most prominent ethnic organisation lobbying for a tougher US stance towards Soviet influence in Eastern Europe. Apart from symbolic achievements like the establishment by Congress in the 1950s of Captive Nations Week, it is difficult to identify any obvious impact upon policy made by the Assembly. The Assembly certainly was, however, used in the 1950s by the CIA as a means of orchestrating anti-Soviet feeling.[81] Generally speaking – and despite the reaction to Gerald Ford's 1976 gaffe about Eastern Europe not being under Soviet domination – Americans of Eastern European origin do not appear especially concerned with foreign policy when casting their Presidential votes.[82] (On the attitudes displayed by patrician executive leaders to more recently-arrived 'fellow immigrants', one cannot resist quoting a letter written by President Roosevelt to FBI head J. Edgar Hoover in 1942: 'Have you pretty well cleaned out the alien waiters in the principal Washington hotels? Altogether too much conversation in the dining rooms!')[83]

An area of American ethnic politics of special interest to observers in Britain is the Irish lobby. Irish-American opinion is regularly scolded in the British press for its supposed naive indulgence towards Irish nationalism. In Britain, the most famous Irish-American organisation is NORAID (the Irish Northern Aid Committee), although considerable publicity was also given in the 1970s to the republican Irish National Caucus. NORAID has, especially during the 1970s and particularly in New York, collected money fairly openly in support of the provisional Irish Republican Army. Between 1971 and 1978 it actually reported donations of one and a half million dollars. Although NORAID's strength revived during the IRA hunger strikes of the early 1980s, its profile has been lower in recent years, notably after its 1984 registration under the Foreign Agents Registration Act. It is thought not to have been involved directly in arms acquisition, although the provisionals have purchased arms through a separate US network. A contributor to both republican coffers and morale, NORAID has been a not insignificant non-governmental foreign policy actor.[84]

More representative of mainstream Irish-American opinion is the Ancient Order of Hibernians, the traditional Catholic defence body and organiser of the New York St Patrick's day parade. The Ancient Order was instrumental in 1977 in establishing the Congressional Ad Hoc Committee on Irish Affairs, the most active elite group on Northern Irish issues of recent years. Until 1988 the Committee was chaired by Mario Biaggi, New York Congressman and highly decorated ex-New York policeman. (Biaggi resigned his seat in 1988, facing near-certain expulsion from Congress after criminal conviction in the Wedtech defence contracting scandals.) Biaggi did condemn violence on either side of the Northern Ireland divide and has emphasised the priority of economic regeneration as a means to help both Catholics and Protestants.[85] However he has, especially during a trip to Ireland in 1975, sailed very close to outright support for the IRA. Interestingly, as a Congressman for a Bronx-Queens district, he had no substantial Irish-American population in his constituency. The Northern Ireland issue represented primarily an opportunity for visible position-taking, with Biaggi even on occasion indulging in slightly hare-brained attempts at statesmanlike 'mediation'.[86] His Committee, as of 1988, consisted of 116 members (ninety-four Democrats, twenty-two Republicans). About half the membership could be regarded as active, with its core being made up of twenty-five Members of Congress from New York. Its principal achievements were seen to be the successful pushes in 1979 and 1981 for State Department prohibition on arms sales to the Royal Ulster Constabulary, and also the pressure that resulted in the economic aid package agreed in 1986.[87] (Biaggi, in fact, expressed some reservations about the package for Northern Ireland, arguing that aid should be tied to a satisfactory British review of 'shoot-to-kill' policy allegations.)[88]

Conspicuously absent from the membership list of Biaggi's Ad Hoc Committee were the names of the US Congress's three most famous Irish-American politicians: Senator D. P. Moynihan of New York, House Speaker 'Tip' O'Neill and Senator Edward Kennedy. (Congressman Joseph Kennedy Jr was a highly active member of Biaggi's Committee.) Together with former New York governor Hugh Carey, Moynihan, O'Neill and Edward Kennedy constituted the 'Four Horsemen' group:[89] organised eventually around the Friends of Ireland, and close both to the government of the Irish Republic and (to lesser degree) the Catholic Social Democratic and Labour Party (notably John Hume) in the North. The 'Big Four' were effectively enlisted by the Irish government, largely through the agency of ambassador Sean Donlon, to support Republic initiatives and to counter the influence of Sinn Fein and the Irish National Caucus.[90] In the mid-1980s, the 'Big Four's' energies were channelled primarily in support of the Anglo-Irish agreement of 1985. The agreement was welcomed in virtually all Irish-American and US governmental circles, not least by the 'Irish' American' President Reagan. To Senate Foreign Relations Committee chairman Claiborne Pell, the agreement, remained even in 1988 the 'best hope of ending the violence'.[91] US economic support for the Anglo-Irish agreement represented the first occasion for direct US Administration involvement in Anglo-Irish relations.[92] In a strange echo of sentiments expressed by Enoch Powell, the Washington correspondent of the *Irish Times* described the (pan-Irish) aid package as threatening to turn the Irish Republic into a US 'client state'.[93]

The Irish lobby has been successful in publicising criticisms of British policy and has been a factor in mobilising US backing for 'power-sharing' solutions in Northern Ireland. Such activity, especially Congressional criticism of British policy, is represented in the British press as ignorant and offensive. In fact, it raises important issues. It represents the articulation of a perspective rarely heard on the British mainland, particularly since the imposition of media controls on republican statements. It should also be noted that, in many areas, the Congressional Irish lobby is very hostile to 'official' US policy. Extradition to a justice system characterised by juryless trials is one such area. (The US Senate ratified a new extradition treaty with Great Britain in July 1986.) Congressman T. J. Downey of New York protested the decision of Attorney-General Meese to deport Joseph Doherty to the UK in the following terms: 'Now you know ... that if he were an Afghan Mujahidin, a Cuban, or a Contra, Mr. Doherty would be granted asylum at the drop of a hat.'[94] Joseph Kennedy added: 'The Attorney General is suggesting that the principles and values of the United States judicial system should be set aside in order to avoid ruffling the feathers of Margaret Thatcher.'[95] The feeling that US policy is distorted by the desire to support its British ally is widespread. The Gibraltar IRA deaths of March 1988 (described by Joseph Kennedy as 'state-sponsored killings'[96]) evoked the following response from Biaggi: 'Official United States policy for the twenty years I have been involved with the Irish issue is support the British Government first, ask questions later.'[97]

The Irish lobby has managed, at the state level, to gain significant acceptance of the MacBride proposals: fair employment practice requirements for US-owned firms operating in Northern Ireland. However, as with other ethnic influences, it is all too easy to exaggerate their actual impact on policy. The lobbying organisations and their allies in Congress can rarely draw on sustained grass-roots activism. Ethnic loyalties, as at the New York St Patrick's day parade, very often operate primarily at the symbolic level. Sean Cronin estimates that only about one hundred thousand Irish-Americans out of forty millions have any serious, sustained interest in Irish politics.[98] As with the Eastern European ethnics, there is little evidence that US policy towards the land of origin is a major determinant of their voting preferences.

The future for ethnic group influence would seem to lie in two directions. Firstly, traditional attempts to influence policy, especially through Congress. Despite the traditionally low priority attached to foreign policy concerns by black Americans, the African American lobby has had an impact in this way on US policy towards South Africa. The apartheid issue and South Africa generally has high saliency for black elites, and indeed the general black American population. The involvement of the African American lobby in future African policy – a Marshall Plan for Africa? – has long been a subject of speculation.[99] Given demographic forecasts, Hispanic participation and influence is bound to increase;[100] although, given the composition of the US Hispanic population, the precise impact of this on American policy towards Latin America is uncertain. Secondly, in an interdependent, disaggregated world, ethnic groups may seek to operate as non-governmental forces, intervening directly in foreign politics. A recent example of this would be the National Association for the Advancement of Colored People's Legal Defence and Educational Fund, a free legal aid service for South African blacks established in 1978.

6 The media and foreign policy

It is common currency that the media have both a tendency to distort the news, and considerable political power in their own right. James Reston referred in 1967 to the 'tyranny of technique', encouraging 'a startling, even a breathless, presentation of the news, featuring the flaming lead and the big headline'.[101] Broadcasters are regularly accused of trivialisation and 'pack journalism'. The media (especially television) emerged from the Vietnam war and Watergate with a reputation for being able to topple Presidents. Lyndon Johnson himself, on the day following his 31 March 1968 speech announcing that he would not seek re-election, addressed the National Association of Broadcasters in accusatory tones. Historians had only to guess, declared LBJ, the effect 'television would have had during earlier conflicts ... during the Korean War, for example, at the time our forces were pushed back to Pusan, or World War II, the Battle of the Bulge ...'. As David Halberstam put it: 'They had beaten him, those cameras and all those punk kid reporters in Vietnam.'[102]

Johnson may well have had a point in implying that media coverage of the 1968 Tet offensive had a distorting effect.[103] There is no question as to its impact; like Nixon's 1972 visit to China, it was one of those foreign affairs reporting events with an almost instantaneous domestic political repercussion. The post-Vietnam notion that public opinion swung away from the war because of crusading journalism and vivid photography is, however, little more than romantic myth. Some newspapers, like the *New York Times* and *Los Angeles Times*, did exhibit schizophrenic attitudes to the war, with, for example, the official *Los Angeles Times* pro-war line being undermined by editors like Jim Bellows.[104] In general, however, the media were instinctually solidly pro-war and only shifted attitudes when sharp elite divisions on the issue had become apparent. D.C. Hallin has calculated that only 22 per cent of all film reports from Southeast Asia before 1968 showed actual conflict. Many of these images were highly ambiguous, many involving very little evidence of violence.[105] Johnson's own communication failures – his inability to invoke an effective 'rhetoric of limited war' – were more damaging to the war cause than activities of crusading journalists.[106]

Foreign affairs coverage in the American media is of a high standard, although it is largely confined to what is generally thought of as 'elite' or 'prestige' segments of broadcasting. The *New York Times, Los Angeles Times, Washington Post, Chicago Tribune, Wall Street Journal, Baltimore Sun, Christian Science Monitor*, the leading news magazines, the *MacNeil-Lehrer Report* on public television and *All Things Considered* on national public radio are traditionally included under this label. The crucial role played by the leading wire services (notably Associated Press and United Press International) should also be mentioned. Doris Graber has estimated that only 11 per cent of newspaper stories, measured over the long term, relate to foreign affairs.[107] To the extent that the general public is uninterested in foreign policy, the media is – apart from 'set pieces' like Nixon's China trip – unlikely to have much effect. However, the public agenda-setting function of the mass media (generally in concert with governing elites) is widely recognised.[108]

The foreign policy media have been seen, on the one hand, as instruments of elite manipulation; and, on the other – especially if one includes journals like *Foreign Affairs* and *Foreign Policy* – as instruments of intra- and inter-elite communication. Parenti sees newspapers and television as consciously used vehicles for elite propagation of anticommunism. In the Gramscian tradition, the media exist to disseminate and reinforce the dominant hegemonic ideology;[109] they seek to 'correct' the degree to which personal, everyday experience tends to contradict the (anti-communist) hegemonic ideology. In the absence of clear external censorship in the American context, the press may be seen as practising a variety of self-censorship. This operates at the level of ownership. It also, however, involves the degree to which the media is structured so as to keep information and comment within 'acceptable' bounds. Hallin points out that early Vietnam protesters often only gained quasi-sympathetic coverage if they could be presented as stout individualists, acting (however misguidedly) out of eccentric conscience. A 1967 CBS report on an Indiana schoolteacher, fired for anti-war activities, ended with the line: 'In a small town, its difficult to be different.'[110] Self-censorship may also operate, especially under conditions of shifting elite consensus, to stifle criticism of Presidential initiatives. In the early Reagan years, only Jack Anderson, among 'prestige' journalists, appeared willing seriously to challenge the new Administration's foreign policy.[111]

Sections of the media appear to exist in order to service foreign policy governing elites as much as to serve the general public. The State Department uses press briefings as a way of communicating with Congress and other executive agencies. 'Leaks' and trial balloons are similar devices of elite communication. 'Prestige' journalists and foreign policy managers tend to drink at the same informational fountain, and tend to define problems in similar terms. In this sense, the media operate to transmit elite perceptions of 'reality' beyond the relatively narrow band of people directly concerned with foreign policy questions.[112]

The relationship between governments and broadcasters is formally adversarial. Their immediate interests appear opposed, as will be observed by anyone attending a White House press conference. Executive spokesmen seek to confine journalists' attention to pre-set tracks; journalists look to open out the themes of discussion. Yet the relationship is also symbiotic.[113] Presidents, for example, cannot afford to ignore Patrick Anderson's aphorism: 'What a President does may matter less than what the people think he is doing.'[114] The Nixon Administration embodied an attempt to intimidate and 'take on' the press. To an extent, this attitude was replicated under the Reagan Administration, with the broadcasting media after the 'honeymoon' period frequently being characterised as unpatriotic and destructive. In 1983, Reagan set up the 'Outreach Working Group on Central America', deliberately designed to exclude the press from the process of information dissemination from the Administration to elite groups.[115] Such attitudes and devices, however, are ultimately counter-productive. Neither the Watergate affair nor Irangate were products of a media conspiracy. Nonetheless, neither may be understood outside the context of a pre-existing breakdown in the mutually supportive Presidential-press relationship.

Notes

1   Cited in M. Small, 'Public opinion', in A. De Conde, ed., *Encyclopaedia of American Foreign Policy*, New York, 3, 1978, pp. 844–5. (See W. Lippmann, *Public Opinion*, New York, 1922.)

2   W. Lippmann, *The Public Philosophy*, London, 1955. The context of Lippmann's argument was set by McCarthyism (see *The Public Philosophy*, p. 55).

3   See S. Welch, 'American public opinion: consensus, cleavage and constraint', in D.P. Forsythe, ed., *American Foreign Policy in an Uncertain World*, Lincoln (Nebraska), 1984, pp. 21–47, pp. 22–3.

4   *Meeting the Communist Threat*, New York, 1988, p. 80.

5   See S. J. Rosenstone, 'Economic adversity and voter turnout', *American Journal of Political Science*, 26, 1982, pp. 212–32.

6   W. R. Schneider, 'Rambo and reality: having it both ways', in K. Oye *et al.*, eds., *Eagle Resurgent*, Boston, 1987, pp. 41–75 at p. 49. See also W. R. Schneider, 'Conservatism, not interventionism: trends in foreign policy opinion, 1974–82', in K. Oye *et al.*, eds., *Eagle Defiant*, Boston, 1983, pp. 33–64; and P. Geyelin, 'The Adams doctrine and the dream of disengagement', in S.J. Ungar, ed., *Estrangement: America and the World*, New York, 1985, pp. 193–224, p. 202.

7   See generally, J.E. Rielly, ed., *American Public Opinion and U.S. Foreign Policy 1987*, Chicago, 1987.

8   See L.S. Wittner, *Cold War America*, New York, 1978, ch. 2.

9   See, e.g., T. W. Smith, 'American attitudes toward the Soviet Union and communism', *Public Opinion Quarterly*, 47, 1983, pp. 277–92.

10   T.W. Smith, 'Nuclear anxiety', *Public Opinion Quarterly*, 52, 1988, pp. 557–75.

11   *Ibid.*, p. 560.

12   See, e.g., the table reproduced in W. LaFeber, *The American Age*, New York, 1989, p. 636.

13   R. B. Levering, *The Public and American Foreign Policy, 1918–1978*, New York, 1978, p. 103.

14   See Schneider, 'Conservatism, not interventionism'. Also R. Rose, *The Postmodern President*, Chatham (New Jersey), 1988, p. 228.

15   J. E. Mueller, *War, Presidents and Public Opinion*, New York, 1973.

16   See B. Russett, 'The revolt of the masses: public opinion on military expenditures', in B. Russett, ed., *Peace, War and Numbers*, Beverley Hills, 1972, pp. 299–319; L. Kriesberg and R. Klein, 'Changes in public support for U.S. military spending', *Journal of Political and Military Sociology*, 10, 1980, pp. 275–97.

17   See, e.g., F. L. Klingberg, *Cyclical Trends in American Foreign Policy Moods*, Lanham (Maryland), 1983; M. Roskin, 'From Pearl Harbour to Vietnam: shifting generational paradigms', *Political Science Quarterly*, 89, 1974, pp. 563–88.

18   N. A. Graebner, 'Public opinion and foreign policy: a pragmatic view', in D.C. Piper and R.J. Tercheck, eds., *Interaction: Foreign Policy and Public Policy*, Washington D.C., 1983, pp. 11–34, p. 16.

19   J.R. Lee, 'Rallying around the flag', *Presidential Studies Quarterly*, 7, 1977, pp. 252–6; also P. J. Canover and L. Sigelman, 'Presidential influence and public opinion: the case of the Iranian hostage crisis', *Social Science Quarterly*, 63, 1982, pp. 249–64. See also D. Morgan, *The Flacks of Washington*, New York, 1986.

20   R. Y. Shapiro and B. I. Page, 'Foreign policy and the rational public', *Journal of Conflict Resolution*, 32, 1988, pp. 211–47

21   A. Campbell *et al.*, *The American Voter*, New York, 1960; V.O. Key, *The Responsible Electorate*, New York, 1966.

22   Key, The Responsible Electorate, p. 8.

23   'Foreign policy and the rational public', p. 244 (V. O. Key, *Public Opinion and American Democracy*, New York, 1961). Shapiro and Page criticise the argument of G. A. Almond, *The American People and Foreign Policy*, New York, 1950. See also J. E. Holmes, *The Mood/Interest Theory of American Foreign Policy*, Lexington (Kentucky), 1985.

24   'Foreign policy and the rational public', pp. 214, 239.

25   See M. K. Jennings and R. G. Niemi, *Generations and Politics*, Princeton, 1981, pp. 386–91.

26   *War, Presidents and Public Opinion.*

27   See B. B. Hughes, *The Domestic Context of American Foreign Policy*, San Francisco, 1978, pp. 23–5; J. A. Nathan and J. K. Oliver, *Foreign Policy Making and the American Political System*, 2nd ed., Boston, 1987, p. 205. Possibly one or two per cent of 'opinion leaders' may be active in public affairs.

28   J. S. Nye, 'The domestic environment of U.S. policy making', in A. L. Horelick, ed., *U.S.–Soviet Relations: The Next Phase*, New York, 1986, pp. 111–26, p. 115. See also B. Russett and D. DeLuca, ' "Don't tread on me": public opinion and foreign policy in the eighties', *Political Science Quarterly*, 96, 1981, pp. 381–99.

29   'American public opinion' p. 39. See also R. Oldendick and B. Bardes, 'Mass and elite foreign policy opinions', *Public Opinion Quarterly*, 46, 1982, pp. 368–82; K. A. Lamb, *The Guardians*, New York, 1982, pp. 178–91; W. O. Chittick and K. R. Billingsley, 'The structure of elite foreign policy beliefs', *Western Political Quarterly*, 42, 1989, pp. 201–24.

30   See M. Mandelbaum and W. Schneider, 'The new internationalisms', in K. Oye *et al.*, eds., *Eagle Entangled*, New York, 1979, pp. 34–88; M. A. Maggiotto and E. R. Wittkopf, 'American public attitudes towards foreign policy', *International Studies Quarterly*, 25, 1981, pp. 601–31; O. R. Holsti and J.N. Rosenau, *American Leadership in World Affairs: Vietnam and the Breakdown of Consensus*, Boston, 1984, ch. 4.

31   See J. E. Rielly, 'The American mood: a foreign policy of self interest', *Foreign Policy*, 34, 1979, pp. 74–86.

32 B. Sussman, *What Americans Really Think*, New York, 1988, p. 5.

33 See R. Sobel, 'Public opinion about United States intervention in El Salvador and Nicaragua', *Public Opinion Quarterly*, 53, 1989, pp. 114–28. See also E.C. Ladd, 'Where the public stands on Nicaragua', *Public Opinion*, 9, 1987, pp. 2–4, 59–60.

34 Sobel, 'Public opinion', p. 115.

35 See T. L. Deibel, 'Reagan's mixed legacy', *Foreign Policy*, 75, 1989, pp. 34–55, p. 37.

36 See M. Smith, 'The Reagan Administration's foreign policy, 1981–1985: learning to live with uncertainty?', *Political Studies*, 36, 1988, pp. 52–73.

37 R. W. Tucker, 'Reagan's foreign policy', *Foreign Affairs*, 68, 1989, pp. 2–27, p. 12.

38 'Reagan's mixed legacy', p. 52.

39 B. C. Cohen, *The Public's Impact on Foreign Policy*, Boston, 1973, pp. 58–70.

40 See E. den Oudsten, 'European attitudes on nuclear defence', in C. Marsh and C. Fraser, eds., *Public Opinion and Nuclear Weapons*, London, 1989, pp. 37–56, at p. 37.

41 See J. Dumbrell, 'Congress and the antiwar movement', in J. Dumbrell, ed., *Vietnam and the Antiwar Movement*, Aldershot, 1989, pp. 101–12, at p. 108.

42 Shapiro and Page, 'Foreign policy and the rational public', p. 237. See also L. A. Kusnitz, *Public Opinion and Foreign Policy: America's China Policy, 1949–1979*, Westport (Connecticut), 1984.

43 See, e.g., W. G. Jacoby, 'The impact of party identification on issue attitudes', *American Journal of Political Science*, 32, 1988, pp. 642–61; R. B. Levering, 'Public opinion, foreign policy, and American politics since the 1960's', *Diplomatic History*, 13, 1989, pp. 383–94, p. 391.

44 'Reagan's foreign policy', p. 5.

45 See N. J. Ornstein and M. Schmitt, 'The 1988 election', *Foreign Affairs*, 68, 1989, pp. 40–2, p. 46.

46 *Guardian*, 11 October 1988.

47 W. Schneider, 'The November 4 vote for President', in A. Ranney, ed., *The American Elections of 1980*, Washington D.C., 1981, pp. 212–62, p. 233.

48 Ornstein and Schmitt, 'The 1988 election', p. 41.

49 In 1984, men split 62–37 for Reagan against Mondale, women 56–44; in 1988, the Bush' Dukakis split was 57–41 for men, 50–49 for women. (See P. Norris, 'The 1988 American elections: long, medium and short-term explanations', *The Political Quarterly*, 60, 1989, pp. 204–21, p. 210.)

50 E. Klein, *Gender Politics*, Cambridge (Massachusetts), 1984, p. 160; T. L. Brewer, *American Foreign Policy*, 1986, p. 64; R. Gatlin, *American Women since 1945*, London, 1987, p. 242.

51 Y. King, 'All is connectedness: scenes from the Women's Pentagon Action USA', in L. Jones, ed., *Keeping the Peace*, London, 1983, pp. 40–63, p. 59. See also J. Brenner, 'Beyond essentialism: feminist theory and strategy in the peace movement', in M. Davis and M. Sprinker, eds., *Reshaping the U.S.*

Left, London, 1988, pp. 93–113.

52 The Council published *A Guide to Women Foreign Policy Specialists: Directory*, Washington D.C., 1987.

53 S. E. Bennett, *Apathy in America*, Dobbs Ferry (New York), 1986, pp. 73–4; R. B. Rapoport, 'The sex gap in political persuading', *American Journal of Political Science*, 25, 1981, pp. 32–48. See also K. Beckwith, *American Women and Political Participation*, Westport (Connecticut), 1986.

54 J. Hoff-Wilson, 'Of mice and men', in E. P. Crapol, ed., *Women and American Foreign Policy*, Westport (Connecticut), 1987, pp. 170–86, p. 170 (also p. xii).

55 See H. L. Calkin, *Women in American Foreign Affairs*, Washington D.C., 1977; M. S. Olmsted *et al.*, *Women at State*, Washington D.C., 1984.

56 Statement of Representative Patricia Schroeder, House Committee on Foreign Affairs, Committee print: *Women's Perspectives on U.S. Foreign Policy* (Women's Foreign Policy Council informal Congressional hearing, 19 November 1987), Washington D.C., 1988, p. 4.

57 Hoff-Wilson, 'Of mice and men', p. 176.

58 *Ibid.*, pp. 179–82.

59 *Women's Perspectives*, p. 13.

60 *Ibid.*, p. 17.

61 See, e.g., E.M. Schreiber, 'Anti-war demonstrations and American public opinion on the war in Vietnam', *British Journal of Sociology*, 27, 1976, pp. 225–36; J. P. Robinson, 'Balance theory and Vietnam related attitudes', in D. Nimmo and C. M. Bonjean, eds., *Political Attitudes and Public Opinion*, New York, 1972, pp. 338–61, at p. 353.

62 M. Small, *Johnson, Nixon and the Doves*, New Brunswick, 1988, p. 21. See also P. Burstein and W. Freudenberg, 'Changing public policy: the impact of public opinion, antiwar demonstrations, and war costs on Senate voting on Vietnam war motions', *American Journal of Sociology*, 84, 1978, pp. 99–122.

63 See A. Cockburn and J. Ridgeway, 'The freeze movement versus Reagan', *New Left Review*, 137, 1983, pp. 5–21; W. Kaltefleiter and R. L. Pfaltzgraff, eds., *The Peace Movements in Europe and the United States*, London, 1985; D. C. Waller, *Congress and the Nuclear Freeze*, Amherst (Massachusetts), 1987; F. B. McCrea and E. Markle, *Minutes to Midnight*, London, 1989.

64 Shapiro and Page, 'Foreign policy and the rational public', p. 243.

65 R. Osgood, *The Nuclear Dilemma in American Strategic Thought*, London, 1988. See also H. Cleveland and L. P. Bloomfield, *Prospects for Peacemaking: A Citizen's Guide to Safer Nuclear Strategy*, London, 1987 (on the 1984 'Minnesota experiment' involving dialogue between Minnesota citizens and defence specialists).

66 Waller, *Congress and the Nuclear Freeze*, ch. 8.

67 *Ibid.*, pp. 300–01.

68 See J. Castell, *The Bishops and the Bomb*, Garden City (New York), 1983; C. Rose, *Campaigns against Western Defense*, London, 1986, ch. 11.

69 M.T. Hayes, 'Incrementalism as dramaturgy: the case of the nuclear freeze', *Polity*, 19, 1987, pp. 443–63, p. 444. See also P. Watanabe, 'Giving peace a chance', in P. Davies and F. A. Waldstein, eds., *Political Issues in*

America Today, Manchester, 1987, pp. 215–27.

70 See P. Solo, *From Protest to Policy: Beyond the Freeze to Common Security*, Cambridge (Massachusetts), 1988 for the view that public pressure forced Reagan's hand on arms control. See also a critical review of this book in *Orbis*, 33, 1989, p. 128 (A. Garfinkle).

71 J. Trinkl, 'Struggles for disarmament', in Davis and Sprinker, eds., *Reshaping the U.S. Left*, pp. 51–62, p. 55.

72 See L. E. Ambrosius, 'The President, the Congress and American foreign policy: the ethnic factor', in G. Rystad, ed., *Congress and American Foreign Policy*, Sweden, 1981, pp. 62–89; A. A. Said, ed., *Ethnicity and U.S. Foreign Policy*, New York, 1977; M.E. Ahrari, ed., *Ethnic Groups and U.S. Foreign Policy*, New York, 1987.

73 See K. R. Legg, 'Congress as Trojan horse? The Turkish embargo problem, 1974–1978', in J. Spanier and J. Nogee, eds., *Congress, the President and American Foreign Policy*, New York, 1981, pp. 107–31; P. Watanabe, *Ethnic Groups, Congress and American Foreign Policy: The Politics of the Turkish Arms Embargo*, Westport (Connecticut), 1984, pp. 167–68.

74 See I. A. Lewis, 'American Jews and Israel', *Public Opinion*, 11, 1988, pp. 53–5.

75 P. Findley, *They Dare to Speak Out*, Westport, 1985, p. 25.

76 M. C. Feuerweger, *Congress and Israel*, Westport, 1979, p. 81. See also T. P. O'Neill, *Man of the House*, New York, 1987, pp. 362–63; C. A. Rubenberg, *Israel and the American National Interest*, Urbana-Champaign (Illinois), 1986.

77 W. B. Quandt, *Decade of Decisions: American Policy toward the Arab-Israeli Conflict of 1967–76*, Berkeley, 1977, p. 22.

78 See Ambrosius, 'The President, the Congress', p. 75; also, P. Stern, *Water's Edge: Domestic Politics and the Making of American Foreign Policy*, Westport, 1979.

79 G. F. Kennan, *Memoirs, Volume Two: 1950–1963*, Boston, 1967, p. 286.

80 J. E. Miller, 'Taking off the gloves: the United States and the Italian elections of 1948', *Diplomatic History*, 7, 1983, pp. 35–56.

81 See C. Simpson, *Blowback: America's Recruitment of Nazis and its Effects on the Cold War*, London, 1988, p. 267. Also S. A. Garrett, 'Eastern European ethnic groups and American foreign policy', *Political Science Quarterly*, 93, 1978, pp. 301–23.

82 Garrett, 'Eastern Europe ethnic groups', pp. 314–15.

83 L.M. Lees, 'National security and ethnicity', *Diplomatic History*, 11, 1987, pp. 113–26, p. 113.

84 J. Holland, *The American Connection: U.S. Guns, Money and Influence in Northern Ireland*, Dublin, 1989, p. xiv, ch. 2; A. Guelke, 'The American connection to the Northern Ireland conflict', *Irish Studies in International Affairs*, 1, 1984, pp. 3–40, pp. 32, 38.

85 Interview with Robert Blancato, staff aide to Mario Biaggi, Washington D.C., 14 July 1988.

86 Holland, *The American Connection*, pp. 120, 140.

87 Blancato interview.

88   *Congressional Record*, 17 February 1988, E247.
89   S. Cronin, *Washington's Irish Policy 1916–1986*, Dublin, 1987, p. 313.
90   Holland, *The American Connection*, ch. 4; Guelke, 'The American connection', p. 33.
91   *Congressional Record*, 17 March 1988, S2507.
92   Holland, *The American Connection*, p. 151.
93   Cronin, *Washington's Irish Policy*, p. 326. Powell (as a Unionist Member of Parliament) argued that US policy was motivated by a desire to secure membership of NATO by a united Ireland (see Guelke, 'The American connection', p. 27).
94   *Congressional Record*, 15 June 1988, E2016.
95   *Ibid.*, 16 June 1988, E2050.
96   *Ibid.*, 17 May 1988, E1561.
97   *Ibid.*, 8 March 1988, E566.
98   *Irish Times*, 8–10 October 1984 (cited in P. Bew and H. Patterson, *The British State and the Ulster Crisis*, London, 1985, p. 135); see also G. Moorhouse, *Imperial City: The Rise and Rise of New York*, London, 1988, pp. 49–52; R. J. Thompson and J. R. Rudolph, 'Irish-Americans in the American Foreign-Policy-Making Process', in Ahrari, ed., *Ethnic Groups*, pp. 135–53.
99   See M. Sithole, 'Black Americans and United States policy towards Africa', *African Affairs*, 85, 1986, pp. 325–50, 339, 350. Also M. Weil, 'Can the blacks do for Africa what the Jews did for Israel?', *Foreign Policy*, 41, 1974, pp. 109–21; S. Metz, 'The anti apartheid movement and the populist instinct in American politics', *Political Science Quarterly*, 101, 1986, pp. 379–95; P. Rich, 'United States containment policy, South Africa and the apartheid dilemma', *Review of International Studies*, 14, 1988, pp. 179–94. See also K. Longmyer, 'Black Americans' demands', *Foreign Policy*, 60, 1985, pp. 10–25.
100 See R. Tostade, 'Political participation', in P. S. J. Cafferty and N. C. McCready, eds., *Hispanics in the United States*, New Brunswick (New Jersey), 1985, pp. 235–52. Also B. Richardson, 'Hispanic American concerns', *Foreign Policy*, 60, 1985, pp. 26–51.
101 J. Reston, *The Artillery of the Press: Its Influence on American Foreign Policy*, New York, 1967, ch. 2, p. 15.
102 D. Halberstam, *The Powers that Be*, London, 1979, pp. 429–30.
103 See P. Braestrup, *Big Story*, Boulder (Colorado), 1977.
104 Halberstam, *The Powers that Be*, pp. 532–3, 553–5.
105 D. C. Hallin, *The 'Uncensored War': The Media and Vietnam*, New York, 1986, pp. 129–31.
106 See C. Seymour-Ure, *The American President: Power and Communication*, London, 1982, p. 147; K. J. Turner, *Lyndon Johnson's Dual War: Vietnam and the Press*, Chicago, 1985, p. 6. But see also S.C. Taylor, 'Reporting history: journalists and the Vietnam war', *Reviews in American History*, 13, 1985, pp. 451–61.
107 D. A. Graber, *Mass Media and American Politics*, Washington D.C., 1985, p. 308.
108 See W. Schneider, 'Public opinion', in J.S. Nye, ed., *The Making of America's Soviet Policy*, New Haven, 1984, pp. 11–35; M.E. McCombs and D.R. Shaw, 'The agenda setting function of the mass media', *Public Opinion*

Quarterly, 36, 1972, pp. 203–21; M. Robinson and M. Sheehan, *Over the Wire and on TV*, New York, 1983; M. B. Grossman and M. J. Kumar, *Portraying the President*, Baltimore, 1981, p. 236; M. Linsky, *Impact: How the Press Affects Federal Policymaking*, New York, 1986.

109 See M. J. Parenti, *Inventing Reality*, New York, 1986; C. Mouffe, 'Hegemony and ideology in Gramsci', in C. Mouffe, ed., *Gramsci and Marxist Theory*, London, 1979, pp. 168–204; T. Bottomore, ed., *A Dictionary of Marxist Thought*, Oxford, 1983, pp. 200–03; also W. L. Bennett, *Public Opinion in American Politics*, New York, 1980.

110 Hallin, *The 'Uncensored War'*, p. 196.

111 See M. Hertsgaard, *On Bended Knee: The Press and the Reagan Presidency*, New York, 1988.

112 See E. J. Epstein, 'The selection of reality', in E. Abel, ed., *What's News: The Media in American Society*, San Francisco, 1981, pp. 119–82.

113 Turner, *Lyndon Johnson's Dual War*, p. 7.

114 P. Anderson, *The President's Men*, Garden City (New York), 1968, p. 187.

115 See J. C. Spear, *Presidents and the Press: The Nixon Legacy*, Cambridge (Massachusetts), 1984, pp. 39–43, 291; J. Tebbel and S. M. Watts, *The Press and the Presidency*, New York, 1985, pp. 544–7.

8

Private and regional power

1 Corporations and foreign policy

(a) *Multinationals and American power*   This chapter will attempt to indicate the kind of influence exerted by US-based multinational corporations over American foreign policy. Firstly, however, it is necessary to redeem a promise made in Chapter 1 and address the following question: how far should such multinationals be regarded as an integrated part of 'American' power?

In 1987, it was estimated that forty-one of the world's largest economic entities (countries and corporations) were multinational corporations (MNCs). General Motors had an annual product size significantly larger than that of South Africa, Argentina or Yugoslavia. At 96.37 billion dollars, General Motors' annual product was about one-fifth the size of the United Kingdom's. In the early 1980s, MNCs marketed approximately 80 per cent of trade in the world's market economies. American domination of the multinational enterprise has declined, but as noted in Chapter 1, it is still not inappropriate to speak of American 'hegemony'. In 1965, sixty-nine of the world's leading 100 corporations were American; in 1984 the figure was forty-six. Inward investment into the United States, rapidly accelerating in the period since 1973, also became a significant domestic political issue. So, by the later 1980s, the United States had become not only the world's largest foreign investor, not only the world's largest debtor nation, but also the world's largest host for inward foreign investment.[1]

These changing investment patterns point up the saliency of the interdependency paradigm of contemporary international relations, and should alert us to some of the complex difficulties inherent in a realist interpretation of 'American power'. It should also be remembered that MNCs themselves vary considerably in terms of relationships between the American parent company and overseas subsidiaries. D. H. Blake and R. S. Walters suggest a threefold classification: the 'parent-dominant, subsidiary subservient' type; the quasi – 'international holding company in which the various subsidiaries operate with a high degree of autonomy'; and 'the integrated international enterprise' with the 'parent company's operations as well as the subsidiaries" being 'incorporated into an overall managerial effort'.[2] The third type appears to be increasingly important, with signs also of American MNCs dropping their traditional caution regarding sharing the ownership of subsidiaries with local, host interests.[3].

Such trends indicate some of the problems of attempting too close an identification between MNCs and 'American' power. According to Raymond Vernon's *Sovereignty at Bay* (1971)'[4] MNCs should be seen as genuinely transnational (or 'anational') institutions: rational products of post-war economic conditions – improved international communications, new opportunities to develop economies of scale, and so on – and bastions of an essentially benevolent liberal world order. A similar anationalism was postulated in R. J. Barnet and R. E. Muller's *Global Reach* (1974).[5] But for Barnet and Muller, multinationals are oligopolies; they erode competition and cat against the insterests of both parent and host countries.

Upholders of the 'anationalism' of MNCs would argue that their true character was camouflaged in the post-1945 era by the apparent identity between US security and American business interests. As Bergsten, Horst and Moran put it, in the post-war years, 'restoration of an open, multilateral economic system ranked alongside "no more Munichs" as a cornerstone of foreign policy'.[6] The economic institutions of the Cold War provided the environment for Americanm corporations to expand.[7] With the ebbing of US military and economic hegemony, however, it is possible to argue that American MNCs will survive as more autonomous institutions, 'putting the use of their oligopoly power increasingly at the service of diverse national claimants'.[8]

Against 'anational' interpretations of MNC power are ranged the forces of Marxian theories of economic imperialism and realist (or 'neo-mercantilist') theories of state power. As noted in Chapter 1, Marxian theory is concerned primarily with the structure and power of capital itself, rather than with the power of particular nation states. However, core capitalist interests are generally identified with the

United States, albeit a 'late-imperial' United States.[9] Rejecting pluralist ideas of foreign policy-making, Marxists would see US foreign policy as the product of the desire/need to secure overseas markets, protect business interests and maintain access to valuable raw materials.[10] 'Neo-mercantilists' also tend to discount conventional ideas of pluralism in foreign policy-making. If retained at all, the notion of a pluralist policy-making process tends to serve as an explanation for policies which distort the furtherance of the authentic national interest. 'Neo-mercantilists' would reverse the Marxian insistence on interpreting US foreign policy as a mechanism for supporting US business interests. Rather, the emphasis here is on the 'promotion of international economic power and domestic prosperity' as 'aspects of the larger objective of preserving national strength in relation to other states'.[11] Economic considerations are seen as subordinate to, or at least functioning primarily to support, strategic and security issues.

Where does this leave our enquiry into the relation of corporate multinational to American national power? Certainly, it appears that MNCs, as 'meso-economic' sector, are susceptible to political and economic analysis without constant reference to parent, or indeed, host states.[12] However, any concept of MNC autonomy or transcendent 'anationalism' is wildly overdrawn. Interdependency undermines not only 'hard' realist or 'neo-mercantilist' positions. It also undermines the putative autonomy of any particular actor or sector within the international political economy, including the 'meso-economic' sector itself. By the same token, state policy-making structures should not be considered as autonomous units, unaffected by the wider national or international political economy. Neither, however, should they be considered as inert epiphenomena. (The 'weak' American state[13] is especially susceptible to such treatment.) Marxian ideas of 'relative autonomy' (referred to in Chapter 2) point away from epiphenomenal treatments of the state. So does the growing body of state-centred, 'domestic structures' writing which seeks to carve out an 'independent' role for the state, even in a world of complex interdependence.[14]

Business and governmental elites in the United States overlap and interpenetrate; they share the same liberal values and commitments to mutually reinforcing capitalism and democracy. However, a 'relatively autonomous' state, influenced by its own traditions and bureaucratic histories, does impinge upon business autonomy. It sets trade and anti-trust policies; it may prohibit trade with 'enemy' nations.[15] (Also relevant to the question of MNC autonomy is the clear evidence concerning the enhanced power of host states.)[16] As will become apparent in the following discussion, empirical investigation of the relationship between the American state and American MNCs reveals a tale of complex linkages, overlapping but not identical interests, potential and actual disputes.

(b) *Multinationals and American foreign policy*   Studies of business influence on American foreign policy tend to focus upon foreign economic and trade policy. Again, however, the rise of interdependence has called into question the extent to which policy may be so compartmentalised. Trade policy itself may be both 'strategic' (designed to promote a liberal world order, rooted in free trade) and 'manipulative' (involving devices like sanctions and 'most-favoured' nation-trade relationships).[17] Nonetheless, the 'issue area' approach to this question of business influence still provides at least a hypothetical framework for analysis. Clearly, business is not interested equally intensely in all foreign policy questions; nor do all foreign policy issues offer equal opportunities for the expression of (aggregated or disaggregated) business interests. Conventionally delineated issue areas are regulative, distributive, redistributive and security.[18] Of these categories, security issues are generally regarded as the least domestically divisive, and are more generally settled at an elite, state level.[19] Distributive politics involve the dispersal of tangible benefits where 'everyone who counts politically'[20] gains something. Distributive politics are the stuff of the Congressional pork barrel and the subject of relatively disaggregated business lobbying. Regulative issues involve clear winners and losers and are the subject of more complex governmental and societal interactions. (McGowan and Walker offer, as an example of regulative politics, 'the complex patterns of interactions among governmental and nongovernmental actors' over General Agreement on Tariffs and Trade (GATT) issues 'within and across national boundaries').[21] Redistributive politics involve intense conflict, with fundamental issues of power at stake, with clear winners and losers, and something approaching a mass public mobilisation. Such occasions are rare in modern US history, though Zimmerman cites the domestic conflict over the Vietnam war.[22]

Realist accounts tend either to assume or to argue for the primacy of security issues. Krasner argues that the 'state' – in the American context, the White House or State Department – may be able to redefine distributive or regulative issues into security issues. This has the effect of narrowing the cast of decisional actors to leading state officials. In the 'weak' American state, such redefinition tends to produce negative results; state officials are able to resist business pressure, but not positively to transform it.[23] Krasner's *Defending the National Interest* (1978) demonstrates the possibilities of (real and perceived) divergence between state and business interests, and the ability of the state to achieve its 'security' ends. In concentrating on American MNCs involved in the extraction of raw materials, Krasner assaults those cruder Marxist accounts which postulate clear, determined correlations between such activity and state policy. In fact, it is not especially difficult to find examples of business and state interests diverging, with the state generally emerging victorious. Congressional cancellation, in the mid-1970s post-Vietnam environment, of the Overseas Private Investment Corporation is one such example.[24] Restrictions on free trade resulting from American-Soviet rivalry have also harmed the immediate interests of US multinationals, offering opportunities to rivals. Proponents of close, determined correlation between MNC interest and state policy also have to address questions of policy inconsistency. H. B. Malmgren declared in 1972 that he only wished that foreign economic policy had been as coherent as radical critics claimed.[25] US governmental commitment to free trade has always varied across different sectors of trade policy. Thus, state intervention in the agricultural sector has been sanctioned to a far greater degree than in manufacturing or services. It is difficult to explain such differences entirely in terms of the divergent objective needs of the relevant corporations.[26] (A Marxist rejoinder to all this would invoke the 'relative autonomy' of the state and the shifting structural requirements of capital.)

If the American state does not always pursue policies which are to the immediate, declared interest of giant corporations, then the reverse also is true. MNC currency speculation in the early 1970s and co-operation in the Arab embargo on oil supplies to the US in 1973/74 are cases in point.[27] The governmental-MNC relationship is complex, with occasional disruptions and disfunctions, but with a strong underlying sense of shared interest. MNCs have been used to enforce US foreign policy: for example, by denying the technology needed to develop a French nuclear force in the 1960s. They have been used for intelligence gathering.[28] Private interests have also been involved in grey areas of foreign policy, deliberately kept at one remove from the public domain and subject to the doctrine of 'plausible deniability'. The role of International Telephone and Telegraph in mobilising opposition to the Allende regime in Chile in the early 1970's is now widely acknowledged.[29] David Rockefeller, chairman of Chase Manhattan bank, was an influential actor in US-Iranian relations prior to the 1979 revolution.[30] He had a leading role in organising the Trilateral Commission, an important influence in the foreign policy of the Carter Presidency. Throughout the early 1980s there were repeated reports of corporations channelling money to the *contra* rebels in Nicaragua. Such funding, of course, may occur without official sanction, knowledge or support. Even in this unlikely event, in a disaggregated, interdependent world, it may still be held to contribute to 'American' foreign policy. In the case of the Reagan Administration's Nicaraguan policy, however, there is little doubt about its utilisation of what the Tower Commission called 'private and foreign' (principally Israeli) 'sources'. Colonel North openly solicited money from private sources to fund *contra* operations. According to the Tower Commission, such abuses give 'private and foreign sources potentially powerful leverage in the form of demands for return favours or even blackmail'.[31]

It is clear that, although exact correlation between state policy and MNC interests does not exist, MNCs represent a powerful, and largely unaccountable influence on (and even implementer of) US foreign policy. It is important here to avoid conspiracy theory. Corporations for the most part exert their influence in fairly obvious ways. At one level, their influence is an inherent and inescapable part of the world capitalist system. The early and mid-1980s rescheduling of Third World debts was largely the work of private creditors, and significantly influenced the US government-sponsored Baker plan.[32] In an address given at the conservative Conference Board in 1988, senior economist Steven Malin spoke of foreign policy changes being 'forced' by the operations of the international bond market.[33] This market tends to be regarded by policy-makers as more sensitive and indicative of future trends than the domestic stock market. It has increased in importance not only with the burgeoning US debt, but also with the movement in the American economy towards financial services and away from manufacturing.

At another level, corporate power may be observed in lobbying and political funding activities. Corporate influence-buying philosophy is illustrated in the fact that, in the 1986 Congressional elections, General Electric's political action committee gave funds to thirty-four House candidates who did not even face an opponent.[34] Such activity is clearly tantamount to crude influence-buying, rather than legitimate participation in the democratic process. With their massive lobbying resources, huge corporations are able to embed themselves securely within the 'iron triangles' or 'subgovernments' of policy-making. Through smart footwork and influence in Congress, 130 large corporations managed, in one or more years during the period 1982–85, to avoid paying any tax on profits whatsoever. This prompted Illinois Democratic Senator Paul Simon to point out that 'the janitor at General Electric pays more taxes than GE'.[35]

The business lobby is easily the most powerful on Capitol Hill. However, as pluralists will point out, 'business' should not be regarded as a monolith. Certainly, primarily domestic-oriented business coalitions (like Business Roundtable and the US Chamber of Commerce) do attempt to co-ordinate business pressure also in foreign policy. However, such co-ordination can camouflage both intra-business and even intra-industry disagreements. T. M. Franck and E. Weisband cite the example of the lobbying of Congress in the early 1970s by the US fisheries industry to set up a 200-mile fishery exclusion zone; this was unsuccessfully opposed by tuna and shrimping interests who feared reciprocal action by Japan.[36] Also, as R. A. Pastor has observed, most studies of interest group pressure conclude that 'all groups, regardless of their alleged clout, lose some of the time and win some of the time'.[37] Failure may be due, for example, to unexpected changes of Congressional opinion or personnel, or to the presence of countervailing interests.

Contemporary debate about MNC influence over US trade policy centres on the extent to which protectionism has emerged as an important national (and indeed international) force. American labour (especially the AFL-CIO) was converted to a protectionist position in the early 1970s. Protectionism has for some time been seen as a likely result of the combination of America's 'weak' state and changing public reactions to relative economic decline.[38] Protectionist demands have arisen in the context both of Congressional elections – for example, in connection with the Southern textile industry in 1986 – and in the 1988 Presidential race, especially with the Democratic nomination candidacy of Richard Gephardt. It was widely expected that a degree of protectionism would be written into the 1988 trade bill. In fact, the protectionist character of the 1988 Omnibus Trade and Competitiveness Act was somewhat muted. The Gephardt amendment, which would have mandated retaliation against countries (especially Japan) which failed to reduce their trade surplus with the US, was defeated. J. E. Spero has described the Act as embodying a 'commitment to trade liberalisation through multi-lateral' (GATT) 'negotiations'.[39] Other commentators have been less impressed by the 'free trade' thrust of the 1988 trade bill, and indeed by the claims that the US-Canadian free trade agreement does not really represent a retreat from multilateralism. The 1988 Act contains the retaliatory 'Toshiba' provision, stipulating sanctions against countries in breach of Western strategic control roles. It also, according to J. Bhagwati, provides numerous opportunities for protectionists in the US to tie up foreign rivals in lengthy investigations into 'breach of fair trade' complaints.[40]

The 1988 trade bill did, no doubt, to some degree bear the imprint of Congressional, extra-corporate, even popular, protectionist sympathies. However, it also reflected changing MNC preferences. It tends to be assumed that multinationals will always favour low tariffs, with business preference for protection being confined to smaller, national firms in competition with imports. Yet many MNCs now tend to steer a new path between protectionism and free trade towards 'strategic trade policy'. The American semiconductor industry has lobbied for a closure of domestic markets to Japanese corporations who do not purchase US microchips.[41] Increasing numbers of American MNCs seem to favour 'strategic' initiatives to retaliate against perceived abuses of fair trade. Milner and Yoffie argue that such demands reinforce American governmental ideas of fair play in trade policy, resembling a strategy of specific reciprocity. As such, they threaten to undermine the current GATT regime, with its basis in 'diffuse reciprocity in the form of unconditional most-favoured-nation status'.[42] MNC demands for a 'level playing field' in trade relations greatly influenced the negotiations pertaining to the US-Canadian free trade agreement. They are likely to be taken up by US governments and may underpin future conflicts with economic rivals. An interesting sidelight on this issue was displayed in a September 1989 speech given by CIA Director William Webster to the World Affairs Council in Los Angeles. Webster appeared to be staking out a role for the CIA in a world of fading Cold War rivalries. Warning that our 'political and military allies are also our economic competitors',

Webster hinted that such competitors were becoming increasingly important targets for US intelligence activity.[43]

(c) *Organised labour as a countervailing force?* Pluralist theory would suggest that organised labour operates as a countervailing force to the power of the multinational corporations. Such an assertion has never been especially convincing, but is particularly unpersuasive in the face of recent evidence of the declining influence of American labour unions. The late 1970s and 1980s were a disastrous period for union membership and influence within the Democratic party. The percentage of American workers belonging to unions declined from thirty-five in 1954 to under twenty by 1984.[44] Various explanations may be offered for this decline: from shifts in American economic activity towards Southwestern areas of traditional union weakness to labour's failure to adapt organisationally to a service and information-based economy. Labour clearly has declined in the face of an employers' offensive[45] and suffered because of the ability of American MNC's to use profits from foreign operations to undermine the bargaining position of American unions.[46]

The AFL-CIO conversion to a protectionist (or 'fair trade') position in the 1970s involved the articulation of a number of charges against economic internationalisation and multinational enterprise. MNC activity was seen as detrimental to the American balance of payments. Above all, multinational corporations were accused of exporting American jobs. For AFL-CIO head George Meany, the answer was 'fair trade, do unto others as they do to us'.[47] The defeat of labour-sponsored legislation to regulate MNCs (the Burke-Hartke bills) in the 1970s indicated the relative weakness of labour, even before the decline of the 1980s. As noted above, gains for 'strategic trade policy', to the extent that they have been incorporated into recent trade legislation, derived from changing MNC preferences rather than from the influence of organised labour.

As well as a reputation for corruption and violence, American labour has – from a European perspective – a reputation for hawkishness on foreign policy. The official AFL-CIO line on the Vietnam war was one of support for Administration positions. In his 1967 biennial 'State of the Union' message, Meany described the AFL-CIO view on Vietnam as neither 'hawk' nor 'dove' nor 'chicken'.[48] Since its battering by McCarthyism, American labour has been exceedingly anxious to establish impeccable anti-communist credentials. The AFL-CIO's

American Institute for Free Labour Development, for example, operated as a more or less overt instrument of Cold War propaganda.[49] Labour was not an enthusiastic supporter of detente in the early 1970s and by the end of the decade was supporting increased defence spending.[50]

Labour hawkishness is, of course, not the whole story. The Vietnam war divided labour just as it divided the whole country. The (impeccably anti-communist) Walter Reuther, leader of the United Auto Workers, opposed Meany's view on the war; the UAW broke from the AFL-CIO labour umbrella in the late 1960s. Anti-war labour organisations, such as the Labour Leadership Assembly for Peace which met in Chicago in 1967, were formed both within and without the AFL-CIO.[51] The AFL-CIO itself has opposed aid to rightist dictatorships and, for example, importation of chrome from white-led Rhodesia in the 1970s. Lane Kirkland, Meany's successor, tended to embrace traditional Cold War positions;[52] nonetheless, the American labour movement strongly opposed Reagan Administration policies of sacrificing social spending to the needs of the defence sector.

2 Foreign policy elites

The interpenetration of government and business elites in the United States has been well documented.[53] What tends to surprise Europeans is the extent to which such an elite (or elites) dominates both Democratic and Republican Administrations. President Carter's Cabinet contained at least three people who had been on the board of International Business Machines.[54] The Council on Foreign Relations, the best known of all foreign policy elite organisations, tends to be associated with policies advocated by the Democratic party. Its offshoot, the Trilateral Commission, provided ideas and personnel to the Carter Administration. It might be assumed that the Council lost influence in the early 1980s to organisations like the Committee on the Present Danger and the institutions of the New Right.[55] Yet Reagan's second Secretary of State, George Shultz, was a former CFR director. Vice President George Bush, Secretary of Defence Weinberger, CIA Director Casey and Shultz's predecessor, Alexander Haig, were CFR members as well.[56]

Such elite continuity fuels conspiracy theory, and the Council on Foreign Relations has been attacked from the left as an imperialistic Rockefeller interest, and from the right as an instrument of Wall

Street-Kremlin plans for one world government.[57] Transnational elite groups, like the Bilderberg meetings, have been similarly caught in a right-left pincer movement.[58] Of course, in a country like the United States, with a strong consensual commitment to free enterprise capitalism, the existence of strong links between government and business personnel is scarcely surprising. Influential foreign policy 'think tanks' (like Kissinger Associates) also exist primarily to make a profit. Business elites may show a slight disposition to hawkish foreign policy attitudes, but there is little evidence for the assumption that they are driven in these attitudes by narrow formulations of business interest.[59] There is no question that many elite foreign policy figures are motivated by the ideal of public service.[60]

Yet it is the continuity and narrowness of the foreign policy elite which, especially in a country as diverse as the United States, is disturbing. (The term 'elite' here is used in the radical populist 'power elite' sense; it may be held to encompass both elites which make crucial foreign policy decisions and – in Noam Chomsky's words – 'groups in managerial positions in the political and economic institutions' including 'the ideological institutions, the editorial positions and other positions of control within the media').[61] Since 1945 (and, indeed, before), top foreign policy positions have been dominated by white men from legal and/or business backgrounds and ready access to the 'revolving door' which separates the public from the private sector. Isaacson and Thomas's study, *The Wise Men* traces the interlocking backgrounds and careers of six central figures in the foreign policy elite of the 'American Century': Dean Acheson, Charles Bohlen, Averell Harriman, George Kennan, R.A. Lovett and J.J. McCloy. Such figures tend to dismiss the notion of a foreign policy 'establishment': 'Skull and Bones, Groton, that sort of thing.'[62] McCloy, sometime chairman of Chase Manhattan bank, Council of Foreign Relations director and president of the World Bank, was born in relatively humble circumstances in Philadelphia in 1895. Certainly, the foreign policy elite is, in the words of Isaacson and Thomas, capable of absorbing talented outsiders 'who are eager to accept its cultivating process'. McCloy came to embody elite attitudes of public service, Wall Street-governmental partnership, and the primacy of continuity over political partisanship. 'Damn it, I always forget,' President Franklin Roosevelt remarked upon being reminded that McCloy was not a Democrat.[63]

The elite is riven by fashions and factions. Various organisations –

RAND, the Brookings Institution, the American Enterprise Institute, the Hoover Institution – experience fluctuations in prestige and influence.[64] The left-leaning Institute for Policy Studies has also had an influence on the Democratic party agenda. In particular, the quasi-apolitical 'managerialism' characteristic of so many 'defence intellectuals' in the 1950s and 1960s, goes in and out of fashion. The Council on Foreign Relations clearly underwent significant opinion change in the 1970s.[65] The Reagan Administration saw the introduction of a seasoning of Westerners with New Right antecedents ('cowboys' rather than 'Yankees'), but the mixture at the top was not fundamentally altered.[66] (In considering the 1980s foreign policy elite, it should also be remembered that Reagan in 1987 appointed the first black National Security Adviser, Colin Powell.)

As Jerry Sanders has shown, the changing foreign policy environment of the late 1970s and early 1980s was shaped not so much by forces from the Sunbelt and the New Christian Right as by 'establishment' figures on the Committee on the Present Danger. Formed originally in 1940, the CPD represented an alliance of corporate (mainly Eastern Republican) and scientific-technocratic elites. Paul Nitze, principal author of NSC-68 and leading CPD figure throughout its history, shared a background and many associations with Isaacson and Thomas's 'wise men'. Emanating itself from the foreign policy elite, the CPD was able to accomplish an effective assault from the right on 'managerialism'. Its effectiveness was signalled with the 1981 publication, under Council of Foreign Relations auspices, of the hawkish study (co-authored by Nitze), *The Soviet Challenge: A Policy Framework for the 1980's.*[67]

The developing foreign policy agenda is regularly punctuated by such publications: 'think tank' documents setting out options and recommendations for the next Administration(s). On the right of the political spectrum, both the Hoover Institution and the Institute for Contemporary Studies (an American Enterprise Institute offshoot) competed with the CPD in attacking 'managerialism'. The Hoover Institution in 1988 produced another agenda-setting volume aimed at an incoming GOP Administration.[68]

Again, conspiracy metaphors are inappropriate. Such agenda-setting is open and observable. The suppression of information rather than its dissemination is characteristic of a conspiracy. The publication of new ideas by business-funded 'think tanks' is not the problem. What does raise anxieties is the narrowness of the range of policy options offered by the most influential of the foreign policy research institutions.[69] Competing foreign policy positions also manifestly do not form the stuff of popular politics: of, for example, George Bush's 'lowest common denominator' and *ad hominem* 1988 Presidential campaign. Democratic politics do not benefit from the existence of a narrow, relatively exclusive foreign policy elite.

3 Defence contractors and the 'military industrial complex'

Defence contracting firms constitute a special case of corporate power. Since the end of the Second World War the United States has been a 'warfare state'. In early 1946, the Joint Chiefs of Staff declared:

United States foreign policy should continually give consideration to our immediate capabilities for supporting our policy by arms if the occasion should demand, rather than to our long-term potential, which, owing to the length of time required for mobilisation of the nation's resources, might not be sufficient to avert disaster in another war.[70]

Defence spending did drop after the Second World War, but the Korean war saw it racing again to new heights. By the early 1950s, annual defence budgets were easily exceeding the fifteen billion dollar target set in the late 1940s. Defence mobilisation was defended through continual appeals to 'national security', a concept which sustained massive spending levels during an apparently endless Cold War.

The 'warfare state' created the kind of unaccountable, vested interests about which President Eisenhower warned in 1961. Figures released by the US Census Bureau in 1985 indicated how these interests had prospered during the Reagan Administration's military build-up of the early 1980s. In 1984, the ten largest defence contractors achieved an average 25 per cent return on equity. This should be contrasted with the average corporate figure of 12.8 per cent. Lockheed's profit as a percentage of equity was forty-two, and General Dynamic's thirty. The ten companies reported pipeline governmental orders for over eight billion dollars.[71]

The explanation for massive defence contractor profits does not lie in their greater efficiency relative to non-defence corporations. It lies in the privileges accruing to leading actors within the 'military industrial complex'. The Pentagon regularly compensates contractors who tender unsuccessful, even unsolicited, bids. Defence firms are able to defer paying taxes on profits, often for several years.

General Dynamics paid no taxes at all in the period 1972–85. (In 1984, it achieved profits of 683.6 million dollars.) The whole system is lubricated by frequent personnel interchange between the Pentagon, defence contractors and various research agencies, which act as 'transmission belts' between the contractors and its governmental client. A familiar Cold War joke was that the Pentagon runs the world's second largest planned economy after the Kremlin.[72]

Problems of vested interest have long been recognised: by a host of critical academic and journalistic commentators[73] and by numerous political and military figures since Eisenhower. In 1967, Secretary of Defence Robert McNamara alluded to the strong domestic pressures to deploy new weapons systems 'out of all proportion to the prudent level required'.[74] Admiral Hyman Rickover declared that, under the Reagan Administration, 'defence contractors have *carte blanche*. They can do anything they wish.'[75] Scientific opinion, from the anti-ballistic missile deployments of the 1960s to the 1980s Strategic Defence Initiative, has also mounted intermittent protest.[76] Academic 'biographies' of weapons systems regularly illustrate the role of invested interest (both contracting interests and inter-service rivalries).[77] Yet, although cruder versions of conspiracy theory should be rejected, corruption, inefficiency, and distorting effects on US foreign policy remain.[78] In April 1985, forty-five of the largest 100 contractors were under criminal investigation. A series of military procurement scandals broke out in the summer of 1988. Part of the problem seems to reside in the defence industry's (and, indeed, the Pentagon's) perception of 'feast' inevitably being followed by 'famine': calls for retrenchment, 'new looks', and defence cutbacks. The Reagan years saw the defence industry determined to enjoy the feast while tables were fully laden. Reagan's navy secretary, John Lehman, began a campaign to deregulate the industry and encourage competition. He attempted, for example, without success, to encourage another contractor to compete with General Dynamics to build nuclear-powered missile submarines. (The defence industry attempted to turn the new deregulatory climate to its advantage by lobbying against Congressional attempts to centralise oversight of weapons development.) During the Reagan years, Congressional investigations regularly uncovered examples of fraud and inefficiency: for example, the use of sub-standard components.[79] Defence contracting interests also frequently underpin American ties with various rightist regimes. An example would be the collusion between the CIA and Rockwell International to sell the IBEX electronic communications system to the Shah's government in pre-revolutionary Iran.[80]

The sheer scale of Pentagon spending and contracting is staggering. Reagan's spending requests for the period fiscal 1986 to fiscal 1988 amounted to over one trillion dollars.[81] Major General Perry Smith makes the scarcely credible estimate that fifty thousand governmental defence contracts are signed every day![82] The notion, however, that the entire US economy is sustained and inextricably bound up with 'military Keynesianism' and the 'permanent arms economy' is probably overstating the case. Military spending may be used as an instrument of counter-cyclical policy; but, because of the huge time-lags involved, and the fact that the major slice of the economy is non-military, it is not a very reliable instrument.[83] Experience of the 1980–85 military build-up (only slightly smaller than the one associated with the Vietnam war) suggests that its inflationary impact was less than expected, but that it did have a substantial effect on deficits.[84] The militarised American economy in the Second World War, of course, performed marvellously. But the manifest functionality of high levels of military spending to effective capitalist performance should not be assumed too lightly. The manifest inefficiency of much of the defence industry is a case in point. High military outlays also divert funds from more productive investment, tend to create less employment than other governmental expenditure, and distort research priorities.[85] Post-Cold War, post-imperial demilitarisation of the United States would not, of itself, solve every economic problem; yet it would release energy and resources for more socially and economically productive areas.

4 Foreign policy by state and local governments

The 1980s witnessed a major expansion in the foreign policy activity – 'initiatives' or 'interference', depending on one's point of view – of state and local government. At one level, this represented an aspect of disaggregation of the foreign policy process in a world of interdependence [86] It also, however, reflected the opposition of many liberal local, especially city, governments to the policies of the Reagan Administration. The Local Elected Officials project, the leading information network for this new liberal municipal activism, grew out of the nuclear freeze movement.[87] (In 1987, the project began publishing its own journal, the *Bulletin of Municipal Foreign Policy*.)

Also in 1987, the city of Seattle set up its own Office of International Affairs with a quarter of a million dollar annual budget. Among other tasks, the office was concerned with maintaining relations with Seattle's thirteen sister cities, including Managua, capital of Nicaragua. A sample of headlines from 1988 and 1989 issues of the *Bulletin* indicates the range of activities involved in this new activism: 'Detroit Endorses INF Treaty'; 'San Francisco urges Pope to Recognise Israel'; 'Alaska Officials battle Plutonium Flights'; 'The Viability of Nuclear-Free Zones'; '39 Mayors sign Anti-*Contra* Initiative'; 'Missouri and the MX'; 'Jersey Town Fights Rights Abuses in Brazil'.[88]

Much of this kind of activity is not new. Local elected officials have often taken high-profile positions on foreign issues, especially when this may generate support among local ethnic voters. A significant proportion of local foreign policy falls into the category of symbolic or 'consciousness-raising' activity. As of 1988, fifty-seven American cities had 'sistering' arrangements with towns in Nicaragua. State and local governmental influence over education may also have a 'consciousness-raising' foreign policy dimension. High schools in New York and Milwaukee ran 'peace study' courses during the 1980s; Alabama required its teachers to emphasise 'ways to fight communism'.[89] As this latter example indicates, local activism does not have to be in a liberal direction. Local communities have regularly also taken anti-Soviet initiatives. The District of Columbia's alteration of the address of the Soviet Embassy to 'One Andrei Sakharov Plaza' is the best known example. In 1982, Glen Cove (on New York's Long Island) protested Soviet action in Afghanistan by banning Soviet diplomats from its beaches and golf courses.[90]

The influence of state and local government has also traditionally been felt in the areas of trade and cross-border policies. Demands for trade protection tend to surface at the regional or state level; for example, as noted above, demands to protect the Southern textile industry against imports became a significant issue in the South during the 1986 Congressional election campaign. The increasing perception of greater world economic interdependence has encouraged state governments to organise their lobbying for changes in trade policy more effectively.[91] The Senate's role in treaty ratification also tends to increase regional leverage in trade (and indeed other) issues of particular local concern. Some state governors base much of their appeal on a commitment to an active pursuit of their state's trading interests which effectively ignores any need for federal co-ordination.

In 1988, for example, Booth Gardner (Governor of Washington state and chairman of the National Governors' Association Committee on International Trade and Foreign Relations) declared that states did not need any leads from the Department of Commerce: 'I see Commerce being a facilitator. I see states being the line of action.' Washington state has its own office in Tokyo, promoting the state's trade, investment and agricultural interests.[92]

Several border cities and regions of the United States take pains to emphasise their participation in cross-border regional economies. One such is the Paso del Norte region which includes the city of El Paso (Texas) and Juarez (Mexico). Its economic integration is based largely on the controversial *maquiladora* industries (US plants operating in Mexico and taking advantage of low wages and pliable regulatory regimes).[93] State and local government influence over binational questions in areas such as environmental pollution, immigration and boundary disputes may also be strong.[94]

More controversial are unilateral actions taken by subnational governments with clear foreign policy objectives. The ability to lift such action beyond the realm of the purely gestural derives largely from the financial power of state and local governments. Their investment portfolios may be collectively estimated at around five hundred billion dollars.[95] State governments are financial actors on the world stage, and have contributed to the globalisation of capital. State bonds are increasingly sold on the world market.[96] During the mid-1980s, over a hundred state and local governments decided to sell investments related to the South African economy. About twenty billion dollars in stocks and bonds were thus divested. In 1988, Michigan became the first state to adopt an anti-apartheid selective purchasing policy. Massachusetts began moves to withdraw pension funds from financial institutions indirectly involved in Britain's Northern Ireland policy. (The campaigns to enact the MacBride proposals at state level were mentioned in the previous chapter.) Subnational governments have also refused to cooperate in federal military research and federal nuclear emergency planning.[97]

The legal and constitutional status of local foreign policy is complex and problematic. The Constitution's 'supremacy' or 'kingpin' clause (Article 6) would seem severely to limit local initiatives. Constitutional disbarring of subnational obstruction of foreign commerce would appear to have a similar impact. Several Supreme Court decisions, notably *Zschernig* v. *Miller* (1968),[98] suggest that federalism stops at the water's edge. Less daunting is the 1799 Logan Act, hostile to local participation, but effectively moribund. Legal and constitutional arguments, however, do not all point in the same direction; proponents of local foreign policy have taken heart from various court successes at the state and local level. Some self-styled 'sanctuary cities' offer assistance to refugees, especially from Central America, and refuse to implement or co-operate with federal deportation laws; they have appealed to international laws and agreements on human rights as legal justification.[99]

It is unlikely that the 'problem' of local foreign policy will find ultimate resolution in the court system. As Michael Shuman has noted, subnational initiatives in the 1980s involved not only a protest against the policies of the Reagan Presidency. They also represented a democratically oriented disillusionment with the traditional foreign policy process: 'Critics of municipal foreign policy put their faith in a small, largely unaccountable elite in Washington, D.C., the same "best and the brightest" who brought us Vietnam, a covert action every 16 months since 1900, and an unending nuclear arms race.'[100]

Even Shuman, however, is forced to acknowledge that unchecked local foreign policy may become anarchic and 'dangerous'. Yet it is worth remembering that many of the non-constitutional, efficiency-based, arguments against local initiatives recall the arguments proferred against a strong Congressional role. The claim that US foreign policy must always speak with one voice may always be countered by Shuman's comment: 'America has *never* spoken in one voice in foreign policy – and never will.'[101]

Notes

1 Statistics from C. W. Kegley and E. R. Wittkopf, *World Politics*, 3rd ed., New York, 1989, pp. 159–65; D.H. Blake and R. S. Walters, *The Politics of Global Economic Relations*, 3rd ed., Englewood Cliffs, 1987, pp. 90–4. See also R. T. Kudrle and D. B. Bobow, 'U.S. policy toward foreign direct investment', *World Politics*, 34, 1982, pp. 353–79; E.A. Brett, *The World Economy since the War*, London, 1985, pp. 85–6.

2 Blake and Walters, *Politics of Global Economic Relations*, pp. 98–9. See also S. Gill and D. Law, *The Global Political Economy*, Brighton, 1988, p. 194.

3 Blake and Walters, *Politics of Global Economic Relations*, pp. 98–9.

4 New York, 1971.

5 New York, 1974. See also C. F. Bergsten *et al.*, *American Multinationals and American Interests*, Washington D.C., 1978, pp. 329–35.

6 Bergsten *et al.*, *American Multinationals*, pp. 309–10.

7 See N. Hood and S. Young, *The Economics of Multinational Enterprise*,

London, 1979, p. 18; also J. A. Nathan and J.K. Oliver, *United States Foreign Policy and World Order*, 3rd ed., Boston, 1985.

8 Bergsten *et al.*, *American Multinationals*, p. 328. See also J. A. Nathan and J. K. Oliver, *Foreign Policy Making and the American Political System*, 2nd ed., Boston, 1987, p. 288.

9 M. Davis, 'The political economy of late-imperial America', *New Left Review*, 143, 1984, pp. 6–38.

10 See especially H. Magdoff, *The Age of Imperialism*, New York, 1969.

11 Bergsten *et al.*, *American Multinationals*, p. 324. See also R. Gilpin, *War and Change in World Politics*, Cambridge, 1981 and *The Political Economy of International Relations*, Princeton, 1987; S. Krasner, *Defending the National Interest*, Princeton, 1978; G. J. Ikenberry, 'The irony of strength: comparative responses to the oil shocks', *International Organisation*, 40, 1986, pp. 105–37; G. J. Ikenberry *et al.*, 'Introduction: approaches to explaining American foreign economic policy', *International Organisation*, 42, 1988, pp. 1–14 (pp. 9–14).

12 See, e.g., S. Holland, *The Socialist Challenge*, London, 1975, and *The Global Economy: From Meso to Macroeconomics*, London, 1987.

13 See Ikenberry *et al.*, 'Introduction', p. 3; P. Katzenstein, ed., *Between Power and Plenty*, Madison (Wisconsin), 1978.

14 See P. B. Evans *et al.*, *Bringing the State Back In*, Cambridge, 1985; also J. Zysman, *Governments, Markets and Growth*, Ithaca (New York), 1983; M. Evangelista, 'Issue-area and foreign policy revisited' *International Organisation*, 43, 1989, pp. 147–172.

15 See Blake and Walters, *Politics of Global Economic Relations*, p. 108.

16 See Bergsten *et al.*, *American Multinationals*, p. 322; S. D. Krasner, *Structural Conflict: The Third World against Global Liberalism*, Berkeley, 1985, p. 195.

17 See I. M. Destler, *Making Foreign Economic Policy*, Washington, D.C., 1980, p. 7; R.N. Cooper, 'Trade policy as foreign policy', in R. M. Stern, ed., *U.S. Trade Policies in a Changing World*, Cambridge (Massachusetts), 1988, pp. 291–322.

18 See T. Lowi, 'American business, public policy, case-studies, and political theory', *World Politics*, 16, 1964, pp. 677–715 and *The End of Liberalism*, New York, 1969; W. Zimmerman, 'Issue-area and foreign policy process', *American Political Science Review*, 67, 1973, pp. 1204–12; W. C. Potter, 'Issue area and foreign policy analysis', *International Organisation*, 34, 1980, pp. 404–20; P. McGowan and S. G. Walker, 'Radical and conventional models of U.S. foreign economic policy making', *World Politics*, 35, 1981, pp. 347–82, pp. 366–9; M. Evangelista, 'Issue area'. See also S. D. Cohen, *The Making of United States International Economic Policy*, New York, 3rd ed., 1988.

19 See W. Hanrieder, 'Dissolving international politics', *American Political Science Review*, 72, 1978, pp. 1276–87.

20 Zimmerman, 'Issue area', p. 1206.

21 McGowan and Walker, 'Radical and conventional models', p. 368.

22 *Ibid.*; Zimmerman, 'Issue area', p. 1209. For a critique of the issue area approach, see Kudrle and Bobow, 'U.S. policy', p. 358.

23 Krasner, *Defending the National Interest*, especially pp. 55–90; see also

R. M. Price, 'U.S. policy toward Southern Africa,' in G.M. Carter and P. O'Meara, eds., *International Politics in Southern Africa*, Bloomington (Indiana), 1982, pp. 45–88 (on the balance between 'security', 'economic' and 'credibility' interests).

24 See Kudrle and Bobow, 'U.S. policy', p. 370.

25 H. B. Malmgren, 'Managing foreign economic policy', *Foreign Policy*, 6, 1972, pp. 39–51.

26 See J. Goldstein, 'The impact of ideas on trade policy: the origins of U.S. agricultural and manufacturing policies', *International Organisation*, 43, 1989, pp. 51–71; also, R. M. Fraenkel *et al.*, *The Role of U.S. Agriculture in Foreign Policy*, New York, 1979.

27 See Blake and Walters, *The Politics of Global Economic Relations*, p. 116; K. L. Teslik, *Congress, the Executive Branch and Special Interests: The American Response to the Arab Boycott*, Westport (Connecticut), 1982.

28 On the foreign policy role of giant corporations, see A. Said and L. R. Simmonds, ed., *The New Sovereigns*, Englewood Cliffs, 1975; R. W. Mansbach *et al.*, *The Web of World Politics*, Englewood Cliffs, 1976; P. Taylor, *Nonstate Actors in International Politics*, Boulder (Colorado), 1984, pp. 203–12.

29 See, e.g., Kegley and Wittkopf, *World Politics*, p. 170.

30 See J. Marshall *et al.*, *The Iran Contra Connection*, Boston, 1987, p. 151.

31 *The Tower Commission Report*, New York, 1987, p. 98.

32 See C. Lipson, 'Bankers' dilemmas', *World Politics*, 38, 1985, pp. 200–25.

33 Conference Board, Third Avenue, New York City, 28 June 1988 (session attended by the author).

34 P. M. Stern, *The Best Congress Money Can Buy*, New York, 1988, p. 31.

35 Stern, *The Best Congress*, p. 10.

36 *Foreign Policy by Congress*, New York, 1979, p. 195. On business diversity, see R. Bauer, I. S. Pool and L. A. Dexter, *American Business and Public Policy*, Chicago, 1972.

37 *Congress and the Politics of U.S. Foreign Economic Policy 1929–1976*, Berkeley, 1980, p. 7.

38 See, e.g., Zysman, *Governments, Markets and Growth*, p. 274.

39 J. E. Spero, 'The mid-life crisis of American trade policy', *The World Today*, 45, 1989, pp. 10–14, p. 11. See also P. Nicolaides, 'Trade warfare: the quest for fair trade', *The World Today*, 44, 1988, pp. 119–23.

40 J. Bhagwati, 'The United States and trade policy: reversing gears', *Journal of International Affairs*, 42, 1988, pp. 93–108. See also J. Bhagwati, *Protectionism*, Cambridge (Massachusetts), 1987.

41 H. V. Milner and D. B. Yoffie, 'Between free trade and protectionism: strategic trade policy and a theory of corporate trade demands', *International Organisation*, 43, 1989, pp. 239–71.

42 *Ibid.*, p. 240.

43 *Guardian*, 21 September 1989.

44 R. H. Ziegler, *American Workers, American Unions, 1920–1985*, Baltimore, 1986, p. 193.

45 See M. Goldfield, *The Decline of Organised Labor in the United States*, Chicago, 1987.

46 See K. Cowling and R. Sugden, *Transnational Monopoly Capitalism*, Brighton, 1987, p. 73. See also R. W. Cox, 'Labor and the multinationals', *Foreign Affairs*, 54, 1976, pp. 344–65.

47 Blake and Walters, *The Politics of Global Economic Relations*, p. 28 (see also pp. 114–16).

48 *Labor Relations Yearbook – 1967*, Washington D.C., 1968, p. 297.

49 See G. K. Wilson, *Unions in American National Politics*, London, 1979, p. 128. Also R. Radosh, *American Labor and United States Foreign Policy*, New York, 1969; W. Peck, 'The AFL-CIA', in H. Frazier, ed., *Uncloaking the CIA*, New York, 1978, pp. 226–65.

50 See R. Godson, *Labor in Soviet Global Strategy*, New York, 1984, pp. 71–3; Nathan and Oliver, *Foreign Policy Making*, p. 270.

51 On labour opposition to the war, see P.S. Foner, *American Labor and the Indochina War*, New York, 1971; also J. West, 'Labor and peace', *Political Affairs* (theoretical journal of US Communist Party), 46, 1967, pp. 22–8; G. Mayers, 'Labor speaks out for peace', *Political Affairs*, 47, 1968, pp. 53–7. Also, J. Windmuller, 'The foreign policy conflict in U.S. labour', *Political Science Quarterly*, 82, 1967, pp. 205–34.

52 See the symposium on 'Labor's international role', *Foreign Policy*, 26, 1977, pp. 204–48.

53 See, e.g., T. R. Dye, *Who's Running America?: The Conservative Years*, Englewood Cliffs, 1986; R. Brownstein and N. Easton, *Reagan's Ruling Class*, New York, 1983; P. H. Burch, *Elites in American History*, New York, 1980.

54 See Gill and Law, *The Global Political Economy*, p. 206.

55 See R. D. Schulzinger, *The Wise Men of Foreign Affairs: The History of the Council on Foreign Relations*, New York, 1984, pp. 236–9. On the Committee on the Present Danger, see A. Tonelson, 'Nitze's world', *Foreign Policy*, 35, 1979, pp. 74–90; J. W. Sanders, *Peddlers of Crisis*, Boston, 1983; P. Nitze, *From Hiroshima to Glasnost*, New York, 1989.

56 C. W. Kegley and E. R. Wittkopf, *American Foreign Policy: Pattern and Process*, 3rd ed., New York, 1987, p. 266.

57 The point about the CFR being attacked from left and right was made strongly in an address given on the Council's behalf by Gregory Treverton (Senior Fellow) at the CFR New York City headquarters, 27 June 1988 (session attended by the author). For an attack from the left, see L. H. Shoup and W. Minter, *Imperial Brain Trust*, New York, 1977; also P. Thompson, 'Bilderberg and the West', in H. Sklar, ed., *Trilateralism*, Boston, 1980, pp. 157–89, p. 188 (note 57, on right-wing conspiracy theory).

58 See Thompson, 'Bilderberg'.

59 See B. M. Russett and E. C. Hanson, *Interest and Ideology*, San Francisco, 1975, pp. 244–50. NSA Brent Scowcroft and Deputy Secretary of State Eagleburger worked for Kissinger Associates before joining the Bush Administration. Questions in Congress have also been raised over the company's influence over Bush's Foreign Intelligence Advisory Board.

60 See W. Isaacson and E. Thomas, *The Wise Men*, London, 1986, p. 27 (remarks of Henry Kissinger).

61 D. Barsamian, 'Interview with Naom Chomsky', *Radical America*, 22, 1989, pp. 29–39, p. 29; also C. W. Mills, *The Power Elite*, New York, 1956.

62 Isaacson and Thomas, *The Wise Men*, p. 27 (remark of J. J. McCloy). 'Skull and Bones' is a Yale University elite club, and Groton a Connecticut private school.

63 *Ibid.*, pp. 66, 29.

64 The RAND corporation was a leading Cold War 'think tank' originally primarily concerned with air force security research. The American Enterprise Institute and Hoover Institution are research bodies of a generally conservative orientation. Brookings is a Washington D.C. research body best known for liberally inclined domestic policy research.

65 See R. Kolkowicz, 'The strange career of the defense intellectuals', *Orbis*, 31, 1987, pp. 179–92; C. Gershman, 'The rise and fall of the new foreign-policy establishment', in C. W. Kegley and E. R. Wittkopf, eds., *Perspectives on American Foreign Policy*, New York, 1983, pp. 175–81.

66 See M. Raskin, 'Democracy and the national security state', in M. Levine *et al.*, *The State and Democracy*, New York, 1988, pp. 168–97, p. 187; M.J. Parenti, *Democracy for the Few*, 4th ed., New York, 1983, p. 227. But see also B. Rubin, *Secrets of State*, New York, 1987, p. viii.

67 Sanders, pp. 70, 310; Commission on U.S.-Soviet Relations (CFR), *The Soviet Challenge*, New York, 1982. See also T. Bodenheimer and R. Gould, *Rollback: Right-wing Power in U.S. Foreign Policy*, Boston, 1989, pp. 167–9, on rise of the New Right.

68 See J. G. Peschek, *Policy-Planning Organisations: Elite Agendas and America's Rightward Turn*, Philadelphia, 1987; C. D. Heatherly, ed., *Mandate for Leadership*, Washington D.C., 1981 (published by the Heritage Foundation); A. Anderson and D. L. Bark, eds., *Thinking about America*, Stanford (California), 1988.

69 See Thompson, 'Bilderberg', p. 159.

70 *Foreign Relations of the United States, 1946*, I, Washington D.C., 1972, pp. 1165–6.

71 See K. W. Ryavec, *United States-Soviet Relations*, New York, 1989, p. 119; S. McLean, *How Nuclear Weapons Decisions are Made*, London, 1986, pp. 73–4.

72 See Kegley and Wittkopf, *American Foreign Policy*, pp. 268–75; G. Adams, *The Politics of Defense Contracting: The Iron Triangle*, New Brunswick, 1982; J. Goodwin, *Brotherhood of Arms: General Dynamics and the Business of Defending America*, New York, 1985, B. Gross, *Friendly Fascism*, New York, 1980, pp. 191–95.

73 E.g. A. Yarmolinsky, *The Military Establishment*, New York, 1971; R. Kaufman, *The War Profiteers*, New York, 1972.

74 L. Freedman, *The Evolution of Nuclear Strategy*, 2nd ed., London, 1989, p. 336.

75 Ryavec, *United States-Soviet Relations*, p. 120.

76 Freedman, *Evolution*, p. 336; Union of Concerned Scientists, *The Fallacy of Star Wars*, New York, 1984.

77 E.g. T. Greenwood, *Making the MIRV*, Cambridge (Massachusetts), 1975; P. Hayes *et al.*, *American Lake*, Harmondsworth, 1987 (ch. 14: 'Missile in search of a mission', on the sea-launched Tomahawk cruise missile).

78 See S. Sarkesian, ed., *The Military-Industrial Complex: A Reassessment*,

Beverley Hills, 1972; S. J. Rosen, *Testing the Theory of the Military-Industrial Complex*, Lexington (Massachusetts), 1973.

79 Ryavec, *United States-Soviet Relations*, p. 120. See also C. Coker, *U.S. Military Power in the 1980's*, London, 1983, pp. 80–5 (on labour shortages and technical problems in the defence industries); *Congressional Quarterly Weekly Report*, 1988, pp. 1723–5 (on the 1988 procurement scandals).

80 See Marshall *et al.*, *The Iran Contra Connection*, p. 153.

81 See R. A. Stubbing, *The Defense Game*, New York, 1986, ch. 2.

82 P. M. Smith, *Assignment: Pentagon*, Washington D.C., 1989, p. 169.

83 See V. R. Berghahn, *Militarism*, Leamington Spa, 1981, p. 88; F. Halliday, *The Making of the Second Cold War*, London, 1983, pp. 126–33. See R. Smith, 'Military expenditure and capitalism', *Cambridge Journal of Economics*, 1, 1977, pp. 132–67, for a critique of 'military Keynesianism' theories.

84 See J. Schor, 'Warning-military spending may *not* be bad for your economic health', *Radical America*, 21, 1987, pp. 47–53, p. 52; Gill and Law, *The Global Political Economy*, p. 120.

85 See S. Melman, *Pentagon Capitalism*, New York, 1970; R. W. De Grasse *et al.*, *The Costs and Consequences of Reagan's Military Buildup*, New York, 1982 and De Grasse, *Military Expansion, Economic Decline*, New York, 1983.

86 See S. P. Mumme, 'State influence in foreign policymaking', *Western Political Quarterly*, 38, 1985, pp. 620–40, p. 620; also W. F. Hanrieder, 'Dissolving international politics', *American Political Science Review*, 072, 1978, pp. 1276–87; *Publius*, 14, 1984 (special issue, ed. I. D. Duchacek).

87 See M. H. Shuman, 'Dateline Main Street: local foreign policies', *Foreign Policy*, 65, 1986–87, pp. 154–74, p. 157.

88 *Bulletin of Municipal Foreign Policy*, 2 (Spring) 1988; 3 (Summer), 1989.

89 Shuman, 'Dateline', p. 160.

90 See J. Dull, *The Politics of American Foreign Policy*, Englewood Cliffs, 1985, p. 114.

91 See J. M. Kline, *State Government Influence in U.S. International Economic Policy*, Lexington (Massachusetts), 1983.

92 Interview, *Business America*, 15 February 1988, p. 14.

93 In 1987, the *maquiladora* industries produced nearly one billion dollars in cash flow through El Paso banks: Institute of Manufacturing and Materials Management, University of Texas at El Paso, *Paso del Norte Regional Economy*, 12 May 1988.

94 See Mumme, 'State influence'.

95 See P. J. Spiro, 'Who should conduct foreign policy? (taking foreign policy away from the feds)', *Bulletin of Municipal Foreign Policy*, 2 (Spring) 1988, pp. 6–21, p. 17.

96 See J. Leigland, 'States sell bonds worldwide', *Journal of State Government*, 61, 1989, pp. 137–41.

97 See Spiro, 'Who should conduct foreign policy?', p. 16; *Bulletin of Municipal Foreign Policy*, 3 (Summer) 1989, pp. 33–4 (on MacBride proposals).

98 U.S. 429. See also *U.S.* v. *Pink* (1942), 315 U.S. 203.

99 For the various legal and constitutional arguments, see L. Henkin,

Foreign Affairs and the Constitution, New York, 1972, pp. 230–48; Spiro, 'Who should conduct foreign policy?'; Shuman, 'Dateline', pp. 163–9; K. Lewis, 'Dealing with South Africa: the constitutionality of state and local divestment legislation', *Tulane Law Review*, 61, 1987, pp. 469–517.

100 M. H. Shuman, 'Spiro's impossible quest', *Bulletin of Municipal Foreign Policy*, 2, (Spring) 1988, pp. 7–13, p. 13.

101 *Ibid.*, p. 9.

9

Two case-studies and conclusion

This chapter offers two case-studies: U.S.-British relations during the period of the escalation of the Vietnam war, and President Carter's human rights policy (with particular reference to Argentina). Some implications of the case-studies will be considered in Section 3 below, with Section 4 being devoted to some general conclusions about American foreign policy and its future.

1 Case-study: Anglo-American relations and the Vietnam war, 1964–68

(a) *The United States, Britain and Vietnam* Between 1964 and 1968, the British Labour government, led by Harold Wilson, offered consistent support for US policy in Vietnam. Wilson and his foreign ministers braved stormy House of Commons debates on the subject, as well as severe intra-party criticism up to and including Cabinet level. Edward Short, Chief Whip to the Wilson government, has described Vietnam protest as his 'most troublesome political problem' in the mid-1960s.[1]

Despite its generally positive orientation towards the American role in Vietnam, the Wilson government did not enjoy a harmonious relationship with Washington over the issue. For one thing, there was always the danger that backbench protest might cause offence. Short's account is disarmingly frank: 'Our reliance on United States support for sterling forced us to refrain from any overt criticism.... nothing could be said or done which would upset Washington. Most of our MP's grasped this, but a sizable minority refused to understand, as did the non-ministerial members of the National Executive.'[2]

Secondly, Wilson, driven at least partially by intra-party protest, did attempt to act as a restraining influence on the Americans. A February 1965 attempt to counsel against precipitate retaliation for a Vietcong attack provoked a tirade of Johnsonian anger, delivered over the telephonic 'hot-line'. In June 1966, Wilson dissociated his government from the bombing of Haiphong and Hanoi. Both Wilson (on 17 May, 1966) and Defence Minister Denis Healey (on 23 June 1966) also declared that arms would not be sold to the US or Australia for use in Vietnam. The American President again responded furiously, this time via the telex machine in the British Embassy in Washington.[3] Thirdly, conflict was liable to erupt over the extent to which the 'perfidious British' (in the phrase used by Congressman Gross of Iowa) maintained shipping links with North Vietnam.[4]

Above all, however, there was the issue of British troop commitment. There was a strong American desire to secure substantial allied troop commitment, a desire which was certainly not satisfied by deployment of Australian, South Korean and other smaller forces. 'Getting more countries represented in Vietnam' appeared on a Tuesday luncheon agenda as early as April 1964. The call for 'more flags' and the so-called 'third country problem' were highly prioritised concerns, albeit defined largely in symbolic/propagandistic terms. David Bruce, American Ambassador in London during these years, later recalled the widespread Washington view that British participation – even British deaths – would be very useful to the United States.[5]

Direct requests for troops were made in December 1964, at the Washington meeting between LBJ and Wilson; they were also made on several occasions during 1965 and 1966 – certainly in April and August 1965. In July 1966, at the height of the sterling crisis, a personal request for troops from Johnson was directed to Wilson.[6] Barbara Castle's diary quotes Wilson in dinner conversation describing another request made in April 1967: 'In Bonn, at Adenauer's funeral, Johnson had told me that if only I would put troops into Vietnam my worries over sterling would be over. Yes, I retorted, and I would be finished too.'[7]

On at least two occasions, it was made clear that a token force would suffice. According to Patrick Gordon Walker (who, as Foreign Secretary, accompanied Wilson on the December 1964 trip), Johnson would have been content with the simple raising of the Union Jack. In July 1966, LBJ requested 'a platoon of bagpipers'. In October

1966, unsuccessful soundings were made as to the possibility of using the British Gurkha Brigade.[8]

All these requests were met by refusal or evasion. There is some suggestion that Washington may have had hopes of recruiting Defence Minister Healey to the cause of troop commitment.[9] However, the Johnson Administration can really have had little doubt as to the strength of British resolve on this issue. In September 1965, Under-Secretary of State George Ball sought to extract a promise that American support for sterling would be balanced by the retention of British military commitments in the Far East. National Security Assistant McGeorge Bundy reported to LBJ that the 'one thing' which Wilson was determined to avoid 'was a liability in Vietnam'.[10] British troop commitment in Vietnam was a political impossibility as far as Wilson was concerned. It would have set off uncontrollable explosions within the Labour party. Moreover, from the British point of view, little had changed since the Eisenhower Administration's (possibly disingenuous) request during the 1954 Dien Bien Phu crisis had been rebuffed.[11] A Vietnamese conflict involving British soldiers and British casualties would have been difficult to sell to the public, and would probably have destroyed the Commonwealth.

The record of the Johnson Administration reveals an extended debate on the question of how best to handle the issue of British troop commitment. George Ball advised LBJ in December 1964, before the talks with Wilson: 'we might suggest that consultation is meaningful only when there are joint ventures, joint risks, and joint responsibilities. This could lead delicately into a discussion of "jointness" in Southeast Asia.'[12]

Some wished simply to trade sterling support and loans for troops. Francis Bator, a National Security Council staffer, wrote in July 1965: 'Vietnam is our paramount problem and what they say and do about it is bound to influence Washington's view of Anglo-American relations. How concrete should we be on what we would like from them?'[13]

McGeorge Bundy provided his answer on the same day (28 July 1965) in a memorandum addressed directly to the President. Bundy noted that a collapse of the pound would be in no one's interest ('we will all be losers'). But he continued:

My own interests, and those of Bob McNamara and Dean Rusk are wider. We are concerned with the fact that the British are constantly trying to make narrow bargains on money while they cut back on their wider political and military responsibilities. We want to make very sure that the British get it into their heads that it makes no sense for us to secure the Pound in a situation in which there is no British flag in Vietnam, and a threatened British thin-out in both east of Suez and in Germany. What I would like to say to Trend myself, is that a British Brigade in Vietnam would be worth a billion dollars at the moment of truth for Sterling.[14]

(Bundy's references were to Defence Secretary McNamara, Secretary of State Rusk and British Cabinet Secretary Burke Trend.) Bator summarised what he called the 'Fowler-McNamara and Ball' position as follows: 'U.K. troops in Vietnam, while not strictly a necessary condition for us to be forthcoming on sterling, would greatly improve the odds.'[15] (Fowler was US Treasury Secretary.)

But troops were not committed, while sterling was supported, both throughout 1965 and during the major sterling crisis of 1966. The key to this was the American desire to avoid devaluation of the pound, a measure which it was thought would expose the dollar to predatory speculation and possibly endanger the whole Bretton Woods financial system. (When Britain eventually did devalue, in November 1967, the dollar did indeed come under severe pressure.)[16] Paradoxically, the very weakness of sterling gave Wilson some leverage in his dealings with Johnson. He could exploit the threat of devaluation, and also put his faith in the hope that – whether or not troops were committed – the US would support sterling. The view that the Johnson Administration gave priority to sterling stability was, in fact, fairly common in Britain in the late 1960s. It was expressed, for example, in places as diverse as Cecil King's diary and in the Campaign for Nuclear Disarmament newspaper, *Sanity*.[17] It surely is significant that even Bundy's rather brutal statement was prefaced by a worry about the pound's collapse. In the event, President Johnson overruled Bundy. Troop commitment was not made the price for supporting sterling. Bundy made the following report on his meeting with Burke Trend: 'In accordance with your instructions, I kept the two subjects of the pound sterling and Vietnam completely separate.'[18]

Part of Wilson's case against troop commitment was that Britain's role as co-chairman (with the Soviet Union) of the Geneva Conference imposed significant limitations on UK policy in Vietnam. The 1966 Washington briefing book for Wilson's visit described this argument as a 'fig leaf'.[19] Soviet determination to keep China out of any eventual settlement in Vietnam tended to negate any hopes of reconvening the Geneva Conference.[20] Nonetheless, Anglo-American relations regarding the war in Vietnam during the later 1960s did largely revolve around a succession of ill-fated British attempts at mediation.

The Vietnam war, of course, represented only one dimension of an increasingly troubled Anglo-American relationship in this period. Other dimensions included the debate over the future of Britain's nuclear force, the various defence reviews and the issue of British military commitment east of Suez, American support for Rhodesian oil sanctions, the decision to schedule – and then partially to cancel – major aircraft purchases from the US, and, above all, the strength of sterling. However, a somewhat narrower focus on the Vietnam war does raise important questions in at least three areas: the style of foreign policy-making within the Johnson Administration, the relevance of this case-study to discussions about various models of policy-making, and also the light it sheds upon the 'special relationship' between Britain and the US.

(b) *Competing interpretations* There are at least four competing interpretations of these events. Firstly, there is Wilson's own account. His argument was, in the words of Tony Benn, that 'public declarations are less effective than private pressure'.[21] Wilson saw himself as resisting Foreign Office pressure to back the Americans even more enthusiastically, and as thereby retaining the degree of independence necessary to act as a credible mediator between the US and North Vietnam. Britain thus operated as a force both for restraint and realism.[22] (Denis Healey has recorded what he calls 'the British view' in the early 1960s as counselling against open-ended support for an unviable government in South Vietnam. He asserts that this view was shared by the State Department.)[23]

A second view would emphasise the importance of the support given by Britain. Under this interpretation, the backing of a docile Labour government helped soften international hostility and hardened American resolve. On the left, Wilson and other Labour leaders were accused of simple cowardice. Some radical leaders saw their role as the mobilisation of a threat of domestic unrest sufficiently strong to deter the commitment of troops.[24] British policy may also be seen as resulting from the simple recognition of national inferiority, compounded by Wilsonian deceit. Tony Benn's diary entry for 1 June, 1967, referred to the Prime Minister being received in Washington: 'with all the trumpets appropriate for a weak foreign head of state who has to be buttered up so that he can carry the can for American foreign policy.'[25]

A similar tone of hurt national pride was expressed in sections of the right wing of the Conservative party. Enoch Powell alleged in March 1966 that Wilson had a secret, craven plan to commit troops to Vietnam.[26]

A third set of interpretations would specifically locate British support for the American line in Vietnam in the context of deals made to secure support for sterling. Richard Crossman appears to have believed that his own government's policy was at least partially the result of clandestine deals between US leaders and Wilson.[27] By August 1966, Foreign Secretary George Brown was offering his view to Crossman that Wilson had effectively sold his soul to the American President.[28] More recently, Clive Ponting has described British economic and defence policy between the spring of 1965 and summer 1966 as essentially the product of secret 'understandings' based on American backing for the pound. Generalised British support in Vietnam, short of actual involvement in the fighting, was part of this 'deal'.[29] (It is worth emphasising that Wilson, Chancellor James Callaghan and Ambassador Bruce have all hotly denied any such arrangement.)[30]

A fourth view would stress the limitations of British support. After all, in concrete terms, what did it amount to? A memorandum from White House staffer for Asian affairs, Chester Cooper, in April 1965 offered a meagre catalogue of British assistance, including an 'English professor at Hue' and a 'typesetting machine'.[31] The official Department of the Army account of allied help, published in 1975, again cited the professor and the typesetting machine, along with a medical team of twenty-six and 2.4 million dollars in economic aid given between 1968 and 1971.[32] This, however, was not the full story. Substantial arms sales were made to the US for use in Vietnam. Such sales involved some collusion between the two parties to cloud the issue of where eventually the arms would be deployed.[33] The inter-locking structure of allied intelligence under the 1947 UKUSA treaty made it inevitable that the United States would gain access to North Vietnamese signals intelligence intercepted in Hong Kong. Again, there was some attempt to camouflage this situation by assigning North Vietnamese intelligence interception to Australian government personnel.[34] Some British advisers – putative experts on counterinsurgency, like Robert Thompson – also helped the

American effort in Vietnam. Less well known is the clandestine role played by the SAS. In June 1969, *Mars and Minerva*, the SAS regimental magazine, featured a photograph of SAS Sergeant Dick Meadows being decorated with the US Silver Star for his service in Vietnam![35]

Despite this, it is perhaps the absence of British troop commitment rather than the extent of British support which requires explanation. Labour leaders, after all, were heirs to the Atlanticist Bevinite tradition.[36] Given the degree of perceived economic dependence on the US – something taken as axiomatic in the Foreign Office during the 1960s[37] – one might have expected a token, public commitment. The explanation lies in Wilson's political difficulties described above, and in American perceptions of his position as described below. Nonetheless, the failure to send troops did incite American bitterness, and not only among Vietnam hawks. Senator Fulbright wrote to *The Economist* (London) in September 1967: 'What puzzles me ... considering your enthusiasm for the war ... is your failure to suggest that your own country would send an army.'[38] Rather alarmingly, anti-war Senator Wayne Morse addressed himself directly to Wilson: 'You do not impress me at all. You would impress me ... if you were in there ... with your own troops and let them do some of the dying.'[39] At a bibulous State Department reception for Dean Rusk in December 1968, the outgoing Secretary of State reportedly admonished the British journalist Louis Heren: 'All we needed was one regiment. The Black Watch would have done. Just one regiment, but you wouldn't. Well, don't expect us to save you again. They can invade Sussex, and we wouldn't do a damned thing about it.'[40]

To what extent was British policy the result of a secret 'deal'? The term 'shared understanding,' within a well defined power relationship, seems more appropriate. By 1970, it was, in fact, common to attribute the delay in devaluing to American influence.[41] A formal deal, with strings, was offered in September 1967, and was rejected.[42] It is of significance that no one suggests that US pressure forced Wilson to do anything he did not want.[43] The Prime Minister, along with most of the tiny Cabinet elite who directed policy, did not want an early devaluation, nor a withdrawal from east of Suez, at least before the 1966 general election. If deflation was the price for a successful defence of the pound, then Wilson was prepared to pay it. Above all, the 'shared understanding' did not involve open British involvement in the Vietnam conflict.

(c)   *US perceptions of Britain and the Labour government*   The bitterness apparent in Rusk's remarks to Louis Heren did occasionally
surface in the more formal Anglo-American exchanges of the period.
Walt Rostow, who took over from Bundy as National Security Assistant in April 1966, wrote to LBJ in the following terms regarding
Wilson's proposed July 1966 visit:

I take it to be our task to make bloody clear to the British Embassy in
Washington and the British government in London that (1) the visit must be
very carefully prepared; (2) the Prime Minister, whatever his pressures at
home, should not come unless *what he says here in public and in private reinforces
your position on Viet Nam*; (3) if this is impossible for him, he must find an
excuse for the visit not to take place.[44]

Johnson wrote personally to Wilson on 14 June 1966, unsuccessfully asking him not to speak in terms of disassociation from American
bombing policies. He suggested that Wilson state publicly that:
'Britain is satisfied that U.S. forces have no designs against civilian
populations and are taking every possible precaution to avoid civilian
casualties.'[45]
Despite the occasional expression of impatience, even bitterness,
American leaders were not so embarrassed by a richness of allied
support as to be ungrateful for such as they had. Even rhetorical
backing was welcome. George Ball drew attention in August 1965 to
the need to avoid exacerbating 'anti-Americanism in Britain'; this
might stimulate a major retreat in UK defence commitments, leaving
the US 'more than ever the policeman of the world'.[46] Administration
spokesmen took every opportunity publicly to proclaim the strength
of allied support in Vietnam.[47] David Bruce later recorded his view
that LBJ was genuinely grateful to Wilson.[48] American perceptions of
the British stance were also affected by the contrast with France. Rusk
declared at a March 1966 Cabinet meeting that the 'last few years' had
not only demonstrated the divisions in the communist world; the
West also was 'in disarray and General De Gaulle must bear a large
share of the responsibility'.[49]
Gratitude to Wilson, especially between 1964 and 1966, was
associated with sensitivity to his problems in containing left-wing
criticism from within his own party. Rusk, in March 1965, urged
Johnson to meet Foreign Secretary Stewart, writing that the British
had 'despite pressure from the left wing of the Labour Party, maintained solid support' for American policy in Vietnam.[50] Even Bundy
advised LBJ in April 1965 that UK support had 'been stronger than

that of our other major allies'.[51] Bruce's cables from London vividly described the pressure on Wilson from 'within the parliamentary Labour party and within the active and militant Labour left in the constituencies'. The Minister had to confront 'left wing hard core, soft left wing (pacifists, liberal woollies, disarmers) and some moderate centrists'.[52] Even after 1966, with relations somewhat chillier, a background paper prepared for Rostow asserted that Wilson had 'demonstrated great skill in keeping the vigorous critics of American policy under control'.[53]

Bruce's elegant and incisive cables fed Washington's perception of the situation in Britain. The Ambassador regarded the Wilson government as essentially reliable and supportive, if only for reasons of 'self interest'.[54] The tone of Bruce's analysis was set in his generally positive assessment of the Labour government as it took office in October 1964. He saw Wilson as presenting 'well on television' but as having problems in ridding himself of his reputation for being 'tricky and unreliable'.[55] The State Department was informed that Wilson's early appointments were of 'dominant moderate complexion', enlivened by 'leftwing spice'.[56] Bruce advised in April 1965 that there was 'no chance of persuading HMG to provide its military forces to SEATO for use in South Vietnam'.[57]

The existence of a socialist government across the Atlantic does not appear to have sent alarm bells ringing in Washington, although the CIA may have entertained conspiratorial theories concerning Wilson.[58] Henry Kissinger was later to note that Wilson came from a 'generation of Labour Party leaders' which was 'emotionally closer to the United States than were many leaders of the Conservative Party'.[59] As early as March 1964, shadow Defence Minister Healey, on a visit to Washington, had offered support for the American stance in Vietnam. He urged the US 'to create a strong military posture ... from which a disengagement could be negotiated'.[60] (It is interesting that Edward Short dates the Anglo-American 'understanding' that, in return for sterling support, Britain would not devalue the pound, to 'well ahead' of the 1964 election.)[61] Bundy wrote in March 1964 that, although Wilson had simply 'invited himself to' John F. Kennedy's funeral, his 'political line is friendly ... except for reservations appropriate for a Socialist leader'.[62] Rusk told LBJ in March 1965 that the US had already achieved an 'excellent degree of understanding and cooperation' with Wilson's government.[63] As for the Conservative party, the briefing paper for Wilson's visit to Washington in July 1966 noted that their support 'has not always carried a tone of conviction'.[64]

American leaders were prepared to keep the British Cabinet elite informed on Vietnam, at least within the limits imposed by diplomatic exigency. The record of the Johnson Administration also reveals a willingness to protect Wilson and his foreign secretaries from avoidable embarrassment over Vietnam. The President referred in his 14 June, 1966 letter to Wilson to their mutual agreement that 'there should be a good deal of blue sky between your visit and possible action in Viet Nam'.[65] In March 1965, Bundy portrayed Rusk as wanting 'to keep the British just happy enough to hold them aboard' on Vietnam.[66] For his part, Wilson clearly wanted to maintain cordial relations with LBJ – short, naturally, of committing troops. This attitude took him on occasion to the brink of sycophancy. Francis Bator, for example, in January 1967, relayed Wilson's excuse for meeting Robert Kennedy. Wilson, so Bator informed LBJ, 'wanted to be sure you understood the circumstances. He felt he could not say no to the Senator's request.'[67]

Perceptions of Britain, as expressed within the Johnson Administration, tended to reflect two basic attitudes. Firstly, it was accepted as axiomatic that, to quote an October 1966 background paper for George Brown's visit to Washington, 'problems of the economy transcend all other difficulties confronting the British Government'.[68] LBJ himself felt it inevitable that the UK would be heavily mortgaged.[69] Secondly, there was a persistent feeling in Administration circles that British political culture was permeated by a kind of defeatist and disenchanted apathy. This made British advice slightly unreliable, and certainly unimaginative, but also militated against any radical shift away from the now traditional pro-Americanism. The briefing book for Wilson's July 1966 visit pointed to the British public's 'defeatism' over Vietnam. The British, it asserted, 'do not see how the struggle in Vietnam can be won by the anti-Communist forces'.[70] Walt Rostow wrote to LBJ that the British had 'an attitude of mind which, in effect, prefers that we take losses' rather than risk 'sharp confrontation'.[71] Bruce, during the cataclysmic summer of 1968 saw British opinion as characterised by 'disappointment, discouragement and disillusion'. British apathy made it unlikely that 'an explosion like that across the Channel' would erupt.[72]

A series of attitudes and considerations, therefore, shaped US approaches to the crucial question of turning British support into something more substantial than rhetoric: genuine gratitude for even verbal support in an increasingly hostile world; sensitivity to Wilson's political problems; and a view of the UK which stressed problems associated with the economy and national morale. There clearly was a concern that American clumsiness might provoke Britain into precipitate devaluation and withdrawal from east of Suez. Also of significance, although to a lesser extent, were two other facets of the case made by Wilson against troop commitment: the action in Malaysia and the putative importance of Britain's role as mediator in Vietnam.

Ambassador Bruce later asserted that there was an Anglo-American understanding over the division of responsibilities in Malaysia and Vietnam.[73] LBJ apparently told Wilson in February 1965: 'I won't tell you how to run Malaysia and you don't tell us how to run Vietnam.'[74] Wilson's argument that the British effort in Malaysia was complementary to, and supportive of, US policy in Vietnam, was always rather precarious. For one thing, there were enormous disparities between the situation in Malaysia and in Vietnam.[75] It is also the case, as the briefing book for Wilson's July 1966 visit asserted, that, by this time, British commitments in Malaysia were 'disappearing as confrontation draws to a conclusion'.[76] Nonetheless, the understanding over the division of responsibilities does appear to have carried weight.

American attitudes towards British attempts at mediation varied from outbursts of Johnsonian anger to the kind of stoic tolerance expressed in an August 1965 study of such initiatives prepared by staffer Benjamin Read. This study described attempts to reconvene the Geneva Conference, Patrick Gordon Walker's efforts to reach Hanoi, the 'stillborn' Commonwealth mission and Harold Davies's mission of 1965.[77] Such activities were treated with some coolness, even in public.[78] The Pentagon Papers negotiating volumes refer to the 'eagerness of the British leaders to participate with maximum personal visibility'.[79] Even George Brown, who exploded with anger at his treatment at the hands of Washington during the 'Phase A/ Phase B' fiasco of February 1967,[80] later acknowledged: 'We were too anxious to be intermediaries.'[81] Wilson was also regarded as excessively garrulous in public about his mediation.[82] Nonetheless, in line with the general Administration attitude towards the Wilson government, British initiatives were normally tolerated. Britain played a role in the SUNFLOWER initiative, as well as in less ambitious projects making use of, for example, the UK Consul in Hanoi, General Colvin.[83]

2   Case-study: President Carter's human rights policy with special reference to Argentina

(a)   *Administration accounts of the policy*   The human rights commit-ment within Jimmy Carter's foreign policy statements emerged slowly and cautiously during the 1976 Presidential campaign.[84] It was articulated in the context of a general commitment to human rights, which included domestic concerns; and also was expressed as part of a general invocation of a post-Vietnam, post-hegemonic world order. After Carter's election, Administration descriptions of the policy concentrated on its range of application, the precise tactics to be adopted, the place of human rights *vis-à-vis* competing priorities, and on problems of definition. Both during and after the Carter Presi-dency, defenders of the policy pointed to its putatively beneficial impact on the behaviour of foreign governments.

The moral basis of the policy made it difficult for the Administra-tion to justify its application on anything other than a global basis. Patricia Derian, the first Assistant Secretary of State for Human Rights and Humanitarian Affairs, told human rights workers in October 1978: 'our policy is global. It is not aimed at any one country or government but at the goal of creating a common condition where full liberties are respected and exercised by all.'[85]

Though embracing globalism in the abstract, the Administration readily acknowledged that progress on human rights could, in practi-cal terms, be achieved only on the basis of a case-by-case approach. It was necessary to appreciate the 'unique political, social, cultural, and historical realities'[86] of countries whose behaviour the United States was attempting to influence. The US did not enjoy equal leverage with all countries, but would – in the words of Mark Schneider (Derian's deputy) – 'do as much as we can wherever we can'.[87]

This tension between globalism and pragmatism was central to the Carter human rights policy, as was an ambivalence about the policy's putative post-hegemonic assumptions. One the one hand, there was a desire, especially in the early Carter years, to stress that the days of unmitigated Kissingerian *Realpolitik* and 'spheres of influence' were over. Robert Pastor, chief NSC staffer for Latin America, wrote to his boss Zbigniew Brzezinski: Instead of viewing Latin America as our 'region of influence' or as a homogenous region, this Administration recognises Latin America's diversity and views the countries in the region as important actors in world affairs.'[88]

On the other hand, and particularly with regard to Latin America, the Carter policy – at least to the degree that it was based on unilateral American action – had hegemonic overtones. After all, prospects for success in the region depended precisely upon America's ability to exploit its hemispheric hegemony. Congressman Tom Harkin, a leading Capitol Hill human rights activist, put the point well in 1978: 'We always hear it said, "Well, we don't want to interfere in those countries. We don't want to go in there and mess in their internal affairs". I don't see why not. We have been doing it for a hundred years anyway ... We are going to influence Latin America ... The question is how.'[89]

Representatives of the Administration frequently declared that the policy should not be confined to punitive measures against offending countries. Deputy Secretary of State Warren Christopher emphasised, in March 1977, the need also to 'inspire, persuade and reward'.[90] Later in the same year he outlined a range of tactics at America's disposal: 'frank discussion', 'symbolic acts', 'public comment', 'appropriate action' (including punitive measures such as the suspension of aid), mobilisation of 'international support', and the compilation of a 'human rights data base' (the annual State Department country reports).[91]

The operational definition of unacceptable human rights practice was provided during the Carter years by the language of the 1974 Foreign Assistance Act: 'consistent pattern(s) of gross violations' of 'internationally recognized human rights' including: 'torture or cruel, inhuman, or degrading treatment or punishment; prolonged detention without charges; or other flagrant denials of the right to life, liberty and the security of the person.'[92]

Such a definition, of course, raised yet more definitional problems. As White House staffer Lynn Daft wrote to Stuart Eizenstat (Director of Domestic Policy Staff) in 1977: 'The trick, of course, is in defining a "consistent pattern of gross violations of human rights" and, once defined and the countries identified, figuring out a way to deal with the "hit list" diplomatically and constructively.'[93]

Definitional problems also revolved around the question of whether 'human rights' should be taken to embody economic categories – the right to '800 calories a day', for example[94] – as well as civil and political liberties. Most famously, in his Georgia Law School speech of April 1977, Secretary of State Cyrus Vance attempted a threefold definition of human rights: 'integrity of the person'; the 'right to fulfilment of such vital needs as food, shelter, health care and education'; and 'civil and political liberties'.[95] In a speech to the United Nations General Assembly in December 1978, Andrew Young (American Ambassador to the UN) identified poverty as 'the basic obstacle to the realisation of human rights for most people.'[96] Such a broadening of the concept of human rights involved an impressive attempt to address global issues, to transcend Cold War paradigms, and to overcome the ethnocentric assumptions of much pre-existing American foreign policy. As a guide to practical policy, however, such definitions inevitably raised difficulties and opened Pandora's boxes. The sheer vastness of the hopes of its defenders evoked the possibility that the policy would become merely symbolic. The argument put forward by Sandy Vogelgesang, a senior career Foreign Service Officer in the Carter Administration, was well directed: better to take aim at a few egregious violators of civil liberties than to indulge in scattershot symbolism![97]

In the event, the Carter Administration was arraigned on two contradictory counts: not only impractical idealism, but also the cynicism of applying its human rights policy to areas (notably Latin America) where national security considerations would not be compromised. On this latter point, it is worth recalling that even Derian, generally portrayed as a firebrand for human rights, was prepared to admit the claims of what Warren Christopher called 'overriding U.S. national security interests'.[98] As she told human rights workers in 1978: 'human rights objectives do not determine each and every foreign policy decision. They are, however, considered along with other vital U.S. interests such as promotion of national security, trade and arms control.'[99]

Ultimately, the policy would be vindicated not by its consistency, nor even by its moral base, but by its tangible effects. Quantifiable success was difficult to come by; nonetheless, concrete results were regularly invoked as a means of maintaining the policy's momentum. Efforts to erode the brutality of the Argentine military dictatorship were regarded as an important part of this success. In May 1979, Derian pointed to a 'significant reduction' in the number of 'disappearances' of opponents of the Argentine military.[100] In their memoirs, both Brzezinski, and Jimmy Carter himself pointed to important successes in Argentina.[101] In 1986 Cyrus Vance even claimed a significant role for the policy in returning Argentina to democracy.[102]

(b) *Origins and evolution of the policy* The Carter human rights initiative was advanced as an integral part of a new post-Vietnam consensus: an alternative both to *Realpolitik* and to a moralistic foreign policy driven by an inordinate fear of communism. At the institutional level, it was part of the early 1970s Congressional resurgence in foreign policy.

The human rights initiative in foreign policy could, indeed, be described as a creation of the House of Representatives. It was generally opposed by the Nixon and Ford Administrations in the name of the need for executive flexibility; and originally it drew only mild support from the Senate.[103] Hearings held and reports issued by Donald Fraser's subcommittee of the House International Relations Committee in 1973 and 1974 put the issue of Congressional concern for a focus on human rights near the heart of the foreign policy debate. Between 1973 and 1976 Congress moved to establish a human rights office in the State Department and to subject various aid programmes to human rights tests.[104]

This Congressional activity was sustained and informed by various policy institutes and pressure groups which came together in the mid-1970s to form an influential human rights lobby. A shared background in the civil rights and anti-Vietnam war movements gave a strong common feeling to many of the activists. A seminal figure was Jacqui Chagnon, former civil rights and anti-war activist, who moved from the organisation Clergy and Laity Concerned to co-ordinate, with Brewster Rhoads, the Human Rights Working Group of the Coalition for a New Foreign and Military Policy. Various church and labour organisations also had a role, as, notably, did Amnesty International. Among the most effective organisations were those concentrating on particular geographic areas: for example, the Washington Office on Latin America (which helped Representative Harkin draft many of his legislative proposals) and the New York and Californian Argentine Information and Service Centers.[105] Policy proposals also emanated from the liberal 'think tank', the Institute for Policy Studies. Its 1976 report, *The Southern Connection*, became especially influential within the Carter Administration in 1977 and 1978.[106] A December 1976 report emanating from the Commission on United States-Latin American Relations (Centre for Inter-American Relations) reviewed the Congressional human rights achievements and, in effect, offered a blueprint for the Carter policy. The report's principal author was Robert Pastor, soon to become Carter's NSC staff chief for Latin America.[107]

The building materials for the policy were thus clearly in place well before Carter entered the White House in 1977. The new President saw himself as responding both to a new domestic mood, and to the promptings of conscience and international law. It should not be forgotten that the Administration continually emphasised the international dimension of the policy, and tried (generally unsuccessfully) to gain Senate ratification to various international human rights treaties.[108] However, more mundane domestic political interests were also of relevance to the policy's adoption. During 1976 it proved a useful vehicle for uniting right- and left-wing functions within the Democratic party.[109] In December 1977 domestic policy adviser Hamilton Jordan wrote to the President:

I agree with Zbig that we need to be more visible and active on the human rights issues. Of our numerous foreign policy initiatives, it is the only one that has a broad base of support among the American people and is not considered 'liberal'. With Panama and SALT II ahead of us, we need the broad-based, non-ideological support for our foreign policy that human rights provides.[110]

A 1978 memorandum from Brzezinski and Anne Wexler similarly invoked the Strategic Arms Limitations Talks. It held that a 'White House event on human rights would be 'particularly valuable to offset the emphasis that will be placed on SALT'.[111] Late in the Administration, White House personnel Steve Aiello, Al Moses and Bernie Aronson urged that the human rights momentum should be maintained: 'To groups like the Poles, Ukrainians ... and others human rights is the single most important political issue in the field of foreign policy ... The issue is of major importance to groups like the Coalition For a Democratic Majority in the (Henry) Jackson-Moynihan wing of the Democratic Party.'[112]

The policy was seen as a cement with which to bind different ends of the Democratic party spectrum. The Congressional coalition which sustained human rights causes regularly included both aid-cutting and anti-Soviet conservatives as well as liberals. To succeed in these terms, however, it was necessary to appear to apply the policy to friend and foe alike. Jessica Tuchman (NSC staffer) judged in July 1978 that the policy's 'seriousness vis-à-vis the Soviet Union' represented its 'bottom line'.[113] In its actual application, the policy did not evolve consistently. By 1979–80 it had become overshadowed by the growing retreat into Cold War orthodoxy and the general crisis atmosphere.[114] Even before this, it exposed itself to the charge made by Jeane Kirkpatrick, and indeed (albeit obliquely) by Brzezinski himself, of being directed overwhelmingly at right-wing 'friends' rather than left-wing 'foes'.[115] In fact, any accusation of being 'one-sidedly anti-rightist' was unfair. The central fact, as Derian herself all but acknowledged, was that any remotely persuasive invocation of 'national security' would cause 'human rights' to be shunted into second place. This could benefit not only 'left-wing' dictatorships, as in mainland China, but also regimes like South Korea, the Philippines under Marcos and the Shah's Iran. Muravchik, writing from the Democratic party's right wing, put the point well (if somewhat tendentiously):

Because we were trying to make new friends in black Africa, because we needed oil from the Near East, because we wanted detente with the U.S.S.R. and wanted to encourage polycentrism within the Warsaw Pact, because in Asia we were trying to build new relationships with some communist governments while continuing to protect non-communist countries ... practically the only place left was Latin America.[116]

The gradual intrusion of 'national security' and the accelerating Cold War dynamic within the Administration thus represented the main influences underpinning the evolution of human rights policy. Also important, however, were procedural and institutional influences: notably, the bureaucratic tensions discussed in the next section, and the continuing strong Congressional input. By 1979, of course, Congress itself was becoming less interested in the initiatives of mid-decade. Yet sections of Congress remained highly active both on their own behalf, and as supporters of activists within the Administration. (Derian quoted a comment made to her by an Under-Secretary of State: 'Look, we can't do anything with you. We know you've got the whole Hill with you.')[117] Mower offers three examples of positive legislative influence: the eventual trade embargo on Uganda, confrontational human rights reports on the Soviet Union, and a decrease in military aid to the Philippines.[118] The principal executive-legislative confrontation of the Carter years, however, revolved around the familiar concept of executive flexibility and good faith, especially in the context of aid and assistance disbursed through international financial institutions. Some members of Congress also became uneasy about executive implementation and interpretation of the human rights tests which Congress had affixed to foreign assistance legislation. A major effort was also mounted to prevent American tax dollars being delivered to repressive regimes through the mechanism of bodies such as the World Bank, the (US) Export-Import Bank and the International Monetary Fund. Only Carter's promise to oppose such loans and grants to 'gross violators' derailed what the Administration saw as improper legislative interference in the executive's conduct of policy.[119]

(c) *The bureaucratic dimension*   One of the chief goals of the human rights lobby was to secure the institutionalisation of human rights considerations within the executive decision-making process. To some extent this was achieved in the installation within the State Department of Derian's Bureau of Human Rights and Humanitarian Affairs, along with the appointment of human rights officers to regional bureaus and to embassies abroad.[120] Traditional, clientistic State Department attitudes did not, however, disappear with the appearance of new bureaucratic actors. They remained entrenched within the regional bureaux (the Policy Planning Staff seem to have acted as a buffer between Derian's Bureau and the remainder of the Department). Traditional attitudes were well summarised in 1973 by Jack Kubisch, Assistant Secretary of State for Inter-American Affairs in the Nixon Administration:

It is one thing for our newspapers or for private citizens to make charges or make complaints .... It is something else for U.S. government officials ... to lean hard publicly on a regime since to do so might make them feel that they are required to dig in their heels and resist us publicly, or not have anything to do with us.[121].

In December 1976, the State Department told Congress that it wished to continue military assistance to Argentina 'to preserve a professional relationship with the Argentine Armed Forces and demonstrate our interest in constructive overall relations'.[122] This traditional attitude tended to advance the claims of 'quiet diplomacy' over supposedly more strident and disruptive pressure on repressive governments.

Against attitudes such as these Derian and her associates waged virtual all-out bureaucratic warfare. Something of a classic bureaucratic 'outsider', Derian frequently collided with the career bureaucracy, who tended to resent what they saw as her arrogance and amateurism. As D.C. McGaffey, a Foreign Service Officer, put it: 'No-one in the Foreign Service assumed that President Carter was politically naive, or totally cynical. Unfortunately, the human rights policy as enunciated did not give sufficient guidance or definition to determine exactly where between these extremes the real, desired policy would fall.'[123]

Casualties of the bureaucratic battles included Terence Todman, a regional bureau head transferred to Spain. An inter-agency group, chaired by Warren Christopher, was established to adjudicate conflicts and consider human rights issues on a case-by-case basis. Providing an arena for conflict, the Christopher Group gradually established working precedents – not least the practice of regularly deferring to 'national security' considerations. Within these confines, decisional outcomes were often unpredictable. Much, according to Derian, 'depended on whether your paper was compelling enough ... whether you were really hot that day'.[124] On occasion, the Christopher Group itself could become a bureaucratic actor. In 1978, for example, the Department of Agriculture unilaterally announced – in direct opposition to a Christopher Group decision – a major loan to Chile.[125]

The history of the Carter human rights policy clearly bears the imprint of these bureaucratic battles. Derian's Bureau conflicted not only with other factions within the State Department, but also, for example, with the Department of Commerce over proposals to sell crime-control equipment to Latin American regimes.[126] Tensions between Derian and Brzezinski are evident in a 1979 NSC staff memo referring to ' a considerable amount of history' between the two 'on the subject of Argentina'.[127] A Congressional delegation reported in 1978 that it was widely felt among Foreign Service Officers that the Christopher Group did not 'adequately use the input from our diplomats' in Latin America.[128] White House aide Joyce Starr informed Eizenstat in 1978 that White House coordination of human rights issue was virtually non-existent.[129]

Bureaucratic interpretation of statutory language had a major impact upon the policy's implementation. Most statutes (notably section 502B of the Foreign Assistance Act) allowed exceptions to aid cut-offs or reductions in the case of countries having poor human rights records. These generally related to 'extraordinary circumstances' or to funds intended to alleviate immediate popular distress. While reasonably fastidious in comparison with other Administrations, the executive branch under Carter was capable of sharp practice in interpreting this loophole language. The failure to restrict Indonesian military aid, despite the regime's brutal record in East Timor, was one such example.[130]

(d) *Criticisms of the policy* Many possible criticisms of the policy emerge from the previous discussion. Others are inherent in common perceptions and interpretations of the Carter Presidency as a whole: for example, the putative failure to speak with one voice or the supposedly precipitate reversion to Cold War orthodoxy in its latter stages.[131] However, criticisms of the human rights policy may be divided into those emanating from different points on the ideological spectrum.

Some leftist critics were prepared to condemn the whole policy as an expression of Trilateral Commission 'world order' liberalism. James Petras wrote in 1977 that morality was the 'recurring ideological expression of U.S. imperialism in a period of crisis'.[132] Curbing egregious excess might also be a way of stabilising right-wing dictatorships and demobilising popular struggles. Interestingly enough, this point surfaced in an Administration reply to a complaint from Paraguay about the destabilising effect of the policy: 'we believe that a policy of promoting a wide range of human rights can help a government achieve a broader base of popular support and this can serve to enhance, rather than detract, from the stability of that government'.[133]

From a left liberal perspective, the policy tends to be regarded as well-intentioned, but deeply flawed. It appears inconsistent – even, as in Carter's famous toast to the Shah of Iran in 1977,[134] hypocritical – and always likely to collapse before the juggernaut of 'national security'. There is substance to this charge. Yet, as noted above, it should be stressed that any comprehensive list of countries which 'escaped' the human rights policy would be very ideologically heterogeneous. It would include, for a long period at least, Cambodia as well as South Korea. Defenders of the policy frequently found themselves performing logical gyrations. Anne Wexler, for example, wrote in 1980 of the Turkish government 'conscientiously' seeking to 'subdue' domestic political violence, while 'remaining true to its democratic principles'.[135]

The Administration's occupation of the moral high ground inevitably exposed it to charges of dishonesty. An NSC staff memo of November 1978 opposed a State Department proposal for an international amnesty for prisoners of conscience on the following grounds: 'If one ever tried to actually implement it ... it would be a nightmare. Who would decide who is a prisoner of conscience? Are the Wilmington 10?'[136]

(Andrew Young, of course, spoke of 'hundreds, perhaps even thousands' of 'political prisoners' in the United States.)[137] Latin American targets of the human rights policies were quick to condemn the interfering arrogance of a hegemonic power which could not even keep its own house in order. Irish-American groups were met with evasions when they raised the question of the British human rights record in Northern Ireland.[138]

On the right, criticism was often articulated within the realist tradition. Carter himself countered that 'moral principles' were the 'best foundation for the exertion of American power and influence'.[139] Ed Muskie, who succeeded Vance at the State Department in 1980, asserted that 'emphasis on human rights serves our national interests'.[140] But, as Dean Rusk pointed out, a truly consistent human rights policy that went beyond simple exhortation was tantamount to isolating the US from the outside world.[141] As the section below on Argentina will illustrate, powerful business interests were concerned to resist any such outcome. Business generally saw the policy as potentially an improper obstacle to free trade.

The Reaganite assault on the policy was largely vacuously polemical. The Carter initiative did not dismiss the virtues of 'quiet diplomacy', nor was it cripplingly devoid of pragmatism. Derian herself attempted 'quiet diplomacy' during visits to the Ivory Coast, the Philippines and Argentina; Vice-President Mondale met South African Prime Minister Vorster in Geneva.[142] It was the 'pragmatic' concern for 'national security' which ultimately restricted the policy's cutting edge to Latin America and (to some extent) South Africa. Aid was cut off during the Carter years in only eight countries: Argentina, Bolivia, El Salvador, Guatemala, Haiti, Nicaragua, Paraguay and Uruguay.[143] The Administration was also extremely reluctant either to consider widespread economic sanctions or to interfere with private investment practices. The policy may justly be accused of being merely symbolic, but surely not of being rigidly unpragmatic,

Did the policy make any difference? Initial surveys, including a Congressional Research Service study, suggested that it mitigated brutality only at the margins. The CRS study (1981) found only 'five or six instances' where 'actual or explicitly threatened reductions in aid' may plausibly be said to have effected human rights improvements.[144] The outstanding, and most frequently cited, example was Argentina.

(e) *Argentina* The extent of officially sanctioned brutality in Argentina was common currency when Carter entered the White House. It had been the subject of extensive Congressional hearings and campaigns by the human rights lobby. (The Argentine military attempted to counter this publicity in a campaign organised by the US public relations firm, Marstellar. In April 1977, a year after the military coup, President Videla appeared on American television to proclaim a 'year of peace'.)[145] Despite this, Vance's February 1977 announcement that aid to Argentina would be cut, from thirty-two million (President Ford's figure) to fifteen million dollars, was less than might have been expected. Jessica Tuchman warned Brzezinski in early February that Congress would not rest content with rhetorical gestures. Administration credibility depending on '*individual country by country budget items for security assistance*' cuts.[146] Even so, Congressional human rights activists – no longer confined to the House – mounted a campaign to delete all aid. Subsequent aid cuts, and the 1977 termination of US military training aid, were essentially the work of Congress.[147]

The question of arms sales loomed large in this debate. Again, the significant action was taken by Congress. From October 1978, sale of munitions list items was banned to Argentina. There were, however, significant loopholes and slippages. Several Chinook helicopters were sold immediately before the ban took effect. Argentina obtained American arms via its allies, and had no difficulty anyway in purchasing them from non-American sources. The Human Rights Bureau was engaged in a constant struggle over the definition of 'noncombat' items.[148]

Action was also taken through international financial institutions to block loans and grants to Argentina. In all, during the Carter years, US representatives in such institutions voted 'no' or abstained on proposals for Argentina at least twenty-three times. In 1978 the State Department invoked legislation relating to the Export-Import Bank to halt funds for a large Argentinian hydro-electric project.[149] Such initiatives were not simply gestures, and went beyond anything contemplated by other Administrations. Nonetheless, the counter-pressures were considerable and could not always be resisted. Not only were voices within the State Department and the military raised in defence of 'traditional' diplomacy; concerted business opposition also began to emerge. It was estimated that, for 1978, an estimated eight hundred million dollars in contract losses were suffered by US firms as a result of the Argentinian human rights issue.[150] As a 1978 White House staff memo indicated, the policy's effect on 'export sales' stimulated 'numerous calls ... inquiries and discussions'.[151] Members of Congress raised the question of the importance of Argentinian hide imports to the US leather industry.[152] Business pressure, co-ordinated by the gas turbine manufacturers Allis-Chalmers, caused Congress, in effect, by 1979–80 to suspend the policy of using Export–Import Bank credits as sticks with which to beat human rights violators.[153] An interesting expression of Brzezinski's views on these issues is contained in an 1980 letter he wrote to the chairman of Eaton Corporation. The chairman, E. Mandell deWindt, had complained about his company's 'failure to obtain a license for the sale of anti-personnel radar units to Argentina'. NSC chief Brzezinski replied that the implementation of the human rights policy:

entails the sensitive balancing of its several components, which often conflict. The process can and does involve the occasional decision to forego a U.S. grant, loan or sale if our basic foreign policy criteria are not met, as in the case you outlined. In that sense, I could agree there is what you call a 'downside' to the human rights policy. But in fact the great majority of proposals are approved, either because they do not violate clearly established criteria, or fit clearly into an exception. Those judgements are made through procedures which seek to keep our various policy purposes in perspective while carrying out the law.[154].

The record of the Carter Administration reveals diligent casework on behalf of Argentinian political prisoners and the 'disappeared'.[155] The case of Jacobo Timerman is the best known, but was one among many others. Yet the policy did have its limitations. As Patrick Flood, who worked in the Human Rights Bureau, put it: 'There were times ... when the push and pull of bureaucratic forces representing other U.S. national interests produced a mixed message about our priorities.'[156]

One such occasion occurred in the wake of the 1979 Soviet invasion of Afghanistan. Desire to keep Argentina firmly in the anti-Soviet camp seemed to signal a possible relaxation of America's human rights posture, and elicited a resignation threat from Derian.

The cynicism of the Argentinian response to the policy makes it difficult to claim with any great certainty that brutality was lessened as a result of US action. Prisons, for example, were painted in preparation for the 1978 Inter-American Commission on Human Rights (of the Organisation of American States) visit.[157] Nonetheless, most authorities, even hostile ones, would acknowledge that in Argentina the policy did bear some fruit.[158] Vance's 1986 attempt to describe Carter as the father of Argentinian democracy was a wild overstatement. Nonetheless, the case of Argentina may be cited against the notion that the human rights policy was just so much rhetoric and humbug. Congress and elements within the Administration did ensure that, during the Carter years, these issues were firmly on the foreign policy agenda.[159] Limited and incoherent as the policy was, apologists for the Carter Administration are entitled to present it as containing seeds of a genuinely post-hegemonic and post-Cold War foreign policy.

3   Reflections on the case-studies

The two case-studies relate to significantly different periods, and comparisons between them should take due note of this. The failure in Vietnam separates the two examples and inaugurated the policy environment which shaped the whole human rights initiative. The two studies also involved different types of decisions. The Johnson Administration study revolved around a negative decision: the decision (ultimately made by LBJ himself) to stop short of forcing Britain into committing troops by holding the pound as hostage. The key Johnson decision did not require implementation in the conventional sense. The first case-study illustrates that decisions *not* to do things may be as important as positive decisions. The Carter example, on the other hand, involved the assumption by the Administration of the vocabulary of human rights, and the working-out of this policy. It clearly illustrates the value of the 'implementation' perspective. The story of the Carter human rights policy is essentially a story of pragmatic accommodation at the implementation stage, accompanied by familiar 'slippages' and executive flexibility in interpreting Congressional statutes. The Carter example also illustrates the influence private business interests may have over foreign policy implementation.

The Johnson example essentially involved a dispute, eventually adjudicated by the President, among a small policy-making elite. The main actors were National Security Adviser Bundy (and later Rostow) and Johnson. Other important figures were NSC staff personnel Francis Bator and Chester Cooper, Defence Secretary McNamara, Secretary of State Rusk, Under-Secretary Ball, and Treasury Secretary Fowler. Only David Bruce represented (as a career diplomat) a perspective outside this narrow, highly-politicised elite. The force with which LBJ was urged to blackmail Britain into committing troops was tempered by the general Washington perception of Harold Wilson's predicament. Nonetheless, the importance of the President's adjudicatory power is underlined by the fact that only Bruce (and eventually LBJ) unequivocally opposed, ultimately, forcing Wilson's hand.

The Johnson Administration policy-makers correctly assumed that there was no significant Congressional or public opposition to a policy of encouraging British troop commitment. In the long term, failure to mobilise allied support might harm the Administration's public standing. Nonetheless, elite domination of policy, and the attendant secrecy, ensured a minimum of detailed public debate on the issue. In effect, decision-makers were released from any urgent need to consider possible non-elite criticisms of how efforts to bring allies into the war were actually conducted. Congress, interest groups, informed and sensitised public opinion: these were simply not of immediate concern to LBJ and his advisers. What was of concern, ironically, was the likely effect of troop commitment on *British* public opinion.

Carter's human rights policy was, in contrast, deliberately made as public as possible. Only thus could a new, post-Vietnam foreign policy consensus be established. Congressional and interest group activity were central to the initiative, and, indeed, emphatically predated the President's advocacy of foreign policy based on human rights. In a sense, the policy was shaped by public opinion. More accurately, however, it represented an attempt to respond to (and mould) perceived post-Vietnam shifts in public opinion. The policy was also the product of what Patrick Flood called the 'push and pull of bureaucratic forces', with the warring State Department factions performing a crucial role. As noted in Chapter 2, the 'bureaucratic politics' approach can explain policy outcomes only within certain confines. It does not address itself to questions of bias within the system as a whole. It sheds relatively little light on highly elite policy processes which (as in the Johnson case-study) tend to be dominated by the President. As the Carter case-study indicates, however, within its limits, the 'bureaucratic politics' perspective is indispensable.

Why was policy-making in the two case-studies so different? Some reasons are obvious: the wartime, crisis-oriented, secretive context of the Johnson example; the post-Vietnam Congressional reassertion which produced the human rights initiatives. The Johnson case also involved elite leader-to-leader contacts between old allies; the Carter policy was nothing if not multilateral, even global, in its ambitions and applications. Despite the case-by-case approach, policy towards one country (such as Argentina) could not be divorced from debate on the policy as a whole. The first case-study was not entirely a narrow 'security' issue. It had, for example, an economic dimension – the dollar/sterling relationship and the issue of loans to Britain. It clearly, however, was of narrower import than the Carter study. LBJ's policy towards Britain did not involve any major reassessment of US policy, but rather a relatively detached judgement (made easier because of its secrecy) about the feasibility of particular courses of action. Carter's human rights policy, even in the relatively narrow Argentinian context, involved deliberate questioning of basic policy assumptions. The Johnson policy-makers were operating on the back of (soon to be shattered) consensus, rather than attempting to create a new one.

The case-studies illustrate the value of some of the approaches to the study of foreign policy decision-making discussed in Chapter 2. The dominant 'belief system' within the Johnson Administration regarding the United Kingdom provided the backdrop to the first case-study. The hard position taken by McGeorge Bundy may be seen as fitting the 'roles' approach. As National Security Adviser, Bundy was almost bound to take a view which addressed Administration concerns in the narrow sense. He thus stood at the opposite end of the attitudinal spectrum to Ambassador Bruce, who interpreted events from his office in London. Similarly, leading actors in the Carter study – notably Brzezinski, State Department and Congressional personnel – also appeared to be acting out, to a degree, pre-determined 'roles': not in the mechanistic, 'bureaucratic politics' sense, but in a dynamic interplay between personality and position. Nowhere is this better illustrated than in Derian's attempts to lower the expectations of human rights workers on the one hand, while simultaneously battling against traditionalist forces in the State Department.

The case-studies also shed light upon general issues (raised in Chapter 1) concerning America's international position. On the narrow issue of Anglo-American relations, the first study illustrates a phase in the gradual pulling apart of the allies. This pulling apart was to become more pronounced as the US began looking increasingly towards the Pacific and the UK towards Western Europe. The elite interchanges between Johnson and Wilson (and their elite advisers) appear indicative of a 'realist' interpretation of international relations.

Yet American reluctance to see the pound devalued gave Wilson some leverage, and indicated the extent to which the relationship (despite American dominance) had a degree of interdependence about it.

With the Carter human rights policy, we see an Administration (or at least elements within it) consciously struggling to formulate a policy for a post-hegemonic, interdependent world. In accord with such an objective, the policy bore the imprint of an appropriately disaggregated policy process. As noted above, and especially as it affected Latin America, the policy largely remained rooted in hegemonic assumptions. Nonetheless, the complex, multi-faceted interactions with Latin America – and notably the key role played by non-governmental actors – did illustrate the mechanics of interdependent foreign policy. The policy was radically distorted by the constant invocation of 'security' considerations. Yet, rather than revealing the triumph of 'realism' over 'interdependence', the policy should be seen as offering guidance to policy-makers searching in the 1990s for a new post-Cold War consensus.

4 Conclusion

(a) *Democracy and American foreign policy* During his 1976 campaign, Jimmy Carter made the assertion that every 'time we've made a serious mistake in foreign affairs' it was 'because the American people have been excluded from the process'.[160] Such a statement may appear naive, especially perhaps in view of the experience of the Carter Administration. As is implicit in David Barrett's argument in Chapter 3, post-1945 US foreign policy has been shaped by Presidential leadership and the National Security Council system. It is not easy to visualise any alternative to this. The public and also foreign policy elites look to the White House to shape the agenda. Congress does not impress as a force either able or willing to assume leadership. American political parties remain relatively weak and inchoate, despite some signs of regrouping and nationalisation.[161] Nonetheless, it is worth making two points which reflect more optimistically upon the connection between democracy and foreign policy.

Firstly, as noted in previous chapters, the supposed antagonism between democracy and efficiency in foreign policy-making is misleading. Unfettered executive power promotes abuses of power, bureaucratism and the persistence of error. In this connection, Kenneth Waltz has an interesting comparison between British and

American practice, neatly reversing some familiar assumptions. The fact that this comparison appeared in a book published in 1967 should put us on our guard against praise for an American system engaged in mismanagement in Vietnam. Nonetheless, his general points are worth considering. In Britain, the 'fusion of powers and the concentration of responsibility encourage governments to avoid problems'. Whereas decentralised American institutions facilitate 'the quick identification of problems, the pragmatic quest ... for solutions ... the open criticism of policies'.[162] It should also be stressed that Carter's 1976 assertion had more than an element of truth in it. While – as Morgenthau famously pointed out[163] – a popular foreign policy is not necessarily a good one, the failures of post-1945 US foreign relations are hardly the failures of excessive democratic control and participation. Hall and Ikenberry offer the following excellent reply to Morgenthau's point:

it is entirely proper to remember that the American people were perfectly prepared to fight in the 'good' war of 1941–5, and that they, rather than the experts, were right to refuse to continue the war in Vietnam .... Democratic control of foreign policy is ultimately ... a positive resource because of its capacity to weed out poor policies.[164]

Secondly, a new era for foreign relations – an era of interdependence and relaxation of Cold War tensions – opens up new opportunities for democratic foreign policy. Traditional arguments about the inappropriateness of disaggregated democratic participation in crisis/security-oriented foreign policy no longer convince. The emergence of 'local' foreign policy (discussed in Chapter 8) epitomises the new environment.

At least four forces stand opposed to successful and creative adaptation to this new era of possibility for democratic foreign policy. The remainder of this Conclusion will draw brief attention to each of these forces, and then will attempt to speculate upon the future of American foreign policy.

The first force threatening to undermine democratic foreign policy may be termed the 'logic of executive competence': the view that policy made in secret by relatively unitary structures is superior to that made publicly (especially) by legislatures. Various objections to this view have already been made, and the point does not need to be laboured. What may be noted here, however, is the constitutional point argued by Louis Fisher. In separating the executive and legislative powers, and assigning to Congress a foreign policy role, the

Framers sought to advance the causes both of democracy *and* efficiency. Despite Hamilton's doctrine of the strong Presidency, the Constitution does not equate Congressional control of the executive with inefficiency.[165]

The second enemy of democratic foreign policy is public ignorance and elite manipulation of public opinion. As noted in Chapter 7, public opinion is more 'rational' than commonly supposed. The positing of an alarmist, bellicose public opinion is little more than a convenient fiction designed to bolster the 'logic of executive competence'. High levels of public education and access to information are essential to the proper functioning of democracy. In their absence, policy debate becomes constricted and ritualistic: confined, for example, to consideration of marginal changes in the defence budget, or to reactions to Presidential initiatives.[166] Here, it can only be urged that access to information be expanded, notably through liberalisation of the Freedom of Information Act; and that public education be highly prioritised in any post-Cold War ('peace dividend') reallocation of resources.

The third and fourth of these forces threatening to undermine future developments towards democratic foreign policy are inextricably linked. They are the militarisation of the American economy (the 'military-industrial complex') and the unaccountable power of giant, privately-owned corporations. Issues such as Pentagon reform and control of the 'military–industrial complex' have been around so long that they seem almost intractable. Any coherent, democratic post-hegemonic American foreign policy will have to grasp the nettle, and confront vested interests. As to corporate power generally, it was noted in Chapter 8 that its influence is complex and subtle. The need, however, is clear: to make corporate power accountable to democratic processes.[167]

(b) *The future*   It seems almost inevitable that defence cuts in the United States, encouraged by budgetary deficits and the diminution of the Soviet threat, will involve a drawback from conventional military commitments in Europe.[168] James Baker, President Bush's Secretary of State, has made no bones about the need to transform NATO from primarily a military into a political and economic alliance. The 2 per cent overall defence cut, in real dollars, proposed by President Bush in January 1990 was only a modest gesture towards military retrenchment. Nonetheless, the 1990 defence budget, along with Bush's proposals for joint US-Soviet cuts, showed that the retrenchment process had begun. One key question for the future, however, is whether military shrinkage should (or will) embrace neo-isolationism.[169]

As noted in Chapter 1, 'isolationism' ('neo'- or otherwise) is not a very satisfactory peg upon which to hang a discussion of American traditions in foreign policy. A drawback from European military commitments would not constitute a 'return' to isolationism. It was George Kennan who remarked that American troops must leave central Europe some day.[170] Nonetheless, there are strong forces which will tend in the future to inhibit the kind of freewheeling, interventionist liberalism which has characterised US foreign policy since 1945.

The most obvious of these forces are deficits and decline. Military retrenchment is not the inevitable consequence of the massive deficits bequeathed by the Reagan Administration. An alternative would be the switching of resources away from private consumption.[171] But retrenchment is by far the most likely consequence. The debate over national decline in the late 1980s almost reached the level of hysteria. (Christopher Coker has advised the US to follow the advice of the poet Heine and imprison prophets of doom until their prophecies come true.)[172] Nevertheless, the United States is clearly faced with competing and potent economic power blocs: not only in Japan, but also in a Europe possibly dominated by a reunited Germany. America, while still to the fore of technological innovation, has fierce competition in this area too.[173] US foreign policy has to operate in an interdependent world: a world, for example, of import dependence and a world where the reaction of Japanese (and other private) investors in the American economy have to be considered.[174]

The inhibitions upon American foreign policy imposed by these forces of deficit, decline and interdependence are especially difficult to gauge in the case of policy towards the Third World. At one level, one might expect these forces to discourage direct US intervention in Third World affairs. The easing of East-West tension may mean that conflict in the Third World seems of diminished importance to American policy-makers. It would certainly appear to give American clients in the developing world less leverage in Washington. On the other hand, the spread of military (and especially nuclear) technology to developing nations adds great unpredictability to the situation. The demise of Cold War rivalries also, in a sense, gives the United States a free hand. The 1989 invasion of Panama provoked Soviet protests, but did not threaten a resumption of the Cold War.

It was symptomatic of the new era of world politics that the Panamanian invasion constituted the first important use of US military force in the Western hemisphere since 1945 in pursuit of a goal not related (directly) to the containment of international communism. The new agenda is widely held to include problems of drugs, terrorism, environmental pollution and international control of arms and nuclear proliferation. This new agenda would seem to point the United States in the direction of multilateralism rather than isolation. New alliance patterns – for example, with the Pacific rim nations – seemed to be emerging even before the revolutionary upheavals of 1989 in Eastern Europe. After these changes, the whole structure of international alliances seems uncertain. Not only the revolutions in Eastern Europe, but also American responses to Western European integration, seem likely profoundly to influence future priorities. It no longer seems remotely certain, for example, that American policy-makers will increasingly direct their attention towards the Pacific.[175]

As United States opinion responded to events in Eastern Europe and the Soviet Union in 1989 and early 1990, morose introspection about national decline gave way in some quarters to expressions of triumph. What did the revolution in Eastern Europe represent if not the triumph of American liberal (democratic and capitalist) values? Did not the dismantling of the Soviet empire (both inside and outside the boundaries of the USSR) put the supposed decline of American power into true perspective? In other quarters, there was still a hesitancy to pronounce a funeral oration for the Cold War. Richard Nixon advised President-elect Bush in 1989 that Mikhail Gorbachev 'does not want to overturn the Soviet system; he wants to strengthen it'.[176]

American policy-makers should avoid both empty triumphalism and nostalgia for a vanished Cold War. Change in Eastern Europe signals the collapse of the bankrupt system of bureaucratised state socialism, not the vindication of post-1945 US foreign policy. It is also by no means impossible that future Soviet governments will seek to reimpose old certainties. The changes put in train in the Gorbachev era, however, will not and simply cannot be put into reverse.

Like the Soviet Union, the United States has to adjust to an interdependent world and to a new balance between resources and commitments. The success of such adjustment will depend, to some extent, upon the creation of a new domestic foreign policy consensus to replace anti-communism. This may be supplied by the 'new agenda' referred to above. Positive reappraisal of the human rights policies of the Carter Administration would also, as previously suggested, push US policy-makers in the right direction.[177] Success will also depend, however, on their ability to adapt the legacy of American liberal ideology to the needs of a world where hegemony will belong to no single nation-state.

Notes

1 E. Short, *Whip to Wilson*, London, 1989, p. 117. On intra-Labour Vietnam protest, see D. E. Butler and A. King, *The British General Election of 1966*, London, 1966, p. 205; L. Minkin, *The Labour Party Conference*, London, 1978, pp. 294–96; and E. Shaw, *Discipline and Discord in the Labour Party*, Manchester, 1988, p. 157.

2 Short, *Whip to Wilson*, pp. 117–18.

3 See H. Wilson, *The Labour Government 1964–1970*, London, 1971, p. 248; T. Benn, *Out of the Wilderness: Diaries 1963–67*, London, 1987, p. 440; *Hansard*, vol. 728, cols. 1116–22 (17 May 1966) and vol. 730, cols. 921–7 (23 June 1966); and C. King, *The Cecil King Diary 1965–1970*, London, 1972, pp. 78–9.

4 *Congressional Record*, 6 February 1968, p. 2310. On the shipping issue, see *The Department of State Bulletin*, LIV (7 February 1966), p. 192; also, folder 'United Kingdom PM Briefing Book 7/29/66' and 'memorandum for Mr. W. Rostow from Benjamin H. Read: Washington visit of Wilson 6/2/67', both in National Security File (NSF): Country File (CF): Europe and USSR: United Kingdom, boxes 215/216 (Lyndon B. Johnson Library, Austin, Texas).

5 D. Bruce, Oral History (LBJ Library), pp. 23–4. See also NSF: Files of McGeorge Bundy (folder, 'Luncheons with the President', vol. 1, part 2), boxes 18/19; R. Larsen and J. L. Collins, *Allied Participation in Vietnam*, Washington D.C., 1975, p. 2; McGeorge Bundy memo to President Johnson, 15 December 1964, NSF: Memos to the President: McGeorge Bundy (vols. 5–8), box 2 (on appointment of James Rafferty to handle the 'third country problem').

6 Wilson, *The Labour Government*, p. 264; A. P. Dobson, *The Politics of the Anglo-American Economic Special Relationship*, Brighton, 1988, pp. 213–20; C. Ponting, *Breach of Promise: Labour in Power 1964–1970*, London, 1989, pp. 47–56, 220.

7 B. Castle, *The Castle Diaries 1964–70*, London, 1984, p. 282.

8 A. Shlaim *et al.*, *British Foreign Secretaries Since 1945*, Newton Abbot, 1977, p. 186; Wilson, *The Labour Government*, p. 264; Larsen and Collins, *Allied Participation*, pp. 22–3.

9 See B. Reed and G. Williams, *Denis Healey and the Policies of Power*, London, 1971, p. 215.

10 McGeorge Bundy memorandum to President Johnson, 10 September 1965, NSF: Memos to the President: McGeorge Bundy, vol. 14 (cited in Ponting, *Breach of Promise*, p. 53).

11 See M. Billings-Yun, *Decision Against War: Eisenhower and Dien Bien Phu, 1954*, New York, 1988, p. 109; R. R. James, *Anthony Eden*, London, 1986, p. 377; G. Warner, 'The settlement of the Indochina war', in J.W. Young, ed., *The Foreign Policy of Churchill's Peacetime Administration 1951–1955*, Leicester, 1988, pp. 233–60. See also R.J. Wybrow, *Britain Speaks Out, 1937–87*, London, 1989, pp. 40, 86 (on public opinion).

12 Memorandum from Ball, 5 December 1964 ('Subject: The Wilson Visit'), NSF: Memos to the President: McGeorge Bundy, vols. 5–8, box 2.

13 Bator memorandum, 28 July 1965, 'Agenda: Preparation for Trend', (folder, 'Trendex'), NSF: CF: Europe and USSR: United Kingdom, boxes 215/216. This memorandum appears to have been widely circulated.

14 McGeorge Bundy memorandum to President Johnson, 28 July 1965, 'Subject: Your Meeting with Joe Fowler', (folder, 'Trendex'), *ibid.*

15 Baker memorandum to Bundy, 29 July 1965, 'Subject: The UK Problem and Thinking about the Unthinkable', (folder, 'Trendex'), *ibid.*

16 See Dobson, *The Politics*, p. 231.

17 King, *The Cecil King Diary*, p. 107; *Sanity*, May 1965, article by C. Feinstein in R. Murray, ed., *Vietnam: Read-In*, London, 1965, pp. 192–3. See also B. I. Kaufman, 'Foreign aid and the balance of payments problems', in R. A. Divine, ed., *The Johnson Years: Volume 2, Vietnam, the Environment and Science*, Lawrence (Kansas), 1987, pp. 79–109, pp. 93–4.

18 Bundy to Johnson, 2 August, 1965, NSF: Memos to the President: McGeorge Bundy, vol. 13 (cited in Ponting, *Breach of Promise*, p. 51).

19 Folder, 'United Kingdom Briefing Book 7/29/66', NSF: CF: Europe and USSR: United Kingdom, boxes 215/216.

20 See F. S. Northedge, *Descent from Power*, London, 1974, p. 269.

21 Benn, *Out of the Wilderness*, p. 262.

22 Wilson, *The Labour Government*, pp. 86, 247.

23 D. Healey, *The Time of My Life*, London, 1989, p. 226.

24 See 'Interview with Tariq Ali', in J. Dumbrell, ed., *Vietnam and the Antiwar Movement*, Aldershot, 1989, pp. 173–81; also T. Ali, *Street Fighting Years*, London, 1987, pp. 45, 69.

25 *Out of the Wilderness*, p. 501. See also J. Aulich, 'Cartoon representations in the British press', in A. Louvre and J. Walsh, eds., *Tell Me Lies About Vietnam*, Milton Keynes, 1988, pp. 111–33, pp. 114–15.

26 See D. E. Schoen, *Enoch Powell and the Powellites*, London, 1977, p. 18.

27 See R. Crossman, *The Diaries of a Cabinet Minister: Volume 2*, London, 1976, p. 181; also *Volume 1*, London, 1975, p. 456.

28 *Ibid. (Volume 1)*, p. 574.

29 *Breach of Promise*, ch. 3. See also G. Warner, 'The Anglo-American special relationship', *Diplomatic History*, 13, 1989, pp. 479–99, p. 492.

30 Wilson, *The Labour Government*, p. 264; Dobson, *The Politics*, p. 214; Bruce, Oral History, p. 18.

31 Cooper memorandum to McGeorge Bundy, 29 April 1965, 'Free World Assistance to Vietnam', (folder, 'McGeorge Bundy Teach-In'), NSF:

Files of McGeorge Bundy, boxes 18/19.

32 Larsen and Collins, *Allied Participation*, pp. 167–68.

33 Ponting, *Breach of Promise*, pp. 220–21.

34 See J. T. Richelson and D. Ball, *The Ties That Bind*, Boston, 1985; D. Campbell, *The Unsinkable Aircraft Carrier*, London, 1986, p. 142.

35 See Bruce, Oral History, p. 24 and N.B. Hannah, *The Key to Failure: Laos and the Vietnam War*, London, 1987, p. 195 (on British counterinsurgency experts). See Campbell, *The Unsinkable Aircraft Carrier*, p. 142 (on SAS).

36 See R. Edmonds, *Setting the Mould*, Oxford 1986; also H. B. Ryan, *The Vision of Anglo-America*, Cambridge, 1987, p. 123.

37 See W. Wallace, *The Foreign Policy Process in Britain*, London, 1975, p. 157.

38 Walt Rostow memorandum to President Johnson, 20 October 1967 (enclosing a copy of Fulbright's letter), NSF: CF: Vietnam, box 102.

39 *Congressional Record*, 18 July 1966, pp. 16032–3.

40 L. Heren, *No Hail, No Farewell*, London, 1970, p. 231.

41 E.g. *ibid.*, p. 183.

42 See J. Callaghan, *Time and Chance*, London, 1987, p. 211.

43 See Roy Jenkins's review of Ponting, *Breach of Promise* (*Observer*, 5 March 1989). Also Dobson, *The Politics*, p. 213.

44 Rostow memorandum to the President, 17 June 1966, NSF: Memos to the President: Walt Rostow, vol. 6, box 8 (original emphasis).

45 'Personal to the Prime Minister from the President', 14 June 1966, *ibid.*

46 Ball, 6 August 1965, 'British Sterling Crisis', (folder, 'Trendex'), NSF: CF: Europe and USSR: United Kingdom, boxes 215/216.

47 See, e.g., Rusk speech at Boston University, *The Department of State Bulletin*, LIV (4 April 1966), p. 519.

48 Bruce, Oral History, p. 23.

49 Cabinet Papers (folder, 3/13/68), box 13, p. 4.

50 Rusk memorandum to President Johnson, 13 March 1965, NSF: CF: Europe and USSR: United Kingdom, box 207 (memo folder, UK, vol. III).

51 McGeorge Bundy memorandum to President Johnson, 14 April 1965, NSF: Memos to the President: McGeorge Bundy, vols. 9, 10, 11, box 3.

52 Incoming cable to Department of State, 5 April 1965, NSF: CF: Europe and USSR: United Kingdom (cables vol. III, 2/65 – 4/65), box 207 (original in capitals).

53 'Background Paper for Mr. Walt Rostow: Vietnam: UK Position', 15 February 1967, (folder, 2/67), NSF: CF: Europe and USSR: United Kingdom, boxes 215/216.

54 Incoming cable to Department of State, 3 June 1965, NSF: CF: Europe and USSR: United Kingdom (cables, vol. IV, 5/65 – 6/65), box 207 (original in capitals).

55 Incoming cable to Department of State, 15 October 1964, NSF: CF: Europe and U.S.S.R.: United Kingdom (cables, vol. II, 10/64 – 2/65), box 206 (original in capitals).

56 Incoming cable to Department of State, 21 October 1964, *ibid.*

57 Incoming cable to Department of State, 27 April 1965, NSF: CF: Europe and USSR: United Kingdom (cables, vol. III, 2/65 – 4/65), box 207, (original in capitals).

58 See P. Wright, *Spycatcher*, New York, 1988, p. 458; also D. Leigh, *The Wilson Plot*, London, 1988, pp. 102–3.

59 *White House Years*, Boston, 1979, p. 92.

60 Memorandum of conversation: visit of Healey, Shadow Defence Minister, 25 March 1964 (folder, 'United Kingdom memos 11/63 – 10/64'), NSF: CF: Europe and USSR: United Kingdom, box 206.

61 Short, *Whip to Wilson*, p. 37.

62 Bundy memorandum to President Johnson, 1 March 1964, ('U.K. folder: meetings with Wilson 3/2/64'), NSF: CF: Europe and USSR: United Kingdom, box 213.

63 Rusk memorandum to President Johnson, 22 March 1965, 'United Kingdom: Wilson visit 4/15/65', NSF: CF: Europe and USSR: United Kingdom, boxes 215/216.

64 Folder, 'United Kingdom PM Briefing Book 7/29/66', *ibid.*

65 'Personal to the Prime Minister from the President', 14 June 1966, NSF: Memos to the President: Walt Rostow, vol. 6, box 8.

66 Bundy memorandum to President Johnson, 6 March 1965, 'Report of meeting between Bundy, McNamara and Rusk', NSF: CF: Memos to the President: McGeorge Bundy, vols. 9–11, box 3.

67 Bator letter to President Johnson, 26 January 1967, NSF: Name File: Bator, box 1.

68 'Background Paper, Visit of U.K. Foreign Secretary', 7 October 1966, NSF: CF: Europe and USSR: United Kingdom, boxes 210/211/212 (memos folder, UK, vol. IX).

69 Edward R. Fried, Oral History, p. 36.

70 Folder, 'United Kingdom PM Briefing Book 7/29/66', NSF: CF: Europe and USSR: United Kingdom, boxes 215/216.

71 Rostow to President Johnson, 28 July 1966 (folder, 29 July 1966), Diary Backup, box 41.

72 Incoming cable to Department of State, 5 June 1968, NSF: NSC Meetings File, vols. 3–5 (folder, 'NSC meetings, vol. 5 tab 59, 6/5/68: Current issues affecting U.S./U.K. relations') (original in capitals).

73 Bruce, Oral History, p. 24.

74 Wilson, *The Labour Government*, p. 80.

75 See M. Caldwell, 'Luddites and lemmings in South-East Asia', *International Affairs*, 41, 1965, pp. 420–40; A. Short, *The Communist Insurrection in Malaya*, London, 1975, p. 160; Healey, *Time of My Life*, p. 227. The actual 'Malayan emergency' had ended in 1960.

76 Folder, 'United Kingdom Briefing Book 7/29/66', NSF: CF: Europe and USSR: United Kingdom, boxes 215/216.

77 Folder, 'Negotiating Initiatives in Vietnam', Read to McGeorge Bundy, 2 August 1965, NSF: CF: Vietnam, boxes 196/197. See also D. C. Watt, *Succeeding John Bull*, Cambridge, 1984, p. 147; Lord Beloff, 'The end of the British Empire', in W. R. Louis and H. Bull, eds., *The 'Special Relationship': Anglo-American Relations since 1945*, Oxford, 1986, pp. 249–60, p. 256; D.

Reynolds, 'A Special Relationship?', *International Affairs*, 62, 1985–86, pp. 1–20, p. 14.

78   E.g. Dean Rusk's remarks on the Davies mission, *The Department of State Bulletin*, LIII (2 August 1965), p. 187.

79   G. C. Herring, *The Secret Diplomacy of the Vietnam War: The Negotiating Volumes of the Pentagon Papers*, Austin (Texas), p. 396.

80   This was a peace plan communicated to Soviet PM Kosygin in London. The initiative was undermined by policy changes in Washington. For various interpretations see: G. Brown, *In My Way*, London, 1971, pp. 145–66; Bruce, Oral History, pp. 26–30 (also p. 1 of second tape); William Bundy, Oral History, pp. 20–3; C. Cooper, *The Lost Crusade*, London, 1971, pp. 358–9; A.E. Goodman, *The Lost Peace*, Stanford (California), 1978, pp. 48–9; P. Gore-Booth, *With Great Truth and Respect*, London, 1974, pp. 355–62; Herring, *The Secret Diplomacy*, pp. 372–6; Lyndon B. Johnson, *The Vantage Point*, London, 1972, pp. 252–5; Ponting, *Breach of Promise*, pp. 222–6; G. Porter, *A Peace Denied*, Bloomington (Indiana), 1975, pp. 56–7; T. J. Schoenbaum, *Waging War and Peace: Dean Rusk in the Truman, Kennedy and Johnson Years*, New York, 1988, pp. 456–8; and Wilson, *The Labour Government*, pp. 345–66.

81   Brown, *In My Way*, p. 146.

82   Herring, *The Secret Diplomacy*, p. 396. See also NSF: Memos to the President: McGeorge Bundy (vols. 5–8), box 2 (memo, 26 December 1964, on Wilson proposal to address the UN General Assembly).

83   Herring, *The Secret Diplomacy*, pp. 356–63, 372–6, 390–475; also, e.g., Diary Backup, box 90 (folder, 'Feb 8–9, 1968'), (anonymous note on UK mediation during the *Pueblo* incident).

84   See *The Presidential Campaign 1976: Volume 2, Part 2*, Washington D.C., 1978, pp. 709–16 (B'Nai B'Rith speech, 8 September 1976), pp. 993–8 (Notre Dame speech, 10 October 1976).

85   *American Foreign Policy: Basic Documents, 1977–1980*, Washington D.C., 1983, p. 425.

86   Ibid.

87   See J. Muravchik, *The Uncertain Crusade: Jimmy Carter and the Dilemmas of Human Rights Policy*, Lanham (Maryland), 1986, p. 121.88. Pastor memo for Brzezinski, through Jerry Schechter, 4 May 1979, White House Central File (WHCF): Subject File (SF): Countries: box CO-9 (Jimmy Carter Library, Atlanta, Georgia).

89   L. Shoultz, *National Security and United States Policy toward Latin America*, Princeton, 1987, p. 290. See also F. O. Vicuna, 'Domestic policies and external influences', in R.J. Vincent, ed., *Foreign Policy and Human Rights*, Cambridge, 1986, pp. 105–18, p. 109.

90   *Basic Documents, 1977–1980*, p. 407.

91   *Ibid.*, pp. 419–23. See also C. Vance, *Hard Choices: Critical Years in America's Foreign Policy*, New York, 1983, p. 436.

92   D. Carleton and M. Stohl, 'The foreign policy of human rights', *Human Rights Quarterly*, 7, 1985, pp. 205–29, p. 207.

93   Daft memo to Eizenstat, 22 November 1977, Staff Offices, Domestic Policy Staff, Eizenstat, Box 208.

94 Remarks of Jessica Tuchman (NSC staffer), Muravchik, *The Uncertain Crusade*, p. 96.

95 *Basic Documents, 1977–1980*, p. 409.

96 *Ibid.*, p. 433.

97 S. Vogelgesang, 'What price principle? U.S. policy on human rights', *Foreign Affairs*, 56, 1978, pp. 819–41. See also S. Vogelgesang, *American Dream, Global Nightmare*, New York, 1980.

98 *Basic Documents, 1977–1980*, p. 415.

99 *Ibid.*, p. 425.

100 *Ibid.*, p. 1293.

101 Z. Brzezinski, *Power and Principle*, London, 1983, pp. 128–9; J. Carter, *Keeping Faith*, London, 1982, p. 150.

102 C. Vance, 'The human rights imperative', *Foreign Policy*, 63, 1986, pp. 3–19, p. 14.

103 See T. M. Franck and E. Weisband, *Foreign Policy by Congress*, New York, 1979, p. 85; C.W. Whalen, *The House and Foreign Policy*, Chapel Hill (North Carolina), pp. 122–6; J. P. Salzberg, 'A view from the Hill', in D. D. Newsom, ed., *The Diplomacy of Human Rights*, Lanham (Maryland), 1986, pp. 13–20; A. G. Mower, *Human Rights and American Foreign Policy: The Carter and Reagan Experiences*, Westport (Connecticut), pp. 60–6.

104 For details, see Carleton and Stohl, 'The foreign policy', pp. 206–7. See also D. M. Fraser, 'Congress's role in the making of international human rights policy', in D. P. Kommers and G. D. Loescher, eds., *Human Rights and American Foreign Policy*, Notre Dame, 1979, pp. 247–54.

105 See L. Shoultz, *Human Rights and United States Policy toward Latin America*, Princeton, 1981, pp. 74–108; Vogelgesang, *American Dream*, p. 145.

106 See J. Kirkpatrick, 'U.S. security and Latin America', in B. D. Larkin, ed., *Vital Interests: The Soviet Issue in U.S. Central American Policy*, Boulder (Colorado), 1988, pp. 49–71, pp. 53–4.

107 *The United States and Latin America: Next Steps*, WHCF: SF: Countries: Box CO-9. See also Pastor's contribution to J. D. Martz, ed., *United States Policy in Latin America*, Lincoln (Nebraska), 1988.

108 See R. B. Lillich, ed., *U.S. Ratification of Human Rights Treaties*, Charlottesville (Virginia), 1981.

109 Muravchik, *The Uncertain Crusade*, p. 8.

110 Jordan memo to the President, 3 December 1977, Chief of Staff, Jordan, box 34.

111 Brzezinski and Wexler memo to the President, through Phil Wise, 24 October 1978, WHCF: SF: Human Rights, box HU-3.

112 Memo from Aiello, Moses and Aronson for Jack Watson (undated), WHCF: SF: Human Rights, box HU-4 (folder, 8/1/80 – 1/20/81).

113 Tuchman Mathews memo to Brzezinski, 7 July 1978, WHCF: SF: Human Rights, box HU-2.

114 See generally G. Smith, *Morality, Reason and Power*, New York, 1986.

115 Brzezinski, *Power and Principle*, p. 128; J.J. Kirkpatrick, 'Human rights in the Carter years', in Kirkpatrick, *Legitimacy and Force*, I, New Brunswick, 1988, pp. 141–4.

116 *The Uncertain Crusade*, pp. 149–50.

117 Mower, *Human Rights and American Foreign Policy*, p. 82.

118 *Ibid.*, p. 81.

119 See Franck and Weisband, *Foreign Policy by Congress*, pp. 92–3; Shoultz, *Human Rights and United States Policy*, pp. 257–66, also ch. 8; D.P. Forsythe, *Human Rights and U.S. Foreign Policy: Congress Reconsidered*, Gainesville (Florida), 1988, pp. 60–1.

120 See D.S. Spencer, *The Carter Implosion: Jimmy Carter and the Amateur Style of Diplomacy*, New York, 1988, p. 58.

121 Shoultz, *Human Rights*, pp. 120–1.

122 A.G. Mower, *The United States, The United Nations, and Human Rights*, Westport (Connecticut), 1979, p. 102.

123 D. C. McGaffey, 'Policy and practice: human rights in the Shah's Iran', in Newsom, ed., *The Diplomacy*, pp. 69–79, pp. 69–70.

124 Mower, *Human Rights and American Foreign Policy*, p. 73.

125 See Franck and Weisband, *Foreign Policy by Congress*, p. 95.

126 Forsythe, *Human Rights*, p. 53.

127 Thomas Thornton to Brzezinski, 15 June 1979, WHCF: SF: Countries: box CO-10.

128 Report of Congressional delegation (House Banking, Finance and Urban Affairs, and Appropriations Subcommittee on Foreign Operations) on visit to Colombia, Argentina, Chile and Brazil, 16 March 1978, WHCF: SF: Human Rights, box HU-2.

129 Starr to Eizenstat, 6 June 1978, Staff Office, Domestic Policy Staff, Eizenstat, box 208.

130 Forsythe, *Human Rights*, p. 53. See also S.B. Cohen, 'Conditioning U.S. security assistance on human rights practices', *American Journal of International Law*, 76, 1982, pp. 191–231.

131 See generally Smith, *Morality, Reason and Power*; C. O. Jones, *The Trusteeship Presidency*, Baton Rouge, 1988; E. C. Hargrove, *Jimmy Carter as President*, Baton Rouge, 1988.

132 J. Petras, 'President Carter and the "New Morality" ', *Monthly Review*, 1977, p. 38.

133 Valerio L. Giannini to Philip Meyer (Paraguay resident), 31 May 1977, WHCF: SF: Human Rights, box HU-4.

134 See Smith, *Morality, Reason and Power*, p. 186.

135 Wexler to G. D. Karcazes, 25 June 1980, WHCF: SF: Human Rights, box HU-3.

136 J. Tuchman Mathews and L. G. Defend memo for Brzezinski, 20 November 1978, WHCF: SF: Human Rights, box HU-3. See also J. Mayall, 'The United States', in Vincent, ed., *Foreign Policy and Human Rights*, pp. 165–87, p. 181.

137 Cited in H. Sklar, 'Trilateralism: managing dependence and democracy', in Sklar, ed., *Trilateralism*, Boston, 1980, pp. 1–58, p. 30.

138 See correspondence in Jimmy Carter Library (in, e.g., WHCF: SF: Countries, box CO-63).

139 *Keeping Faith*, p. 143.

140 Mower, *Human Rights and American Foreign Policy*, p. 24.

141 Spencer, *The Carter Implosion*, p. 59.

142 Mower, *Human Rights*, pp. 90–1.

143 See Carleton and Stohl, 'The foreign policy of human rights', pp. 215–16.

144 Muravchik, *The Uncertain Crusade*, p. 170.

145 Shoultz, *Human Rights*, pp. 50–2.

146 Tuchman memo to Brzezinski, 3 February 1977, WHCF: SF: Human Rights, box HU-1.

147 Shoultz, *Human Rights*, pp. 259–66; P. J. Flood, 'U.S. human rights initiatives concerning Argentina', in Newsom, ed., *The Diplomacy of Human Rights*, pp. 129–39, p. 131. See generally R. Cohen, 'Human rights diplomacy: the Carter Administration and the Southern Cone', *Human Rights Quarterly*, 4, 1982, pp. 212–42.

148 Shoultz, *Human Rights*, pp. 321–2.

149 Shoultz, *Human Rights*, p. 296; Flood, 'U.S. human rights', p. 133.

150 Vogelgesang, *American Dream*, p. 220.

151 See Lee King memo to Alan Wolff, 11 September 1978, WHCF: SF: Human Rights, box HU-3.

152 E.g. F. Moore to Senator Howard Baker, 2 October 1979, WHCF: SF: Countries, box CO-10.

153 R. R. Fagen, 'The Carter Administration and Latin America: business as usual?', *Foreign Affairs*, 57, 1979, pp. 652–69; Forsythe, *Human Rights*, pp. 155–6.

154 Brzezinski to E. M. deWindt, 6 June 1980, WHCF: SF: Human Rights, box HU-3.

155 E.g. Pastor to Solari Yrigoyen (on banning of Jehovah's Witnesses), 5 July 1977, WHCF: SF: Countries, box CO-10.

156 'U.S. human rights', p. 129.

157 Vogelgesang, *American Dream*, p. 61.

158 E.g. Muravchik, *The Uncertain Crusade*, p. 177; A. J. Pierre, *The Global Politics of Arms Sales*, Princeton, 1982, pp. 251–2.

159 See D. L. Cingranelli and T. E. Pasquarello, 'Human rights practices and the distribution of U.S. foreign aid to Latin American countries', *American Journal of Political Science*, 29, 1985, pp. 539–63; F. Pfluger, 'Human rights unbound', *Presidential Studies Quarterly*, 19, 1989, pp. 705–16.

160 *The Presidential Campaign 1976: Volume 3, The Debates*, Washington D.C., 1979, p. 97.

161 See J. Spanier and E. M. Uslaner, *American Foreign Policy Making and the Democratic Dilemmas*, 5th ed., Pacific Grove (California), 1989, ch. 9.

162 K. N. Waltz, *Foreign Policy and Democratic Politics*, Boston, 1967, pp. 304, 307. See also D. Yates, *Bureaucratic Democracy*, Cambridge (Massachusetts), 1982, pp. 42–59; J. D. Steinbruner, ed., *Restructuring American Foreign Policy*, Washington D.C., 1989, pp. 3–4; S. Smith, 'Reasons of state', in D. Held and C. Pollitt, eds., *New Forms of Democracy*, London, 1986, pp. 192–217.

163 H. J. Morgenthau, *A New Foreign Policy for the United States*, New York, 1969, p. 151.

164 J. A. Hall and G. I. Ikenberry, *The State*, Milton Keynes, 1989, p. 100.

165 L. Fisher, 'The efficiency side of separated powers', *Journal of American Studies*, 5, 1971, pp. 113–31.

166 See J. D. Steinbruner, 'The prospect of comparative security', in Steinbruner, ed., *Restructuring American Foreign Policy*, pp. 94–118, p. 118.

167 See A. Arblaster, *Democracy*, Milton Keynes, 1987, p. 102.

168 For a clear statement of opposition to such drawback, see D. M. Abshire, *Preventing World War III*, New York, 1989; for an influential proposal to cut the defence budget in half, see R. McNamara, *Out of the Cold*, New York, 1989.

169 See S. D. Krasner, 'Realist praxis: neo-isolationism and structural change', *Journal of International Affairs*, 43, 1989, pp. 143–59.

170 Cited in C. Layne, 'Superpower disengagement', *Foreign Policy*, 77, 1989–90, pp. 17–40, p. 40.

171 See A. L. Friedberg, 'The strategic implications of relative economic decline', *Political Science Quarterly*, 104, 1989, pp. 401–31, p. 411. See also F. Rohatyn, 'America's economic dependence', *Foreign Affairs*, 68, 1989, pp. 53–65.

172 *Reflections on American Foreign Policy since 1945*, London, 1989, p. 144.

173 See C. H. Ferguson, 'America's high-tech decline', *Foreign Policy*, 74, 1989, pp. 123–44.

174 See Friedberg, 'The strategic implications', p. 413.

175 See S. M. Walt, 'Alliances in theory and practice', *Journal of International Affairs*, 43, 1989, pp. 1–17; J. W. Saunders, 'America in the Pacific century', *World Policy Journal*, 6, 1988–89, pp. 47–80.

176 R. M. Nixon, 'American foreign policy: The Bush agenda', *Foreign Affairs*, 68, 1989, pp. 199–219, p. 204.

177 See J. J. Shestak, 'Human rights, the national interest and U.S. foreign policy', *The Annals of the American Academy*, 506, 1989, pp. 17–29.

N.B. Archival material cited in notes 4 to 83 may be found in the Lyndon B. Johnson Presidential Library, Austin (Texas); material cited in notes 88 to 155 in the Jimmy Carter Presidential Library, Atlanta (Georgia).

Index